ECO-SPIRIT

A Spiritual Guide to
Healing the Planet

By the same author:

The Aura Coloring Book

ECO-SPIRIT
A Spiritual Guide to Healing the Planet

Levanah Shell Bdolak

You Can Help to Heal the Planet Earth

a **Voyant** Book
Malibu Lake, CA

Eco-Spirit Logo by David Fontana
Photo of author by Joan Laurens
Cover typeset by Corum
Artwork by David Fontana
Computer layout by Tad Cooper
Computer typesetting by Corum
Editing by Anita Wolff
Content Editing by Harold Moskovitz

Printed on 100% recycled paper.

To order this book please see the last page. Discounts are available
for bulk orders.

ISBN: 0-944278-02-7

First Edition
Printed in the United States of America

10 9 8 7 6 5 4 3 2 1

This book is dedicated to Mother Earth

May She
Live Long
and
Prosper

Warning—Disclaimer

This book is a reference work based on research by the author. The opinions expressed herein are not necessarily those of or endorsed by the publisher.

The directions stated in this book are in no way to be considered as a substitute for consultation with a duly licensed doctor, psychiatrist, psychologist, therapist, scientist or ecologist.

The author has provided you with information about how to heal yourself and the planet. She has based this information on personal research and revelations, research by others, and channeled insights which she believes to be accurate. However she cannot and does not guarantee the results. This books offers a doorway to the world of transformation, methods to begin healing the Earth and yourself, and a start towards changing personal and mass consciousness. The responsibility for using it ultimately rests with you.

ACKNOWLEDGMENTS

I would like to thank Clearsight Program graduates Richard Barr and Timothy Tessmer for their many healings, intuitive insights, and spiritual wisdom that helped me bypass the stranglehold of writer's block.

I would also like to thank Tad Cooper for his hours of computer support (without his technical proficiency and assistance this book would not exist) and for sharing his nature wisdom, wilderness insights, and ecological education with me.

Many thanks are also due to Richard Green who gave me the support to verbalize the connection between spirituality and ecology.

And much gratitude to Dennis Pollack for his marvelous insights, help, and information regarding the Eco-Spirit T-Shirts.

Without the many years of discussion, input, and insights about Ritual and the Goddess from my old friend Deborah Frankel the content of this book would have lacked quality.

And much gratitude to Lewis Bostwick for teaching me that you can have your head in the heavens and still have your feet on the ground.

Thanks are also due to the students of the Clearsight Program who have aided and supported this project by helping me find the time to write this book.

And, I wish to say thank you to my editor, Anita Wolff, who has consistently strived to bring clarity to this book and taught me a great deal about the fine art of writing.

CONTENTS

INTRODUCTION

The term Eco-Spirit is a combination of the words ecology and spirit. It is defined as the pursuit of inner self awareness and outer environmental action. This pursuit combines the two most powerful abilities we have: the ability to affect our outer environment and the ability to be in touch with our inner selves, both of which combine to allow us to be in touch with the spiritual nature of the earth.

We are at a turning point in our history when we must make responsible decisions about our environment. We have finally begun to open our thoughts and beliefs to include an ecological viewpoint. With this dawning of ecological consciousness, people have begun to add ECO as a preface to a variety of behaviors. There are eco-baskets, eco-businesses, eco-games, eco-books, eco-shoppers, eco-art, and so on. We are moving into a period of time when everyone wants to make a statement and maintain a level of consciousness about environmental issues within the framework of their daily lives. Ecology is one of the largest issues facing us in this and the next century. And the next ten or twenty years will show us how effective we will be and what we can expect to accomplish.

While everyone is adding the prefix ECO to their lifestyle and material purchases, there is still a need to join the concept of caring, nurturing, and saving the environment to finding a more meaningful purpose in life with our inner sense of spirit. As we are beginning to realize, it is not consumerism or the ability to acquire something new every day that nurtures us and give us pleasure. We are now delving into the real issue of what gives meaning to our lives and how we can express that meaning. We are beginning to see the inter-relationship between our personal lives and the health of the planet.

Eco-Spirit is a call for action and for the combining of ecological awareness, spiritual ability, and the necessity to act upon this joining. This union of consciousness and spirit gives us the opportunity to create something very special: the act of being the expression of nature on a conscious level. The ecological dilemma is not just a problem for us to be aware of and solve. We are a part of nature and, therefore, a part of the problem and a part of the solution. Nature has its own agenda. In the end, nature wins out over man's agenda. For example, look at the most extreme version of ecological disintegration. If we keep polluting and unbalancing the planet in the manner we are doing now, we will cause such disintegration of the world that we will become extinct. Humans will cease to exist because the air will be unfit to breathe, the pesticide-laced foods will be toxic to our systems, the soil will be depleted of all nutrients, the water will be poisoned by chemical runoff, and the ozone layer will no longer be able to protect us from radiation. We will have successfully caused our own demise. But nature will go on! The little niche or nook in nature created by the human species will have become another experiment that did not succeed. But Mother Nature will adapt and adjust and continue in some new vein to start another, perhaps radically different experiment. We will come to an untimely end but Nature will not. She will just turn her path towards a new genetic dawn.

We are a unique part of nature in that we are a "conscious organism." We have minds and spirits which enable us to act out our path in nature while also dissecting from and understanding the consciousness of what we are doing. Because of this awesome combination of the genetic core of nature—our bodies, the mental ability to direct them consciously, our minds and the ability to raise ourselves to a higher consciousness, and our spirit and the determination to direct its will upon the planet—we have the potential to be a truly evolved race of beings. We are the part of nature that can speak to nature. Eco-Spirit addresses the combining of our genetic nature self, our intellectual mind, and our spiritual essence to create within us a more highly evolved being that understands and acts to help rebalance the planet.

The Eco-Spirit tools in this book are gleaned from ancient and present, spiritual systems. They create a means by which anyone can begin to use his/her spiritual consciousness and energy to help heal the Earth. These skills can be used by a novice or a person very advanced in spiritual work. They are skills that can be used by any individual or group, bereft of dogma, and are given freely to enable all of us to come together in a massive effort to heal the good ship Earth.

1

SAVING THE PLANET AND OURSELVES

A CALL TO ACTION

When it comes to the environment, we are all in one boat—the good ship planet Earth. Whether we love or hate one another, help or ignore each other, agree or disagree, we have all inherited the legacy of our actions—actions that cause our environment to be balanced or unbalanced. We all must live with the consequences of our actions. If we choose to pollute our air, foul our waters, poison our food system with pesticides, destroy our forests, disintegrate our protective ozone layer, raise the temperature of the planet to create a greenhouse effect, build and create ecological imbalances that kill off hundreds of species of plants and animals, then we must live with the results. We have nowhere else to go. This is our home. It is the only home that we know and possess. And it is hurting. It does not take superior intelligence to figure out that our planet is fighting its most important battle—the rebalancing of its very vital structure by the balancing of life energy versus death energy.

1

This beautiful green and blue planet, this very bright planet, is beginning to lose its life force as species after species drop out of the planetary life cycle. We are losing species faster than we can name them. We are also losing the gift of life that up to now all humans have taken for granted: clean air; fresh water; green and majestic trees; safe, healthy food; large beautiful vistas of natural land; plants, animals, and insects that populate and create our perfectly-balanced ecological environment; and the joy of living in a beautiful world that you know your children will inherit. This is not a fear about the future. This is now. If you live in a major city you already know about the dangers and ravages of air pollution and acid rain. If you do not grow your own food you will most likely have encountered pesticide abuse and overuse. Many people, not trusting their water sources, buy bottled water or use water filtration systems. We do not live in the trusting, happy, gentle world of yesteryear. We live in the technologically-advanced world populated by too many people, too many polluting cars, buses, planes, and industry, and too much ignorance of the dangers created by our own advanced system. Since we are the head and mind, and a part of the living heart of this planet we call Earth when we destroy the planet we destroy ourselves. And what we do today is what we and our children must live with tomorrow.

Of course most people say immediately, "I know that there is a problem ecologically but what can I do? I recycle. I buy "green" products that are not harmful to the environment. I fund ecological groups to save species, protect the wildlife, and conserve the land." And they also say, "I do everything I know how to do but in terms of the quick pace of ecological degeneration of our environment, I feel powerless. Sometimes I just do not know what to do! And even when there is something that, as

2

a private individual, I can do, I still feel it is not enough. Perhaps it is just up to the corporations and heads of state to care for the environment. Just what can I as a single person really do?"

It is true that the corporations and governments of various countries will have to make giant steps in changing their attitudes and actions if we are to survive on this planet. But the real work has to be done by each person. It is you and I who must understand and learn what we can do to change the course of events. It is the individual person who demands the changes in consciousness of the heads of states or the boards of directors of corporations. It is the collection of many individuals who make up the society and communities we live in. And it is our total society that must learn how actions affect the environment, what to do to change those actions, and how to educate ourselves and everyone around us to understand the ramifications of those actions. We cannot afford to wait for the next guy to do it. And so when people say, "But what can I do?" the answer is simple and direct. Do whatever comes naturally and easily. Do whatever it is possible to do. But whether that action is political, educational, or personal, we must use all of our selves, including the spirit of our inner selves, to create solutions to these problems. For it is by using our spirit, which is the very nature that gives us the spark of life, that will bring the most important part of ourselves to work on the problems.

If anything, it is our spirit that provides us with the very vital connection to the planet, it allows us to intuit (know) how to solve what seems like a mammoth, overwhelmingly incredible situation. It is the spiritual part of our selves that can make the direct connection with the planet, with Mother Earth and Mother Nature, and it is the spiritual part of our selves that can then learn to heal and change this situation.

From time immemorial, people have lent their spirit to heal Mother Nature, to grow their crops, and to husband their animals. It is only within the last 200 years, with the coming of the industrial revolution, that people have gotten out of touch with their own intuitive and natural abilities to communicate with the earth directly, to speak to the plants and animals, to the sky, the wind, and the trees, and to themselves. For example, when was the last time you ran barefoot through a meadow of green grass, or laid beneath a tree, or walked in the light of the full moon, or felt the wind blow through your hair? When was the last time you allowed the spirit of nature within you to shine through and fill your heart and soul?

Many of us have lost contact with Mother Nature. We have lost the connection that allows our bodies to feel truly at home on this planet. However, we can give ourselves permission to make this reconnection. To step outside our doors and walk through the grass barefoot, to take the time to smell the flowers, to listen to the birds, and to watch the cloud patterns are our inalienable rights as human beings—if we take it. The experience of connecting with the earth is part of the gift we are given as human beings. This connection with the earth is actually a part of our gift of health. For without this we are separate and apart from nature, alienated from the very essence that enlivens our minds and fills our hearts with wonderment and awe—the awe we experience when we see a beautiful vista, smell the scents of nature, walk in the forests, or listen to the ocean.

It is our very essence, the spiritual spark of life that fills our body, heart, and soul that gives us the chance to turn the ecological tide of events. We are what a gambler would call a wild card. We are both the destroyers and the creators on this planet

4

and if we choose, we can change the course of events. And we can do this by using our most ignored and yet most powerful tool, our spirit. By using our spirit, by acknowledging ourselves as energy workers who can and will change the face of the planet "in accordance" with nature, we can take the next step in the evolution of the human race.

It does not take years of training to be able to use your spirit to heal or work with Mother Nature. There are many exercises in this book that show you how to work with the spirit of nature. And as you open yourself up to this marvelous and awesome method of touching the incredible divinity within all life, you will naturally and intuitively know how to help the planet to change.

Now is the time when we as a race of humans can take the step to heal our planet and learn to live in harmony with our environment. We have evolved enough to develop technology that can destroy the very fine balance of life force on this planet. So we must now use our abilities to evolve on a positive path engaging our highest capacities as energy transformers to rebalance the scales of nature. It does not take much to be an energy worker. A few hours a week can help to add life and light to the planet we live on. It does not take millions of people to make a change on an energy level. If 10,000 people worked using their spiritual essence and the very spirit of their life force to make a conscious statement, we could turn the tide of degeneration. It only takes a small number of people who are willing to make a conscious statement and back that statement up with their conscious use of energy. Perhaps you will want to be one of the 10,000 who will help to change the face of this planet by being energy workers.

Often people ask what can be done by just using their spirit. Your spirit, the part of you that wakes up in the morning and gives you the impetus to enjoy the day, is your energy. As an energy worker you can indeed cause miracles. These miracles can transform the planet. They might not seem like miracles to you when you first enact them, but as you watch and observe them you will begin to truly understand the nature of working with your energy. As an energy worker you can cleanse parks, land, homes, buildings, and areas of harmful or negative influences; promote the growth of crops, trees, and plants; heal plants and animals; check the tide of rampant ecological degeneration and rebalance the energy of Mother Nature; influence people to make decisions coming from their higher nature; and reconnect yourself and others with the planetary life force of Gaia and the true spirit of Mother Nature.

This book is a call to action. It is a call to all who read it to do whatever they can do, whether it be of small or large consequence.

THE DOMINION OF HUMANS

In the book of Genesis, in both the Jewish and Christian Religions, chapter 1, verse 28, God gave to man, "dominion over the fish of the sea, and over the fowl of the heaven, and over the cattle, and over all of the earth, and over every creeping thing that creepeth upon the earth." Over the centuries many people have interpreted this "dominion" to mean control and domination of the sky, the land, the sea, the animals, and the insects. Perhaps we would be more in tune with our own inner nature and our hidden God force if we interpreted "dominion" to mean that we have the task of helping to balance and being the caretaker for our environment.[1] Having dominion "over" nature means that we are in charge or in control, and/or communicate with nature.

6

But we do not normally communicate with the elementals of nature or the devas of the plants or the spirits of the animals.

The Native Americans and many early tribal cultures have as their underlying belief that they must constantly interact and communicate with the spiritual nature of their environment. To communicate with the spiritual nature of the tree, or the plant in the garden, or the mountain, or the stream, is to take the time and energy to notice the nature or spirit of what they were communicating with. You do the same thing in speaking to the plant in your garden when you take notice of its leaves and stem, of its general health, of its wants and needs, and of its life force as spirit. As your spirit acknowledges the plant's spirit you are reaffirming your own life force. You are communicating with its vibrant nature.

Every morning I feed the wild birds in my area by spreading seed under a large pine tree in the front of my home. As I spread the seed I always speak to the spirit of the tree. And the tree speaks back and tells me of the weather and the nature of the planet. One summer morning it patiently explained to me that a small pine seedling growing on the hillside below needed water. This gave me a chance to interact with the trees, to water them during the drought and to understand their needs. They provide me with shelter from the hot sun, hold the slope in place with their root system, provide a home to many birds and insects, help replenish the air I breathe, enable me to have a green view out of my front window, and fill my life with the majesty and wonderment that only a tall tree can do. In exchange, I water them during the drought, interact with them to exchange love and greetings, and protect them from the people who would carve their trunks, deface them with graffiti, or chop them down for a Christmas tree. (Yes, I live in the country and every year at Christmas time strangers come into the valley and chop down live trees on private property or park land to take home and enjoy for two weeks before they throw them out in the trash!) As an exchange for what the tree gives to me, I give it the love and appreciation it seems to sense and enjoy.

If we see ourselves as having "dominion" over the planet in terms of control then we view ourselves as separate and apart from nature. If we truly did have that type of dominion over nature we would also have had to control the inner workings of nature, speak with the elementals and the devas, cause the rain, stop the floods, control the earthquakes and the volcanoes, and generally be masters of the planet. We are not, however, capable of doing this. But, because we see ourselves as the dominators of nature, we bulldoze the rainforests and strip the land; and we cause the ozone layer to grow thin and create acid rain; and we generally resist and ignore the very basic laws of cause and effect.

Ecologists who are studying the destruction of our system of nature tell us that nature is infinitely more complex than we realize and that everything is interconnected. If you have "dominion" as a dominator then you must understand the complexity of the system of nature or risk unbalancing it. If you have dominion as a "caretaker" then you are capable of caring for, sharing with, and nurturing nature as you interact with it. The decision to change from dominators to caretakers is a major turning point in our evolutionary path. If we choose to be the caretakers of our planet we may be able to preserve many species of plants and animals that are dying and, in turn, preserve our planet as the wonderful home that sustains our race. If we choose

8

to "control" all that is around us then we may find that our skills to run the show are not as advanced as we think, and we will burn out the one resource we cannot replace—this planet Earth.

The choice must be made now for it affects not only the current generation of people but the also the generations to come. Because we are developing very quickly as a race, we are going to see tremendous changes in our lifetime. Whichever path we choose—to control or to caretake—we will have to learn to master both our technological and inner spiritual natures to create an outcome that benefits us as a living race. Neither path is easy. Each one of us has to make a decision about which path we will travel. Years ago I chose to travel the path of developing my inner spiritual nature and put my awareness toward practical applications that affect the outer material world. This book is a result of that choice. It tells you how to travel the path of a caretaker energy worker choosing to help care for the planetary system of which we all are a part.

WORKING WITH ENERGY

If we are going to work with energy to change the planet, then there are certain basic laws of working with energy, of working with the spirit, that we must become aware of and work in accordance with. In order to actually create a manifest change on the physical plane, we must be aware of who and what we are as spiritual beings. We have to learn how our spirit exists in a physical body and how our spiritual or energy nature affects or changes the physical plane. These basic statements, or laws, of working with energy can be found in or deduced from any of the spiritual systems now in existence on the planet. If you have studied any manner of working with energy you may find these statements familiar.

The laws of working with energy in order to cleanse, heal, or change the physical Mother Nature level of the planet could be stated as:

1. "As above, so below." This ancient saying, attributed to Hermes Trisgestus in the 13th century, has a great deal of bearing on how we, as spiritual beings, decide to use our energy to change the planet. Whatever we create as spirit or energy on the higher planes of awareness will come to be reflected, like a mirror, on the lower planes of existence. Therefore, if we create on the spiritual plane a planet free of pollution and living in harmony with itself, then that is the message that the planet "below" on the physical plane will receive.

2. Guilt, morality, and responsibility. Guilt, morality, and responsibility are the three banes of motivation. People use them to set you up to feel bad, and therefore to do something. But usually people feel so badly they do little. We must begin to work from a positive mode.

    Guilt could be likened to a rocking chair. The rocking chair moves a lot but goes nowhere. Feeling guilty does not change a situation nor does it make you feel good! We cannot continue to feel or be guilty for what we have or have not done in the past to create the environmental catastrophe we face today. We have to move onwards away from guilt, to action. Guilt is an emotion that paralyzes people. It does not energize them! We must learn to work from inner creativity, hope, and joy in order to succeed.

    Morality is the method that the authorities (whoever they may be) use to control people. But morality is something you cannot teach people. If people get in touch with their true God force or inner nature, they do what is the loving or "moral" thing to do in a situation. Being told what to do is not the same as doing what comes from your heart. You cannot legislate morality. You can legislate some rules for businesses and corporations to prevent them from taking advantage of the defenseless environment, but in the long run the real answer is to educate our children from a very early age to love and respect the environment that they live in so they will protect it from their heart, from the very inner core of their beings. Until the day when our children grow up these measures are but a stop-gap method of protection or legislated artificial morality. It works, but only in limited doses.

Responsibility is a heavy burden to bear because it means your personal ability to respond. We do have the ability. How we do so, either positively or negatively, is up to us. We cannot be responsible for the next guy. All we can do is be responsible for ourselves. If we think of what we are responsible for in terms of our environmental situation it is overwhelming. Like guilt, if you tell people that they are responsible for something they become paralyzed. But let us say instead that we are responsible to love the planet. People would want to help it survive. Of course, we can only love someone or something else as much as we love ourselves, so we must learn the unselfish love that encompasses all manner of being, the love of life, and for ourselves as well.

3. Using your will to create your reality. You must know what you want in order to get it. You cannot just say, "I

want to have all of the good things in life come to me," and get them. You must be specific and focus directly upon a specific action. To heal the environment we must learn to focus our energy on what is most important to sustain the power of the Earth. In the past we focused on "getting what we want" with no attention to the ramifications of our actions upon the environment. Now we have to learn to work in accordance with nature so that we do not trash it for our personal needs. Using our intention or will power means using the strongest part of our spiritual selves to create harmony and life force in the physical realm.

4. Extrapolating or creating from within—learning to cleanse yourself. All action that comes through you must go through your own essential self. As you learn to cleanse yourself of the emotional and mental debris of your ego, you can bring through you the pure essence of healing light to heal the planet.

5. Understanding the Earth as a whole—what goes around comes around! We must begin to use the concept of cause and effect and learn how all actions, both personal and those performed as part of a group, affect the environment.

6. Discovering your archetypes and acting outwardly from them. Our external actions are based on our inner models of reality and behavior. If we can begin to understand and use our most powerful archetypes to create a positive action, then we heal both ourselves and our planet.

7. Understanding the spiritual nature of creation is a beginning step in creating some affinity with Mother Nature. By using a systematic approach, such as working with the elements of earth, air, fire, water and spirit to get in touch with the planetary realm of nature we initiate the first step in actively attempting to heal the planet. By using specific systems we should be able to start healing the earth and achieving the desired results.

8. Belief in yourself as having the necessary power to heal, change, and be one with the planet. This is the next step in the evolution of humankind on the planet. If you do not believe that you personally can do something to help heal and balance the planet, then do not bother to become involved in the ecological movement. The world is set up in such a fashion now that it is difficult to believe that we, as singular beings, can actually affect a change upon the planetary decay. It leads us to feeling and being powerless. People who do not believe that there is anything they can personally do to change their environment have no power and therefore can do nothing. You must believe that you exist for a purpose and that you are here to act upon that purpose. For each of us there is a personal reason for incarnating as a spiritual being on the planet and there is a greater group or higher purpose that determines why we have come here at this particular time to join in with the stream of humanity on the planet.

AN AGE OF CHANGES

This is a traumatic and telling time to exist. The Earth is going through terrific changes. Our humankind is evolving. We are reaching the first footstep of evolution of the human spirit. We are dealing with the power to "choose" our destiny, to "choose" peace over war, to "choose" technology that will mirror what we feel inside of ourselves, and to "choose" the manner in which we live in accordance with our physical environment. These are not intellectual concepts but "choices" that we will make in the next 30 years of our existence as a race of people. We have a group agreement, a group karma, to work out how we as humankind will deal with the physical planet and the interaction between ourselves. As human beings we can choose to be the physical **rulers** of the planet, and in turn destroy the life force of our planet by decimating the animal population, by destroying the soil and plants with our pesticides, and by polluting the air with our machines which enables us to remain in **control** of the planet. Or we can choose to be **keepers** of the planet and work in accordance with the natural laws and slowly turn the planet from massive decay to interactive growth. As a human race we do indeed have a choice! It is a choice our generation must make now.

Being spiritually minded and living a "good" life is not necessarily enacting or being in accordance with the laws of nature. By just existing we use the planet—we must eat, we must create garbage, we must travel from one place to another, we must live in houses—all of this necessitates making decisions. Do we compost our garbage? Do we recycle our garbage? Do we use a gas-guzzling car? Do we eat foods with or without pesticides used to grow them? Do we eat foods that take an inordinate

14

amount of other foods and water to produce, such as meat? Do we buy fur coats? Do we use animals to test our drugs and cosmetics? Do we vacation by driving into wilderness areas? Do we build houses on pristine land? Do we use our canyons for sewer and waste run-off? Or do we take the time to make a connection with Mother Earth on a psychic, intuitive, feeling level?

Some of these questions are unfortunately answered by necessity. If I do not drive to work I can not get there! Some of these questions are answered by unspoken group agreement. In some cities garbage is recycled...in other cities it is not. These unspoken or undealt with group agreements can be changed by like-minded people taking action, by working within the legislative process, and by writing and speaking and changing ourselves and other people's consciousness and actions.

Some of these decisions are going to be dictated by personal preference. Others will be determined by the situation. Perhaps you use a gas-guzzling car right now but you cannot afford to replace it with a more fuel-efficient car. Soon the auto industry will feel the pressure to produce cars that are more fuel-efficient and eventually you will be able to trade in that old car for a more ecological one. This may not happen overnight, but it will happen. The energy tide is turning.

People are waking up to a new world in which we are more thrifty with our resources. Perhaps we are finally realizing that our resources are finite and that we must not only conserve them but learn to create new and more ecological sources of energy.

This way of thinking is radically different from the philosophy under which people in my generation grew up. When I was a child growing up in the 1950s I was led to believe in the post-war American philosophy that there was plenty for everyone. This greatly contradicted the behavior of my parents.

My father came here from Europe when he was 19 years old because he had heard stories that the streets were "paved with gold" and that there were great opportunities. My mother was born in Ohio of Russian immigrants who brought the family over one by one.

When I was a child we would go to the supermarket and they would package everything in large heavy paper bags. They seemed to use as many paper bags as they could. The more bags you carried out of the supermarket the more prosperous you seemed to be, I guess. My mother, however, would insist on carrying her own bag. It was a smaller bag sewn out of denim or other materials she saved from her sewing scraps. Into this bag she crammed all of her goods. Of course, living European style, both my mother and father never shopped once for the whole week like our other neighbors. We went to the store either every day or every other day so that we would be insured fresh food and so we only had a small amount that would always fit in just one well-packed cloth bag. I remember those days well. As I got older I felt "different" from other people and was all too painfully aware of how my parents seemed to have their own agenda in life. I wished to be involved in conspicuous consumption. I wanted to be able to buy and waste. I remember the first transistor radio my father bought for me. It was made of metal and was small for those days, because you could hold it in one hand. By the time that the radio had broken and needed to be repaired, the technology had advanced so far that it was "better" and more economical to replace it with a new plastic version at half the size and half the price. Conspicuous consumption had arrived! My father attempted to have the radio fixed at every shop in town but it was useless. Planned obsolescence had arrived!

My parents never threw anything out that had some use. It was not that my parents were poor. They were not. Money had very little to do with their lifestyle. It was their culture and their value system that dictated their actions. When they emptied a cottage cheese container they washed it out and saved it. (This, of course, was before the advent of plastic refrigerator storage containers.) Everything that came into our home was used and reused and recycled to become something else. Sometimes, as a child, I felt that I never needed to go to a five and dime store to purchase anything because if I needed something, all I had to do was ask my mother and she would have it salted away in the large drawers of her dresser bureau—her own version of the five and dime.

When I was young I dreamed of being able to buy everything and being able to throw it away when it "wore out" instead of having to repair and recycle it. It was not until six or seven years ago that I realized the value of the lifestyle my parents led. When my mother died, I inherited her cottage cheese cups (about 50 of them), her yarn, spools of thread, buttons, and a wealth of items too vast to mention. My most treasured inheritance, however, was her denim shopping bag. Suddenly I realized the treasure I had so grudgingly received. While I dreamed the American dream of being able to carry home new paper bags that I would immediately throw away, my mother had trained me in the "old country" ways of preserving and conserving. And, although it has taken me four decades to understand it and reintegrate it into my life, that training will last me for the rest of my lifetime and perhaps add to the wealth of my children's education. Now, of course, I am proud to go to the "supers" with my little denim bag and see how our social mores have turned, as some people ask me where they can get one too.

It is not that we have to conserve every single item that we bring into our homes. We will always create garbage. But we do have to learn that being a great country, a great people, or a great world of nations and peoples does not mean having to build on nonbiodegradable landfills. But we do not have to WASTE either. We have a choice now. We can choose the values that we wish to instill in our minds, our culture, our children, and our own lives. We do not have to connect the dream and reality of a good economy with the waste and pollution and ignorant despoiling of our environment. We can choose the good life. And the good life can mean clean air, safe and fresh water, pesticide-free wholesome food, old growth forests to preserve for posterity, beautiful grand vistas of natural undeveloped land, and a good economy. We can choose this by our actions now— if we really want to, that is.

ACTING WITH POSITIVE INTENT

When we look at working with our ecological environment to create a balanced system, the first and most important thing we have to do is balance ourselves. We are the part of the eco-system that needs refinement and work. We are either the glitch or the angel in the system. And the first thing we have to do is balance our minds and our emotional systems.

Take a moment to ask yourself what type of world you want to see and live in and be a part of in the year 2,000. Can you visualize it? Can you see the future as you want it in front of you? Or do you see what you fear? Do you see the terrible predictions: overcrowding; flat barren earth devoid of trees or vegetation; air thick with chemicals; water not fit to drink without massive cleansing; people dying from cancer due to a weak ozone layer that does not protect us; flooding of low lying areas due to the greenhouse affect; food that has little nourishment, that is never ripe and poisons us with its pesticide residue, and is in short supply; a massive lack of wildlife; nuclear accidents that have ravished and destroyed populated areas; and a lack of medicine because the eco-system that produces the plants the medicine is derived from have been killed? Or do you see a world where we have taken the time to solve our energy problems: a world with cleaner air and new forms of non-polluting energy; a world where there is enough food for everyone and the food is ripe, nutritious, and safe to eat; a world where the water is safe to drink; a world responsible for its actions ecologically; and a world where people spend their energy wisely to have beautiful vistas, old growth forests, new growth forests, species saved and helped to sustain themselves, and people who are happy, healthy, and fit for life? What type of world do you visualize? Do you act from your fears, your hopes, or your desires?

To an energy worker, what you think is what you create in life. You get or become what you are. And what you are is what you are creating, thinking, and feeling right at this moment. If you think devastation then you are creating that devastation in your personal universe and in your world at large. If you think that the world is going to be totally polluted and "wasted away" why bother doing anything, because you have already created that reality with your mind and with your spirit. You have already accepted that potential outcome as reality.

This planet has a positive and negative level of consciousness. Many people work with the negative to motivate themselves. When you ask someone what he or she wants, often that person will tell you what they do **not** want. But, in truth, you get what you want. If you constantly focus on what you do not want, then you create that negative reality in your universe and you get it. Many of the newer ecological books will give you these awesome and terrible predictions of what is happening to our planet. They state that if we keep going on the way we are right now that by the year 2,000 this or that will happen. Their extrapolation might be based on great statistics and good probability, but it is leading us down a negative, self-fulfilling prophecy path where we will create what we are afraid of. This type of thinking and acting creates fear and negative thought forms that we feed with energy and therefore create into reality.

The time has come for us to use our 20th century advanced consciousness to create the kind of world we would really like to live in. To create a wonderful beautiful clean world, we have to learn to motivate ourselves from the positive standpoint. In the 1970s, I lived in a small city in Northern California where the general population was extremely politically active. The Peace Movement was an issue and many people spent a good deal of their time speaking about the threat of nuclear war, the bomb, and nuclear power plants. Instead of taking a positive tack, many of the people created a fear mentality by promoting books, leaflets, videos, movies, and held meetings describing the horrors of a nuclear war and what would happen to all living beings when the bomb came! People actually ate, drank, and slept the nuclear threat. They created an extremely anxious situation. As a spiritual counselor, I noticed parents were coming to me to discuss their children's nightmares, fears, and traumas about nuclear war. The children, whose psyches were much more wide open than those of their parents, had accepted all of this nuclear war talk as real and were not only creating it on an energy level but waiting for it to happen. Yes, they were fantasizing and creating their own worst nightmares as a viable reality. When I suggested that the family defuse this immediate anxiety attack and choose to discuss positive and loving events at the dinner table, the children's attacks of anxiety soon died away.

We are responsible for the reality we create around ourselves. If we go to see a horror movie and then go to sleep right afterwards there is a good chance that we will create a horror movie scenario on the dream plane. We are affected by our thoughts, our wishes, and our fears. And what we think and fear on an unconscious level is often what we create on a conscious one.

Two of the strongest motivating emotions on this planet are fear and love. You have a choice in life as to which of these emotions you choose to work with. Fear can "scare" people into action but it can also paralyze them. But most of all, fear creates negative thought forms. Whatever you put your energy into is what you wind up getting in life. When you fear something, such as a nuclear war or an ecologically-devastated world, then you are feeding it, putting your energy into it, creating it. If enough people put their energy into it, then it comes to exist. I am not saying that we should bury our heads in the sand and make believe that everything is okay when it is not. Obviously, it is very noticeable that our planetary ecology is decaying and we have to do something now. But how we do that "something" and what mind set we use to motivate ourselves is very important. Strong positive images create a strong generation of people who know what they want and how to work to get it. Negative images only work to demean and undermine our internal sense of life force and create depression, apathy, and the very reality we are trying to change!

If you work from love, then you create a positive image of what you would like to see and experience in your life here on the planet. Some people call this the power of positive thinking or the power of positive visualization. In the particular system of shamanistic spirituality that I was trained in, it was considered the ability to create with spirit. That spirit, or life force, is the spark of life within you that gives you the energy to get up in the morning, to eat breakfast, go to work, hug your friends and lovers, and accomplish something in the world. It is that same spirit that can heal or transform the planet. You have the spirit to wake yourself up to a positive mode of creating your reality and you also have the spirit to turn around the degenerating forces on the Earth. You have the spirit to communicate with the true Mother Earth and give her the power to weather the changes that a highly industrialized out-of-balance technological society of humans is imposing upon her.

By accessing our higher nature, or the spirit within ourselves, we have the ability to begin the needed transformation of the Earth from a planet that is used and abused by humans to a planet that is interacted with and loved and healed by humans. By using our spirit we use the very part of our selves that helps to create change in human consciousness as well as changes in the natural life force stream of the planetary cycle. Instead of becoming the glitch in the earth master plan, we become the angels. Angel is a word in the Bible that means messenger. Therefore, we become the messengers of light who give the needed love and support to

Mother Nature. We become the caretakers of this green and growing planet. To become the angels in the system, we have to learn to master our minds, to think in the positive mode, to create positive thought forms, to love, and to be loved.

But since the ecological system of our planet is degenerating at such a quick pace, we do not have the leisure to sit back and just work on the problem through the power of positive thinking. We must act to help heal and save the planet while learning to clear our own personal systems of the negative emotional "garbage" we carry with us.

The chapters of this book contain specific exercises for learning to clear yourself and for learning to create a positive method of healing the planet with your higher spiritual nature. But while learning to use the very vital spark of spiritual nature within yourself to connect with Mother Earth to create a healing environment you can also recycle, be politically active, and work within your community. This very vital connection with the planet is what makes the difference between us being an undeveloped race of humans or a race of humans with super consciousness living in a new age of awareness. As we use the spirit of life within us to connect with the Earth, we are developing the connection between spirit and matter that our primitive ancestors utilized every day when they picked nuts and berries and tilled the earth. In some ways we have lost a very important connection with this simple spiritual nature. To communicate with the Earth we must work to redevelop this skill. It is, after all, the missing link between our highly-developed technological society and the simple spiritual nature that gives meaning to our lives.

"Finally, humans, I, Rock, speak to you
I ask you to wake up—
    Wake up, humans, wake up!—
and pledge your allegiance to life.
    Even though others may
    look upon you as traitors,
        speak on our behalf in
        all human meetings
            and councils.
Speak with strength and courage
    and power because you
    represent all of us who,
        in the normal course of
        events, have no voice.
We ask you to give voice on our behalf."

                    —John Seed
                    Council of All Beings

24

2

YOUR ECOLOGICAL MIRROR

Our human race is growing up. We are evolving in consciousness. As spiritually aware people we must begin to understand how we can turn our energy away from the ignorant *Destroyer* mentality back to the life force giving nurturing planetary *Keeper* position we were meant to take.

As we teach ourselves the basic lessons of how to respect and use the planet by conserving and not wasting, and living in harmony with the environment, we must also teach ourselves the lesson of how to actualize our spiritual gifts to heal and work in harmony with the nature of the Earth. We can be the *Destroyers* or we can be the *Saviors* who bring harmony and enlightenment to work in affinity with the powers of nature. In many ways we are the brain of the planet because our species was given both intuitive and analytical functional capacities. As the brain of the planet we can not only work in harmony to fashion a beautifully balanced system but we can also explain how and why it functions that way.

Being spiritual can mean being able to use your energy to channel love, light, and joy to the earth. If this seems far fetched you might want to read some of the books, such as *The Secret Life of Plants*, by Peter Tompkins and Christopher Bird, that have shown how humans can begin to understand and unlock powers that we have to communicate and heal the essence of nature. Many people have done experiments using prayer and communication with plants. In a controlled experiment, the plants that were "prayed over" (or sung to, or spoken lovingly to) grew big and healthy while the plants that were ignored or yelled at with anger withered away and died.[2] There is an innate power within all human beings to turn or channel their inner spiritual nature into an enlightening healing power for the good.

What you do today, in the here and now, in present time, is what creates the future that you will be experiencing. Most of us have good hearts and want to do something to help the planet survive and rebalance itself. But having a "good heart" just isn't enough. We have to **do** something to act upon our ideas and considerations. There are many things you can do to help the planet. Perhaps you have thought about some of them but what have you actually done? It is not good enough to be a busy person with good intentions. Those "intentions" must become "actions."

Focus of energy is what makes actions work. We live in a very complex world. There are so many things to do in order to help change our planet that it can be overwhelming. The overwhelmed person does nothing and gets nowhere but means well. Choose your actions carefully, organize your mind and your time, and know your limitations and you will accomplish something. The following is a list of suggestions of how to organize yourself towards action.

1. BE PRACTICAL. Know Your Limitations. Most of us are modern urban people who are just becoming aware of the terrible toll we take upon our environment to support our lifestyle. Modern urban people are busy people who are constantly trying to accomplish what they should have done yesterday and dreaming about what they will get done tomorrow.

   In order to become a person of action you have to learn about your limitations. Perhaps you would like to support every ecological group that mails you its literature. There are now so many and varied ecological groups that all do very good work that it could and might just bust your budget to bankroll all of them. So you have to pick and choose what you can afford to support. This is one way of knowing your limitations.

   Perhaps you have several ecological action fronts happening in your neighborhood: people are organizing a recycling station, there is a neighborhood homeowners association trying to prevent a massive development on some forested land, and one group of people are organizing to get an initiative on the ballot to prevent oil rigs off the coast near where you live. Before you agree to wholeheartedly work on all of these and later find out you have spread your good intentions and your energy too thin, find out what is involved. Decide which action has a priority for you and which issue you can do the most for. Perhaps you discover that you could sign the petition for the anti-oil rig initiative but do not have the time to actually become politically involved. However you could mention this project to your friends, neighbors, and workmates and vote for it once it gets on the ballot. Maybe you do not have the time to help set up the recycling center but would be one of the people to use it once it is up and going. Sometimes you might only have the time, energy, and initiative to get fully involved in only one project. And that might be the one closest to home, the homeowners' battle with the developers. Here you might go to meetings once a month, help to raise money for the lawyer's fees by donating items to a garage/bake sale, and donate your time and money to other money-raising events and help research and prepare documents to present a competent case in court. It is important to know your limitations, or, as a friend of mine once explained, "to have integrity, to be a person of your word." You should only agree to do something if you really have the time, energy, or resources to carry it out. If you say you are going to do something then keep to your word. If you do not think you can actually do something then do not feel badly or guilty. Do what you can in any given situation.

2. DO SOMETHING. Any action is better than inaction. If you have read some of the recent ecological literature you will realize that the resources of our planet, the forests, the water, and the air, for example, are disappearing and eroding so fast that we are fighting a losing battle.

    Our planet is losing up to three species a day.

    35.2 million acres of tropical rainforests are destroyed every year. Already half of the Earth's tropical forests have been destroyed, burned, or turned over for crops or cattle. At the rate that the rainforests are being obliterated there will be no rainforest left by the end of this century.[3]

It takes nature about ten thousand years to make an inch of topsoil and yet we are depleting our soil at the rate of about 6 billion tons per year.

Literally before our eyes annually we see forest land half the size of California vanishing.

Annually we dump approximately 80 billion pounds of toxic waste into our water system. And so far at least one third of our underground reservoirs of fresh water have been poisoned with contamination that could take 100,000 years to clear.

There are 50,000 toxic dump sites in our country and so far we have cleaned up only 22 of these.[4]

In the time that we take to sit and think about what is happening we are losing our most valuable resources. This means that we have to counter this by doing something.

We have two basic courses of action that work. The first is to find something concrete to do and **do it**. It may not be the long range answer but it is better to recycle than to just sit and watch the evening news and bemoan our situation. Worrying gets you nowhere and accomplishes nothing. Only **action** will change a situation. There is the concrete action of attempting to change the direct environment we live in (recycling, protecting trees and land, using renewable resources, not polluting, conserving, and working on new forms of energy resources), and the spiritual action of putting energy back into the positive reinforcement of the planet. We need to accomplish **both** of these actions.

Instead of sitting and thinking, bemoaning and worrying, or just plain ignoring it in the hopes that the planet will right itself "somehow" we need to take action **now**. Each of us must personally discover what our brand of "action now" is. We have so little time to turn around this planetary disaster that we must begin to act now.

Below is a list of simple, easy to perform actions you can do on your personal environmental front:

A. Recycle everything that you can. Find the nearest recycling center and make the trip to it part of your daily routine. Recycling also means reusing. Be creative: use items more than once and do not use disposable items when you can use reusable ones.

B. Use the energy in your home or office efficiently. Turn lights off when you leave a room, use heating and air conditioning when you really **need** it, lower the thermostat on your water heater, take shorter showers, dry your clothes on an outdoor line in the sun, develop methods of using less water to wash your dishes.

C. Separate garbage for recycling, compost your food waste, and if you have the space, grow an organic garden.

D. Check your home for energy efficiency. Use insulation, energy-saving light bulbs, buy energy-efficient appliances, put a brick in your toilet tank to use less water when you flush or as your appliance gets old replace it with a new water-saving toilet, install a shower head that uses less water, weather strip your doors and windows, put a timer on your garden hose and water before 6:30 a.m. or after 6:30 p.m. and use solar energy products (such as a solar mosquito guard).

E. Use your car wisely. Combine trips to save gas recycle used motor oil (take the used oil to a gas station or recycling center that collects oil or check to see if your mechanic recycles oil); buy a car that is fuel efficient and keep it well tuned (to keep your car well tuned, change the oil and filter every 3,000 miles, check the air filters twice a year, and keep the tires properly inflated). A well-tuned car uses up to 15% less gas. According to Rubber Duck Automotive, the average American driver burns 507 gallons of gas a year pumping 11,154 pounds of carbon dioxide into the air. Boosting your car's mileage by just one mile per gallon will cut your annual carbon dioxide emissions by 528 pounds.[5]

F. Be an ecological voice in your office or place of business. Help to start a recycling program at work. Use paper cups instead of styrofoam at the water cooler/coffee machine. Even better, use washable reusable mugs when feasible. Carpool to work when possible. Influence your business to use ecological products and solutions (such as natural popcorn for shipping insulation instead of styrofoam peanuts). Instead of being instantly recycled, shredded paper could also be used as a packing material.

G. Use your political power. Turn out and vote for what you want. Make sure that you are truly informed about the issues and the ramifications of your vote.

H. Be an informed shopper. Buy ecological products that save our resources. Avoid toxic cleaners, pesticides, and disposable products. Use products made of unbleached recycled paper when you buy toilet paper, paper towels, and facial tissues. Buy foods that support Green Awareness and preservation of species. Write to people who send you junk mail and request you be removed from their mailing list. Take a shopping bag (canvas, net, etc.) with you to the store so that you are not creating more waste.

I. In drought areas plant trees to shade your home and to give the planet more air. Put native plants in your yard that are hardy and need less water. If possible, set up a gray water system for watering your plants. Plant in accordance with your natural environment.

J. If you have a home garden, get in touch with heritage seed companies where you can help to preserve and reintroduce older and hardier seed stock and seeds that are organic.

K. Whenever possible **do not** purchase tropical rainforest products unless they are grown or raised in a sustainable manner. Speak to your local merchants to understand where and in what conditions their products come from. Be especially aware of tropical wildlife species (birds, lizards, snakes), tropical plants, hardwoods, and curios. Do not buy lumber or lumber products that are endangered species or are not cultivated in a sustainable way. Do not purchase beef from countries where you know that the forests have been cleared for pasturing cattle. (For further information about how to help save the rainforests, read *The Rainforest Book* by Scott Lewis or contact the Natural Resources Defense Council.)

L. Be involved. Use all of you—your physical abilities, your mental abilities, and your spiritual self to make a change! Use the Eco–Spirit techniques in this book to heal your neighborhood, your place of business, and your connection to Mother Earth!

3. BE REALISTIC AND HONEST. Confront yourself with the true inner knowledge of realism. In your heart you might wish to do something but there are only 24 hours in each day. Only you can decide when you are actually going to do something instead of just thinking about it. Learn to be honest with your inner self. We call this "speaking with your inner voice"—the internal mechanism that gives you a reality check. If you cannot do something do not tell yourself, or someone else, that perhaps later, you will do it. When you lie to yourself you feel badly inside. The inner creative intuitive part of your self knows when you are deceiving it. Then the lie is an intrusion in your space that trips you up. Face reality head on. Agree to do only what you can do and only what you really want to do. Leave the rest for someone else who **wants** to do it!

4. THE "IF EVERYONE" SYNDROME. Don't get caught in the "if everyone" syndrome trap. I was always an

involved person who tried to change the community and the world around me. After many years of this type of action I noticed that everyone who becomes involved in a movement or cause always gets to the point where they are saying, "*If everyone* would rally behind this cause," or "*If everyone* would financially support this issue" or "*If everyone* would do something about this." I think you get the idea about the "if everyone" syndrome. You will never get a one hundred percent turnout of the "if everyones" in any cause because people do not function this way. After all, the statement that "Necessity is the Mother of Invention" did not become a truism by chance.

By the time most people realize that there truly is an ecological planetary hazard, we will be long past the point where simple actions can have an effect upon the environment. In any given situation where there are limited amounts of time and resources to solve a pressing problem, it gets relegated to the spokespeople, the people who are entranced with a particular cause through their devotion to one specific issue (those who eat, sleep, and drink the cause), the forerunners of every generation, and the consciousness raisers. They rally behind the necessity to make it known to the general public. Even if it is an issue like ecology that does truly affect everyone on the planet, most people do not stop in their tracks and do a one hundred and eighty degree turn around of their lifestyles or ecological processes. Change takes time and is accomplished by small daily adjustments. You do not have to have a turnout of everyone on the planet to change the course of affairs concerning the environment.

It only takes a small percentage of actively involved people to carry the ball for the many people who do not have the time, expertise, or desire to work actively to change things. So, instead of trying to get everyone involved, all you need to do is to involve yourself to the best of your own ability.

5.   BUDGET YOUR TIME. Most of us are creatures of the modern urban environment and the lifestyle that ensues from "fast" living. If you want to do something for the environment, you must dedicate some of your time to achieving your end goal. It is amazing how people who really **want** to get something done, no matter how busy a schedule they have, do manage to accomplish their desire by setting aside a specific period of time.

6.   GIVE YOURSELF PERMISSION. You can be instrumental in helping to save the planet if you give yourself permission to **do** something. It is not how involved you get but the fact that you make your own contribution to the life of the planet in your own special way that matters. You might become an Eco–Spirit energy worker who does work to spiritually heal the energy of the planet. You might also recycle, carry a reusable bag to the grocery store, use biodegradable products, hang out your wash to dry in the sun, change to ecologically sound soaps and cleaning products, and change your lifestyle from the unconscious use of resources to the measured understanding of the cause and effect of your actions upon the environment. What you do is up to you, but giving yourself permission to do something creates a positive statement of intent.

7. BELIEVE IN YOURSELF. Respect yourself! **Believe**... that's right...really **believe** that you can change the planet, because if you do not believe this, then you will do nothing! Maybe what you do will seem to you to be a small drop in the bucket of things, but then again, maybe it will be something major in the scheme of things. Regardless of what your actions actually accomplish, you have to have a genuine belief that your personal actions **do** count for something. The time has come for us to acknowledge the realm of cause and effect on this planet.

8. ILLUSIONS and DELUSIONS. There are many illusions and delusions that you can buy into that lead you down the primrose path of inaction and irresponsibility, such as:

   Illusion...

   > ... Since I am just one person, nothing I do will have any great effect upon the environment.
   > ... It is up to the heads of state and corporate leaders to make significant changes.
   > ... If I donate money to my favorite ecological group then I am doing my best to help the situation.
   > ... Let the gung-ho people, the committed ones, do something. They can do more than I can anyway.

   Delusion...

   > ... Just acting with my spirit will solve everything.
   > ... Soon they will find alternative energy

solutions so I do not have to deal with conserving my electricity or my consumption of gasoline.

… The city will recycle garbage so I do not have to do it in my own home.

… Everything is a trade-off. I do not have to deal with being concerned about what I eat (food with pesticides or meat with unnecessary chemicals or preservatives) because I live in an area where the air is still fairly clean. All people have to die of something anyway. I probably won't get cancer until I am in my eighties. Why should I be concerned now?

These are but a few of the traps into which you could fall if you do not listen to your inner voice of absolute personal truth. If you respect yourself, then you want to take care of your body, your home, and your planet. Therefore you must take the time to care for the environment that you live in as it affects your health, your mental state of being, and your ability to live a quality life style.

*"Unknowingly we plough the dust of stars,
blown around us by the wind, and
drink the universe in a glass of rain."*

—*Ihab Hassah*

3

THE FOUR
ELEMENTS

When we begin to consider what we can do to help rebalance the planet we are basically considering what our place, as a human race, is on the planet. Of course it can be a philosophical or religious issue to define what our purpose is as a race. However, many ancient cultures saw mankind's purpose as guardians or keepers of the planet—people who would care for the planet as if it were a part of their extended family. In the last few hundred years we have done a pretty poor job of caring for our planet. In fact, we have given so little consideration to the planetary condition that we must ask ourselves this ominous question: will the planet Earth continue to support or be here for the race of humans? Of all life forms on the planet, it is humankind who has the ability to wantonly destroy the planet. We have within us equally the wonderful seeds of creation and of destruction. This ability, coupled with our conscious awareness, places us beyond that of the other life forms on the planet.

So, in the midst of this turmoil and change, of pollution, waste, and breakthroughs in biological chemistry that could catapult us beyond our wildest dreams, we have to ask ourselves: what can we do for the planet to give it nourishment so that it can sustain us as a race? We have been taking the planet Earth for granted. We expect clean air, fertile land, good water, healthy forests, and the grandeur of nature. Unfortunately, we cannot take these things for granted anymore. If we do not work to preserve what we have and turn around the destruction of what we are losing, we may lose our foothold on our planet Earth.

Not all of us are ecological activists, ecologists, scientists, or nature experts. Many of us do not have the expertise or time to lend to the current problem. But most of us are concerned and want to do something to help the ecological problems that currently plague our world. Each of us will find our own method, our own path, for lending our energy to this needed cause. Many of us will lend our spirit to helping Mother Nature find her balance in these tumultuous times. And it is spirit, this inner resource that we all have inside of us, that holds the great promise of being able to change our circumstances.

The Ancients perceived the nature of our planet as being divided into the four elements of life: earth, air, fire, and water. These four elements, when combined with the fifth element, spirit, were seen as being the building blocks of life.

As an energy worker I have learned that a balanced planet is a place where the elements are held in equilibrium or ecological balance over a period of time. By becoming aware of the elements and how to balance them, we can clean up our environment on an elemental level. We can use our greatest natural resource, our spirit, to get in touch with the inner essence of the spiritual fabric of the planet and influence it to rebalance itself. We have this ability. All it takes to use this ability is to get in touch with the inner core of our selves (our microcosm), and then translate that information into a larger picture, to mirror it in the outer core, the planet (our macrocosm).

Energy workers have been using the concept of the four elements in order to heal the planet for thousands of years. These techniques are simple and straightforward in their symbolism and action. A child could practice them. An adult who finds the pure innocence of the child within him- or herself can also use them to recreate the paradise we once inhabited on the planet. This earth can be our paradise, a land where we can live in harmony with one another, and with all creatures and in varied environments.

Let us take a moment to visualize our planet as pure energy. See if you can imagine a core of light, right in the center of the planet, that extends outwards and forms a radiant egg-shaped sphere of energy that extends many miles through and around the earth. This is the sphere of energy that forms our planet. The center of this sphere is dense and heavy and as it moves outwards it becomes lighter and brighter. This is the energy blueprint of the planet. There is no up and no down, no in and no out, just energy that forms a sphere. Now imagine dividing the sphere of energy into four sections, like quartering an orange.

In the North Quarter is the earth element. It represents stability, fixed form, density, and inertia. On a human level, the earth element represents the positive side of the personality as patience, endurance, responsibility, and thoroughness. The negative side of the human personality qualities of earth elemental energy are stubbornness, resistance, dullness, depression, and boredom. The North Quarter represents the power of the planet, the storage area or the battery of earth energy which is considered the doorway to the inner planes of awareness by many energy workers.

The East Quarter is the air element. The air element represents movement, the intellect or mind, sound and communication, mutability, and life essence. On a human level, the air element portrays the positive side of the personality with the characteristics of optimism, dexterity, intelligence, diligence, laughter and joyfulness. The negative human personality qualities of air elemental energy are gossiping, boasting, squandering, thievery, and frivolity. The East Quarter of the world is where the sun rises and so it brings light, revelation and the enlightenment of the inner self or the illumination of the soul's purpose here on the planet.

The South Quarter is the fire element. The fire element represents transformation, expansion, purification, action, and the creation of heat and light. On a human level, the fire element portrays the positive side of the personality with the characteristics of courage, willpower, enthusiasm, productivity, energy, and heroic action. The negative human personality qualities of fire elemental energy are lust, anger, jealousy, vengefulness, hatred, and malevolence. The South Quarter of the world represents heat and light, sunshine, and expansion.

The West Quarter is the water element. The water element represents the existence of love, fertility, eternal life, the depths of internal consciousness, fluidity, and contraction. On a human level, the water element represents the positive side of the personality with the characteristics of compassion, nurturing, receptivity, forgiveness, caring, and love. The negative human personality qualities of water elemental energy are inability to commit oneself, lack of backbone, instability, an intense emotional state, and being overly receptive to or impressed by outside influences. The West Quarter of the world represents where the sun sets, and where water collects, so it places us in the depths of the internal and the emotions.

The fifth element is called Akasha. It is the life force or spirit that creates life on the planet. Traditionally, Akasha exists in two places: it is within all of the elements since it is the great motivator that sparks them to life and it also moves through the planet and around it. The band of Akashic energy that surrounds the planet in its outer layers is sometimes called the Akashic Records. This fluid energy has the property of recording everything that is done on the planet. Like the human subconscious it is the camcorder of the energy world that constantly records every action on the planet and stores it for further use. Psychics, clairvoyants, channelers, and energy workers have often consulted the Akashic Records for bits and pieces of a person's history. The Akashic Records are amazing because they contain both the past and the future as well as the present. The Akashic energy that channels through the planet energizes the planetary chakras (energy centers) and creates lines of communication from one energy center to another.

Some of these lines of energy are called ley lines by anthropologists. You can find many pictures of them in books about England and Stonehenge and the various stone menhirs and the lines or narrow pathways that run from one area to another. Ley lines are the lines seen on the surface of the planet that run from one energy center to another. Many of these energy centers are power centers that have not been formally used for generations. Examples of them would be Stonehenge, Machu Pichu, or the many places in Europe, China, South America, and Egypt where there are stone menhirs, stone temples, or pyramids and structures that have been used to work with energy or as temples and spiritual centers. The Akashic energy does not just travel from one energy center to another via the visible ley lines on the surface of the planet. Often the Akashic energy will divert itself into a direct line of energy moving right through the planet directly to another energy center on the other side of the planet. These are the invisible ley lines, the power lines, that channel through the planet. These channels open and close periodically depending on the time of year and the position of the planet.

The places where these ley lines surface, such as Stonehenge or Machu Pichu, are directly centered on earth chakras. Chakra is a Sanskrit word that means "a wheel that spins." When you view a chakra from the front it looks like a spinning wheel. In actuality however, a chakra is a cone of energy. The cone of energy spins in two different directions and the base of the cone looks like a spinning wheel. Earth chakras are the powerful energy centers that open to the sky with energy. Just as human beings have an energy system built into them that mechanically shuffles the energy through chakras and energy channels, the planet also has an energy system that sends energy throughout the planet. The planetary energy system has many more chakras, and changes its energy flow at different times of the year. The ley lines, or channels of energy, that flow through this system and through the chakras, lay dormant for part of the year and are activated at different seasons to channel life force through the planet to various chakras at the appropriate time. Some of these earth chakras are positive and reinforce life force. Others are negative and disintegrate or break down life force.

One of the jobs of the Keepers of the Planet, the energy workers, is to learn to channel this life force energy through the ley lines, to clear the ley lines, and to raise the energy up in the earth chakras at those particular times of the year when the energy surges through. Once you get in touch with how energy is transported through the planet and learn to recognize earth chakras you will be surprised to discover that many of the older churches, temples, monuments, and stepped pyramids or mounds have been constructed on major earth chakras.

THE HOLY GRAIL OF NATURE

Perhaps you have read or heard the legends and stories of the Holy Grail, the cup that Jesus drank from at the Last Supper, or the Holy Cup of Cerridwen, the Celtic version of the cup that represents the womb of Mother Nature, the never-ending cup of life force creation. This legend of a special cup that channels the God force and has special healing and uplifting qualities has been with us in myth and legend since the advent of humankind. Many religions and spiritual groups have stories and versions of the search for and the use of this cup.

There is another way to view the mystery of the holy cup within the framework of nature. The Ancients viewed the entire planet as a living organism representing the flesh, blood, and body of God. They viewed the planet as the feminine aspect of God because the planet created or brought forth life (and anything that "gives" life is seen as feminine). And so they created myths and stories and songs and art based on the concept of the planet as a female goddess, a female aspect of the God force. The planet was seen as the body of the Great Mother who would give life to all. The trees were her hair, the rounded hills her breasts, the caves her womb (where people were initiated into the mysteries of life and death), the animals and humans were her children. Her navel was seen as the center point of the earth and it was here the holy cup of never-ending life was placed. This cup was the bowl of life.[6] It was the valleys, the rounded lakes, the holy parts of the earth which were feminine and womb-like such as fertile valleys and deep lakes that were viewed as the navel of the world. As the Ancients viewed the earth around them and found the Great Mother so they would find her navel or center point where the mysteries of life would be presented and revealed to them. Here, at the center of the earth (spiritually), they would be in the most fertile area.

In many ancient spiritual systems the placement of the Great Mother and the location of her navel would move throughout the seasons and many nomadic peoples would move with it. On an energy level, the Holy Grail of Mother Earth is the metaphysical cauldron of life just as the holy Cup of Jesus also represents not only a physical object but a body of spiritual belief. As such, the Holy Grail moves with the seasons and when it enters the physical plane of existence to shine its light upon the earth, a brilliant golden light shines forth to fill humankind with its knowledge, wisdom, lifeline and fertility.

The earth chakras, where this navel of light surfaces, become major energy centers that draw people toward them and raise the consciousness of all who live near or come into contact with this powerful source of lifegiving energy. I have seen this incredible golden light shine forth in the Santa Monica mountains where I live and I have spoken to other energy workers who have seen it in other areas of the planet. It shifts and it changes with the seasons but it is the pure light of life that channels through this planet to heal and reunify all living matter. The Holy Grail is seen by energy workers as being the lost fountain of youth. Because it seasonally shifts its energy field it has been labeled as being mystical, illusory, otherworldly (existing on the astral plane, the plane of imagination), and as a religious mystical relic. But it is one of the hidden mystical tools that reminds human-kind of our ability to evolve into a more advanced race of energy beings.

As we learn to be aware of our own internal energy systems and the movements of the energies on the ley lines of the planet, we will evolve as beings into a higher plane of consciousness and be able to manipulate and clear the energy channels of the planet. Once we are capable of being able to understand and channel these lines of energy force we will be able to consciously help the planet to rebalance its natural life force. Creating a unified life sphere with the ley lines and the Holy Grail of life force energy is advanced work that will take the skill, knowledge, and focus of energy workers in the future. For now, we can do well just to start healing the planet by working with the four elements of creation and the archetype connections. As we develop and use our skills daily, we will evolve into energy workers who can move the entire planetary energy framework by clearing ley lines and using earth chakras.

USING THE FOUR ELEMENTS

The four elements are the key tools with which we can work to balance and transform the planet. By learning to rebalance areas we perceive as needing help, we enable the entire structure of the planet to come into balance. The four elements—earth, air, fire, and water—are perceived as tiny systems or kingdoms within themselves. Within each one of these systems there are thousands of nature spirits that work to create nature as we know it. For many thousands of years these nature spirits have labored to balance and rebalance the world of their system. Centuries ago these beings interacted with humans, but in the last nine hundred years they have shied away from the human race. To them, the human race is aggressive, violent, and destructive.

These many and varied nature spirits are the spirit of each element. Alone they have no immortal soul because they are completely tied to one another and their respective element. They are a unit and as such they work in harmony and agreement with one another. Because the planet is in such dire straits, these nature spirits will do anything to solve the overwhelming problems that they now encounter. They have made it clear that now they will work with humans to help restructure the energy of the planet. This is a great change both for humans and nature spirits. In the past, nature spirits worked, doing their tasks, independent of the human race on the planet. Although they would communicate with humans, they actually never foresaw or even considered working together with human beings to accomplish their tasks. Now we are on the edge of a whole new evolutionary process which can change the entire consciousness of the human race. We can see ourselves not as separate and apart and controlling the system of nature, but as a living part of the scheme of things wherein we work in harmony and coordination with other energy forms on the planet to create a better world.

The four elements are the building blocks of the planet. As such, one can manipulate them to balance an area where there is an imbalance or a problem.

For example, about nine years ago I was teaching a meditation class. One of my students was a psychotherapist in a local hospital. One evening she came to class very disturbed about what was happening on her floor at the hospital. It seemed that there had been quite a few fires breaking out there during the previous week. This was very unusual and she wondered if there was anything that could be done about it on an energy level. There are many reasons why an area gets out of balance. Sometimes people unconsciously feed their emotional systems with so much intensity that it collects and creates a whirlpool of energy that then attracts the elementals causing an imbalance. After all, being alive is a state in which we are constantly learning to change in order to remain in balance. I chose not to spend a great deal of time trying to understand, or even clairvoyantly see, why the hospital had a problem. Instead I decided to try my hand at just fixing it on the spot. From the many ways to assess and change the situation, I chose to use the skills that are now embodied in Eco–Spirit. I grounded the area contained in the entire floor of the hospital and drained out any excess energy. Then I proceeded to open a doorway to the elemental level of fire and send any excess fire energy back to the elemental level where it belongs and is stored. After that, I balanced the entire floor with an equal proportion of earth, air, fire, and water elemental energy. Once the area was balanced, I brought in soft gold cosmic sunlight and filled the entire area with this cleansing high vibration. The fires stopped and people seemed more at ease with themselves on that floor of the hospital.

You could call this coincidence or mind play, but I call it working with energy. And as this century progresses perhaps we will be able to document our actions and prove our workings. This remains to be seen. The only proof you will have is if you work with these skills and observe the fruits of your labor. Your actions will cause an effect. You will be able to change an area to release an over abundance of energy, such as fire or water, or you will be able to bring in more of that energy when you need it. And of course, it will seem like magic or coincidence or whatever it would be called from a non-believer's or sceptic's viewpoint. But after you work with these skills for a few months and notice that the "magic" always does happen when you apply yourself, you will then begin to understand the use and methodology of these wonderful skills that we all possess.

Do you have an empty lot near your home or office building—a lot that is sitting vacant and perhaps being filled with rubbish and trash? I have seen many of these lots become small neighborhood parks. But the people who live in the neighborhood have to want to spend their energy and time to transform this unsightly area into their local green space. Sometimes an area like this has collected all of the negative energy from the neighborhood. You could, using the Eco–Spirit skills, rebalance this area according to its elemental nature, and recharge it with life force, and cleanse it. Then perhaps the people in the area would suddenly wake up and notice it and want to use it for more than their local garbage dump. It takes so little of your time to transform an area with your energy and your consciousness. In as little as one hour a week you could clean up your local neighborhood.

4

THE BREATH
OF LIFE

What is the one element that we cannot see or consciously touch but which we are truly aware that it exists? Air, of course. The ancient energy workers considered air a mysterious component of life force that could transform people from the unconscious to the enlightened. One of the exercises they developed to do this was called "pore breathing." All of the older spiritual paths use breathing as a technique for getting people in touch with themselves. Perhaps you have encountered this in a stress management, yoga, or singing class. Pore breathing, which was used by some of the saints in Europe and a few of the true breatherians in India, is the lesser known of the breathing techniques that have come down to us through spiritual lore and text. Pore breathing is an invaluable skill for planetary energy workers. If you wish to heal the planet then **you** must have a great deal of energy—be charged—to take on this task. If you are suffering from polluted air, poor diet, unhealthy lifestyle, and a general lack of vibrant energy, then you cannot possibly have enough energy to accomplish some project you are working on that might be infinitely larger than you are in time and space. Pore breathing was developed to assist people to learn to charge themselves up with energy from the invisible (just as invisible as air) life force surrounding them.

We all breathe, otherwise we would not be alive! But the method by which we breathe is what is in question here. Most of us breathe without thought about how we take in this wondrous element that gives us life force and transforms our body. Unconscious breathing supplies us with the normal amount of elemental energy that is necessary to preserve our system. Most spiritual systems instruct people in conscious breathing techniques. This is not the secret of being recharged with life force energy to which I am referring. When we breathe, we are not just breathing in the secret, elusive, unseen item called air. We are breathing in, if we choose to become consciously aware of it, the life force energy of the planet. Some people call this akasha, prana, or etheric energy. It is the vital life force quality of the planet. With this energy we feed ourselves just as we feed our physical energy plants (stomachs) by eating or feeding our eyes by viewing an incredibly beautiful scene.

The following exercise will introduce you to pore breathing.

 EXERCISE-PORE BREATHING

Seat yourself in a comfortable chair with a straight back. Ground yourself and close your eyes. Take a minute to check in with and say hello to yourself. So often, with our hectic work schedules, we do not take the time to check in with our internal self to find out what is happening.

As you breathe, put your attention on your breathing. Ask yourself where you are breathing from. Some people lift their shoulders or their chests when told "to breathe". Your breathing should naturally come from your diaphragm, the muscle located in your solar plexus. When you are asleep and breathing totally naturally, you breathe from your diaphragm. By breathing naturally in this manner, you get the most air in your body. If you breathe from your chest, then a good deal of air does not get any further than your upper chest cavity. To find out whether or not you breathe naturally from your diaphragm when you are awake, place your hand on your diaphragm and feel it move in and out as you breathe. If you do not feel it moving, you may be breathing shallowly from your upper chest. If your diaphragm moves, then you are breathing naturally, normally, and from your whole body as nature intended us.

Pore breathing is not the focus of breathing through the nose or the mouth, but the ability to breathe in through the *whole* body system.

It is not how much air you breathe in but the quality of the air which you are breathing that truly matters.

Our skin is the covering that helps to create us as a whole system. One of its functions is to breathe and eliminate waste.

As you are seated in your chair with your eyes closed, take a breath of air. Imagine that the air surrounding you is this medium of energy that is filled with life force energy. As you breathe in this charged life force energy, allow yourself to breathe it in through your nose and lungs and also see yourself as breathing it in through every pore in your body, every pore in your skin. See yourself pulling in this incredible life force power from your surroundings into yourself. It is like being a paper towel that soaks up the water on your kitchen counter. It readily absorbs the water as you must readily absorb the life force energy. Now keep this life force energy within you as you breathe out. With every breath you inhale, feel the energy come in and fill you as you would fill a glass full of water. Then hold onto the life force. When you exhale imagine breathing out waste or whatever you need to let go of. After a few minutes of pore breathing you should begin to feel charged with a fine but very powerful and sustaining life force energy.

I first learned the skill of pore breathing while going out to the parkland, many years ago, to do Earth nature healing rituals. It is easy to do pore breathing when you are out in nature and the land and the air and the surroundings seemed charged with a natural life force vibration that you can almost feel like electricity in the air. You can, however, accomplish the same intensity or charging force by doing this very same exercise in your living room or office. I would not recommend doing it if you are in an atmosphere that is obviously malignant or unhealthy since then you would be pulling in the negative energy flow. Even when you feel that there is not a lot of life force energy in a given environment, such as an enclosed office on the 30th floor of a high rise building, you will find that if you do pore breathing you can hook into the life force that does exist and recharge yourself with it.

5

IT'S VERY
ELEMENTAL

We already know that everything on the planet is made of the four elements (earth, air, fire, and water) and that the fifth element, akasha or life spirit, is the spark that energizes the four elements into action. Now let us step into the spiritual world of the ancients, of the many wide and diverse cultures and religions, and see the planet from their perspective.

To the peoples of ancient cultures (and that could be almost anything before the 20th century!), the world was populated by a wide and multitudinous variety of life forms. The world was alive! And each thing that was encountered had an identity or a presence of being that could be communicated with. In the Ancient World every tree had a spirit one could communicate with, every stream and brook had its nymphs that could bless it and you, every mountain had its guardian keeper and every sea had its mermaids. The world was populated with the spirits of Nature.

Upon crossing a stream or river people would ask the nymph

of the stream for her blessing and make an offering to her. There were many sacred rivers, lakes, streams, and springs where the people of Old Europe went to cleanse themselves and find solace from their ills. Often they saw these springs as natural healing sites and called to the spirit of the spring and made offerings to get her to appear. This has been seen by folklorists as the origin of the practice of throwing coins into a wishing well or fountain. By throwing the "offering" into the well, the water nymph or healing spirit would come and cleanse the person making the offering and renew them with the sacred spring water. Today we view these customs as superstition, but their origins lead straight back to the understanding of how the ancients worked with the elementals during an earlier time on the planet.

Today when we want to cut down a tree, we simply get an ax or chainsaw and go to it. In older times, because each tree was seen as sacred and a living embodied object with a spirit that died when the tree was cut down, people first went to the tree and spoke with it to explain their need of the wood and to get permission from the tree to cut it down. Trees were seen as the givers of shelter, the keepers of certain medicines (from the bark and leaves), the storers of some food (like nuts), and as sources of protection. When these ancient people did cut down a tree they knew to wait for the proper time of the month when the moon was waning before they cut it down. They knew that the sap rises during a full moon and that trees cut down at that time rot on the ground while trees cut during the waning moon have stronger, tighter wood. In a very short period of time we have come from the era of personalization when we had to explain our need and desire for an object and be responsible for the cause and effect of taking that object, to the era of modern urban living where we walk into a lumber yard and order two by fours with no consideration as to where they came from, how they got there, or what are our responsibilities (other than payment).

Before a person or family built their house, they would situate themselves on their piece of land for a year to watch the wheel of the Seasons turn. This allowed them to observe where the sun and moon rose and set and where water ran on the land. They would speak to the trees and observe the animals that made that land their home. When they had developed both an intuitive and empirical feeling for the land, they would then speak to the spirit of the land itself to ask for permission to build their home. Through this process of observation and speaking with the trees and the land, they built their home in affinity, or accordance, and agreement with all living beings in and on their land. When building their home they would situate it so that the light from the rising sun would fill their rooms with a sense of the holy or the mysteriousness of God and life force and so the trees would protect them from the hot sun of the summer and the winds and rains of the winter.

Because these ancient peoples familiarized themselves with the land before building upon it, they understood the lay of the land and knew where to place their home on ground that was high and would stay dry yet was close to water so a well could be dug. They would speak with the wee little men, sometimes called fairies or elementals, who guarded the treasures in the depths of the earth to learn whether the land was friendly and substantial. They would choose not to disturb the local animal trails or wild life more than they had to. They would seek to be in accord with all life on the land so that their house was an extension of the land and its environs just as they viewed themselves as an extension or part of everything around them. These same practices were used to build many of the prestigious churches and cathedrals in Europe.

This is quite different from modern day urban living where we rent an apartment or buy a house with little thought of having to bless the wood before it is cut or take notice of the local bird population before we move in. It seems our values have switched from being land based to being acquisition or item based. Now we check out the plumbing, the access to the bus route or the freeway, how many windows, how many rooms, how much closet space, and perhaps the view. It seems that, instead of experiencing our living environment as a part of the whole, we are acquiring our living environment as a showpiece of our accomplishments or financial status or a temporary convenience for our busy lifestyle.

We cannot return to the "old ways of living with nature". We cannot go backwards in time to recreate lifestyles through which we have evolved. As modern human beings we have a very different view of the world from the early "ancients" of our planet who sought to live in harmony with Mother Nature. Because they saw a spirit in each living thing they also had a great deal of respect for that object apart from themselves. To them, any object that had spirit within it meant that the object had a piece of God or a piece of the cosmic oneness of the mysteriousness of life within it and for that, it was respected. If today we believed that each physical object had a spirit within it we might be looked upon as being superstitious. Yet, if we did see things, plants, animals, and physical objects, as having a spiritual essence then we might begin to respect and value them To cut down a tree is not seen in our culture as taking life force. It is seen as a purely mechanical means of accessing lumber, a means to an end.

Subsequently, along with losing our superstitious nature and our ability to revel in the mysteriousness of nature, we have lost our connection with the land, with the life force stored in its objects, and perhaps with the spirit within ourselves.

THE FAR SIDE By Gary Larson

While his parents beamed, little Tommy Lundquist, future developer, surveyed the view from his newly constructed treehouse.

Because earlier humans saw life and spirit in all the expressions of nature, they did not exalt themselves as people who could control or run nature. They perceived themselves as a part of the chain of life and were constantly interacting with it.

The elements of earth, air, fire, and water were seen as being invisible communities of intelligent beings who lived in a parallel dimension to the humans. At certain times of the year these beings would make themselves known. Sometimes humans would encounter them along their path of life during the year and be able to see and communicate with them. These encounters with the elemental beings are the basis for many of our fairytales and for many of our "long tales" told over a frothy beer or a glass of wine in the late hours of the evening. These brushes with the elemental beings have left us with a rich literary and musical heritage in such beings as Tinker Bell in J.M. Barrie's book *Peter Pan*, the character Puck in Shakespeare's *A Midsummer Night's Dream*, the bowlers that Rip Van Winkle encountered in the Catskill Mountains in Washington Irving's *The Sketch Book*, the pygmies in Wagner's opera *The Ring of the Nibelunganand*, and the many tales stemming from the Irish tradition of leprechauns and the wee little men. The elemental creatures are fascinating and fun to view, communicate, and interact with. These are the creatures of our fairytales, our myths, our childhood friends, and our dreams.

Perhaps it seems a bit far fetched to the modern 20th century mind to conceive of a world inhabited by invisible elemental spirits who fly and sing in the ether of the air and are fiery glowing balls of light dancing in the fields or over the water and are graceful swimmers in the essence of the waters or building and working in the depths of the earth. It taxes the brain as much as conceiving of the cellular structure of the body or of understanding the newest biological discoveries which explore the keys to our chemical and genetic heritage. What is unseen is not always, however, unknowable. Perhaps some day you, too, will have the privilege of witnessing the elemental play of life. Some of these tiny creatures are a wonder to behold and view. I used to sit for hours in my friend's garden just observing the tiny little elementals who helped the plants to grow and prosper. It was like watching a play of delicate little fairies dancing throughout the garden. It was like returning to my childhood when the stories of fairies and gnomes were acceptable and allowable. Watching the elemental creatures is like taking a peek into the delicate beautiful world of God's creatures where the colors are brighter than life and whole dramas are played out in the space of a foot's length in the garden. We humans all too often take the simplicities of life for granted, choosing instead to create a mundane reality we convince ourselves is our entire reality and so ignore this wonderful drama. To understand the elements and the work of these elemental creatures we have to truly understand the nature of the elemental essence itself.

When we look at an element, such as earth, and postulate that it is a building block of the planet, we are not speaking of the actual earth or ground. We are looking at its elemental essence. The elemental essence of Earth is its spiritual or life force energy, the raw primal essence of what creates the earth element. This is the actual energy that composes and creates the physical matter. This primal energy has a life force of its own and is composed of many different hierarchies of spiritual beings that come together as one soul essence. The element of earth, or the essence of earth energy, has one soul. Within that soul are many diverse spiritual beings simply created of essential earth energy These spiritual beings are the active life force of the earth element and help to make earth energy function. They range from micro-miniature and little "wee" beings an inch and a half or two inches tall to great gigantic earth beings half the size of a hill or a mountain. All of these elemental creatures belong to the essence of earth.

These beings are made entirely of one, and only one, type of energy. Although they might have lively personalities and different forms of dress, they are really created from one element. When they die, they return to the elemental life force stream of energy and consciousness of the earth elemental.

The elementals have what we would call one soul or spirit for the entire realm of that element. So, although you might see or be lucky or talented enough to speak with several elemental creatures as separate entities, they are actually all interconnected through one soul. And when they die or pass on, they return completely to the elemental whole.

Humans are a complex combination of higher spirit and the four elements. Humans have spirit encased in a body composed of the four elements of matter. We are considered balanced entities. And the more balanced we are or become, the more spiritually-advanced we are considered to be. We have individual souls and therefore when we physically die, we continue on as spiritual beings. Elementals are all connected to one group soul of their elemental group form and when they die, they do not continue on with individual consciousness. They merge into the group mass, much as water flows into the ocean, to return to their group soul of Earth, Air, Fire, or Water.

It is the element's essence, and its oversoul, that controls the manifestations on the physical plane. As an energy worker and planetary healer it is the essence of earth, air, fire, or water that you need to communicate with to heal or affect changes to the planet. So, if you were working on cleaning the air, you would be working with the element of air, the actual essence of air. And you would be communicating with the elementals, the creatures that create, make up, and direct the element of air. Since these creatures are pieces of one whole and have one soul or spirit, you would try to communicate with the highest air elemental in the hierarchy, the actual manager or director of the element to assist you. This elemental manager would communicate your wishes and direct the others in moving the energy around.

When you think of a creature made of entirely one and only one element, you will see that it contains only its own elemental essence. Although these beings may appear in human or animal form (ranging in size from tiny to huge) they really are only composed of one essence. They are surrounded by the essence of their medium and therefore they can only communicate within that essence. For example, earth elementals communicate with other earth elementals and are not aware of water elementals. Air spirits communicate with one another but would not communicate with earth, water or fire spirits. Each is contained totally within its own medium or element, it is their whole universe. The elementals behave as families or tribes and therefore stay within their own essence. Because we are a combination of all of the elements and have some of their consciousness within our makeup, we can communicate with each of these beings.

These elementals are not affected or destroyed by the earthly process of change or growth. Elementals are not affected by the material changes of earth, air, fire, and water. When they break down they do not really die. Instead they lose individual consciousness and are taken into the whole. They disintegrate back into the elemental form from which they were made and from which they came. Because the elementals are composed of only one element, they have no interaction and little degeneration. We humans, composed of a balance of the four elements, have friction that eventually causes wear and tear, and degeneration or break down of parts. The elementals have little of this degenerative process and so they often live many years beyond our earthly lives. Perhaps you remember from the tales and myths of your childhood of five generations of a family speaking with an elf or gnome or little wee man who always appeared wizened and elderly but lived on. This creature is an example of an earth elemental (the shortest living of the elementals) whose life could span many generations of humans. It is said that elementals have a life span of 300 to a 1,000 years or more.

EARTH ELEMENTALS

The element of earth is the most solid and stable of the elements. Earth represents the physical plane which is solid, dense, and somewhat fixed in space and time.

The creatures that make up the earth element are called Gnomes. This is a general catch-all term for many elementals that are grouped within the earth elemental level. Gnome appears to be derived from the Greek word *gnome* which means to have knowledge or to know, and the New Latin/French word *gnomus* which means to dwell in the earth.

Gnomes govern the care and well-being of the earth and have dominion over the rocks and boulders, stones, gems, minerals, trees, plants and flowers, and all that is made up of the earthly or material realm. They vibrate in harmony with the dense material of the earth. Some gnomes live in family groups while others are a part of the material they govern. Most gnomes are smaller than humans but there are some that govern mountains, ores, and minerals that are immense and cover a good part of a hillside or mountain. Sometimes they are the giants of our folklore. Gnome clothes appear as homespun rustic material or sometimes seem to be a part of the elemental that grows with him or her.

It is said that the gnomes are the easiest of the elementals to see and speak with because they are the most down to earth, the most dense, and the closest to humankind in stature and likeness.

I live in a rural part of the Santa Monica mountains and I see the earth elementals quite frequently. There are little wizened men with pointed hats and pointed shoes who look like miners or workers. There are creatures who inhabit the rocks and hillsides and appear as trolls or creatures with round bodies and big powerful heads. There are the dancing, happy, fairy-like creatures who cultivate the plants and the bushes and come whenever a chime or a bell is ringing in the wind. There are so many different types of elementals that although there are stereotypes, who look like elves from Santa's workshop, it is too tedious and time-consuming to describe them all. The elementals are as numerous and varied as the rocks and stones that make up the earth. They are intelligent, appear to eat a good deal, and only communicate with humans when you are in their path and they have little choice but to do so.

The earth elementals govern the interlacing matrices of crystal; the formation of gems; the making of mountains; the growing or cultivating of plants, bushes, trees, and the like; and the general overall creation of the physical planetary level.

These earth elementals existed on the planet long before the human race. They are the actual energy structure of the planet. Where you see and perceive elementals, the earth is alive and changing and growing within the organic balance of nature. Where you do not perceive the elementals, the earth has been taken over by the inertia of man, or covered with cement, and is deadened to the natural interaction of the elements. This area might be more "fixed" than Mother Nature would conceive. The elementals cannot exist without the freedom to "work" the planet in its changing form, so when I travel in to the city I see fewer elementals as people have covered the land and fixed its form.

The elemental beings used to be everywhere on the planet. Now they retreat from densely-populated areas, slowly losing ground and moving back into the wilderness. For many years the elementals would not work with nor acknowledge humans. They viewed humans as a destructive race that did not live in accordance or harmony with the higher laws. They have experienced human beings as discordant, unregulated, emotionally-restless creatures. Recently, however, they have come forward to communicate once more with the human race and would consider working with us to re-align nature into its rightful balance.

AIR ELEMENTALS

The element of air is the sense of movement, intelligence, and of the life-giving principle. Air carries life force to all living beings.

Air elementals are called Sylphs. Sylph is taken from the Greek *sylphe* which means butterfly because the Sylphs are often seen as tiny delicate creatures with silvery butterfly angelic wings. I have several friends who have noticed the air elementals and call them "tiny fairies" or "tinkerbells." Often these creatures are winged translucent beings that seem to flutter by quickly like hummingbirds.

Sylphs live totally in the medium of air and have the highest vibration of all of the elementals. Sylphs can be as large as humans but are usually much smaller. They usually appear as winged fairy-like creatures able to change form at will. They are quick, joyful, and somewhat eccentric in nature.

The Sylphs work with the winds and gather the clouds and interact with all manner of gases. Because they clean the air of the planet, the ancients called them the spirits of the air.

Many people contact the air elementals in their dreams when they envision themselves as flying. Some children who have the desire to fly often have air elementals around them. The children unconsciously believe that they can fly like the beautiful ethereal creatures they perceive flying around them. Unfortunately, this is not the case.

I look for the Sylphs on hot windy days when I leave the front door of my home open and the wind blows through and causes my indoor wind chimes to move. Sometimes I will see the air elementals dancing around the chimes in a swirling motion. They always seem joyous and it lightens my heart to watch them. They seem attracted to glass or wood or very delicate chimes that are easy for them to move and produce high-pitched sounds. Of course, there are also air elementals that cause tornadoes and wind storms and these seem larger, more serious, and somewhat dour. Instead of being playful they are being destructive and showing a force of power. Generally, however, the Sylphs are high spirited and will fill you with the love of song and dance if you contact them.

Sylphs are the most difficult of elementals to communicate with because they have such a high ethereal aerial vibration. Most humans take little notice of them at all. They are friendly, however, and if you take the time and effort to communicate with them they might instruct you how to hone or sharpen your creative mind and thought processes.

THE FIRE ELEMENTALS

The element of fire is seen as the power of expansion, the element of action, the giver of heat, the keeper of spirit, and the expression of will.

The fire elementals are called Salamanders. Where the term Salamander came from is still an enigma. The ancients viewed the Salamander as a spirit which dwelt in fire. They described the Salamanders as lizard- or dragon-like in shape and glowing with the heat and color of fire. They always perceived these creatures in the hottest and densest part of the fire, within or on the glowing coals. Fire spirits were also seen as balls of light hovering over the fields and tongues of light dancing over the waters.

The fire elementals are perceived as the strongest and most powerful of all the elementals. The fire elementals govern all fire and heat and transmutation by fire on the planet.

If you sit in front of a wood or coal fire long enough you might be able to see the elemental fire spirits, the Salamanders, writhing and crawling like lizards or newts with tongues of fire curling from them. People usually see these creatures in the hottest part of the fire. Humans have always had this fascination with watching a fire and it is my belief that this is because we unconsciously are taking notice of the fire elementals as they move throughout their medium.

Fire elementals work through the emotional and passionate levels in animals and men. They govern the intestines, the internal organs, and the blood stream. They control and work through heat as change.

The Salamanders are difficult to communicate with and, because they are the element of pure fire, can be dangerous to humans. They can be uncontrollable and are not to be taken for granted in any given situation.

THE WATER ELEMENTALS

The element of water is the power of fertility, the practice of love, and the giver of emotions. It is expandable and contractible in its nature.

The water elementals are called Undines, which is derived from the Latin word *unda* which means waves, because the Undines are spirits of the waves. Every body of water was seen as having its own type of water spirit—the fountain or brook had its nymph, the sea its mermaids, and the ocean its oceanids. These water elementals often took their name from the body of water that they inhabited.

Undines are seen as beings of great grace and beauty, as being very Venusian in nature. Some people see these beings as the size of humans and others see them as barely two or three inches in height. Usually Undines have appeared as females and so we have many myths and stories of fishermen who have seen or even coaxed a mermaid to visit them, although she could not leave her watery element too long or she would die.

Undines are considered to be very emotional in nature and to be friendly towards humans. They spend a good deal of their time frolicking and playing in the water and the waves and caring for all manner of plants and growing things. You might easily learn to see water elementals in your garden when you are watering it or at the ocean as they dance in the waves. The elementals used to come in quite close to shore, but now, because of the polluted beaches, they seem to move further and further out into the ocean making it harder to see them and even more difficult to get them to help clean the water close to shore.

When I first moved to the Santa Monica Mountains I came home one evening to feel a dampness in the air and a mist surrounding the house. In the watery mist were hundreds of dancing, swimming water elementals. I was surprised to see them so far inland as we are at least eight miles in from the beach. It seems they travel in on the ocean air currents that flood through the canyons at night and in the early mornings. It is fun to watch the Undines and I have greatly enjoyed their evening visits.

THE AKASHIC REALM OF SPIRIT

The elementals of earth, air, fire, and water are specific spiritual creatures that some people can see and hear. They are the innate creatures of Mother Nature and it is their job to be the builder and disintegrator, to be the worker of their particular element in life. Akashic energy is pure energy. It is the spark of life force that fills all living beings with the very essence of being alive. Akashic energy has no form, no shape, and no identity. It is the catalyst that impels all other beings to live and change. You could theoretically and philosophically liken the nature of Akashic energy to that of the soul. A human body is not truly alive until the soul arrives and fills the body with life. Akashic energy is part of that soul spark that charges the body with that very special life force that makes the difference between just existing and living.

You can get in touch with Akashic energy by doing a meditation that channels your Higher Self and pure energy through your body. As you learn to get in touch with this energy you will find that you feel more alive, more dynamic, and more charged in life.

"Sit down before fact like a little child, and be prepared to give up every preconceived notion, follow humbly wherever and to whatever abyss Nature leads, or you shall learn nothing."

— *T.H. Huxley*

6

TOOLS
TO USE

To be able to heal the environment spiritually we must understand how to reach the internal side of ourselves as well as the inner core of planetary awareness. To do this we need skills. This book contains a set of simple and easy-to-use skills that show you how to access that wonderful, awesome range of internal visionary capacity that opens the doorway to inner (spiritual) and outer (physical) action.

In order to be an energy worker who heals the planet, you must be able to be grounded within your own self, be able to center yourself, to keep focused upon your particular project, and be able to clear yourself of any extraneous or powerful emotions that clog your productivity. As a planetary healer you must also be able to plug into the archetypal levels of planetary awareness as well as make a connection with the life force energy that charges all of us. This seems like a tall order! But it is possible to accomplish, without effort, and with total consciousness of your actions and your accomplishments.

The latter chapters in this book explain how the planetary energy system works and what you can do as an energy worker to clear and cleanse it. The simple skills described in the following chapters will show you how to help heal the planet we live on, and how to heal yourself.

The tools in this book can be used by anyone, no matter how you define yourself. Whether you see yourself as a spiritual person or an ecologically-concerned person, you can take the skills in this book and use them to make your life work more smoothly and to help heal our planet Earth. These skills do not conflict with any religion or spiritual belief system that you practice or follow. Many of the tools and skills in this book are gleaned from the ancient practices of our ancestors as they learned to integrate their spirit or life force with their abilities to gather nuts and berries, hunt, and develop agriculture to sustain their bodies and souls.

Unlike our present culture, in which everything is divided or "specialized", our "primitive" ancestors communicated with each aspect of life force as they encountered it throughout their lives. They spoke to the spirit of the trees; to the wee deva creatures that helped them to cultivate their crops; to the elemental beings of air to bring wind to pollinate; to the beings of water to bring rain to quench the thirst of their plants; to the spirit of Oneness, or God, on the planet as represented as the goddess and god of the earth and sky to nurture, shelter, and protect them; and to the spirit of nature itself to revitalize them. These skills of interacting with the "energy forms" of the very matter of life itself have not been lost. To some extent they are a part of every religion and spiritual practice that we have today. In some religions they are obvious, while in others they are masked in liturgy and gently removed by history. But they do exist. They are presented once again in this book to remind us that, as an evolving race of humans, we can be in touch with our roots—the very nature of our spiritual and physical beings. We can use these skills to create a unified body of thought and action, a sphere of reference that allows us to perceive and become one with the system of interactive Nature.

The tools in this book are invaluable if you use them. They give you the doorway to the physical and natural realm of humankind evolving as a spiritual self on this planet. They give you the ability to interact with the very cellular and structural nature of physical life. These tools also give you the ability to interact with your own inner nature in a practical way to accomplish specific goals that actually have merit outside of your thoughts. They give you the techniques to enable you to accomplish the goal of the integration of spirit and matter—to heal yourself and the planet Earth.

"In a gentle way, you can shake the world."

—*Mahatma Gandhi*

7

GROUNDING

Your connection with the earth is what makes your body feel real and sustained by its environment. It is also this connection that gives you the ability to be powerful enough to affect and change your environment. When you have made this earth connection, you suddenly have the power of the entire planet to back you up and nourish you. You literally become an extension of the planetary earth force.

Many people go to the woods or the wilderness to try and regain this earth connection that they sense they lose in the urban environment of cement, cars, and big buildings. But you cannot always run off for a weekend of camping, or take a hike in the wilds, or a walk through the woods to sustain your yearning soul when you really need to experience that wonderful solidity of the earth and nature. However, you can learn to use a simple skill, called Grounding, to enable yourself to feel in touch with the earth, empowered by its solidity, and able to function and deal with the 20th century urban environment. Grounding enables you to channel the entire strength of the planet—which is quite useful as an energy worker.

Grounding gives you the ability to create your own reality, to bring your spiritual nature down to earth in order to create a happy, healthy, balanced lifestyle that works for you. Grounding is the ability to make life "real" for yourself. As you learn to make a connection between your self, your body, and the planet, you become able to bring in higher information from your spiritual self into your body to use on a practical everyday level. Grounding empowers you with the ability to still (calm) yourself and know what is right for you in any given situation. The process of grounding also teaches you to be more aware and loving of your primary vehicle on this planet—your body. It is your body that enables you to experience and enjoy life's pleasures.

Without a body we can not use our senses. We can not see, hear, taste, feel, touch, or smell the physical world unless we have a physical vehicle through which to work. It is the act of bringing the spiritual self into the physical body that enables you to actualize your dreams and hone your awareness to a usable state. With your spirit in your body you can begin to access your knowledge and ability to heal the planet.

Grounding is a very simple skill to learn but it is also a very powerful one to know and use. YOUR ABILITY TO GROUND IS YOUR ABILITY TO MAKE YOUR LIFE WORK FOR YOU.

METHODS OF GROUNDING

The ancient method of Grounding was to imagine roots growing from your feet into the earth and reaching deep into the earth and holding onto it. This method works, but it does not work as well as the newer method described later in this chapter. Having roots from your feet grounds your body but it does not completely ground the entire energy system of your body. The newer method of using a grounding cord grounds the entire energy system (chakra system) for you. If you have worked with an older method of Grounding using the root system, you might want to add this newer method to your repertoire.

Some spiritual people have told me that they do not "need" grounding at all! But I have found that if you wish to be connected to the planet, you will also want to learn how to be attached to it and how to understand that you truly are a **part** of it. Grounding gives your body the stability of knowing you truly have the entire power of the Earth behind you and that your physical body is really an expression of the earthly plane.

The following exercise is the newer more modern method of Grounding. I hope you find it interesting and usable on a daily level.

 EXERCISE – GROUNDING

Find yourself a chair with a straight back that you can sit in and have your feet solidly reach the floor. Now, make yourself comfortable. Loosen any tight clothing. Remove your shoes so that your feet make a solid connection with the ground. Take a nice deep breath and relax.

At the base of the spine in men and a little further forward between the ovaries in women, is an energy center we call the First or Root Chakra. Your First Chakra is about the size of a 50-cent piece. *(Chakra is a Sanskrit word that means spinning wheel. It is called this because as you view a chakra from the front it appears as a spinning wheel! The Chakras are shaped like a cone of energy and they are positioned in your body with the base in the front of you and the point at the back of you. Chakras spin simultaneously in two different directions. Chakras are very powerful vortexes of energy that bring in and send out information and energy.)* Now, be aware of your First Chakra for a moment and then connect a cord of energy to the bottom of your First Chakra and send it down, through the chair, through the floor, through the ground, all the way down to the very center of the Earth and hook it on to the center of the Earth. This cord of energy can be like a beam of light that goes down to the center of the Earth and encircles it or like a big redwood tree that has roots that reach down to the center of the Earth and hook on to it, or a chain with an anchor, or a cat's tail that hooks onto the center of the Earth, or whatever works for you. Your grounding cord is your lifeline to the planet.

Perceive for yourself what it "feels" like to be "grounded." You may feel heavier or denser or different. You may be more aware of your body or your energy field. You may feel some tension in your body. If you do feel tension, just send it down your grounding cord. Whatever you send down your grounding cord will go down to the center of the Earth and become neutralized. If it is someone else's energy or problem it will go back to them once it reaches the center of the Earth. If it is your own energy manifested as tension, it will come back to you in a new and more usable form. Any energy you send down your grounding cord to the center of the Earth will go back to it's original source, wherever it came from.

Having a grounding cord for your body and your energy field is similar to having a lightning rod on a house. As you use your grounding cord it will drain off any excess energy from you, as well as releasing anyone else's energy that is in your space.

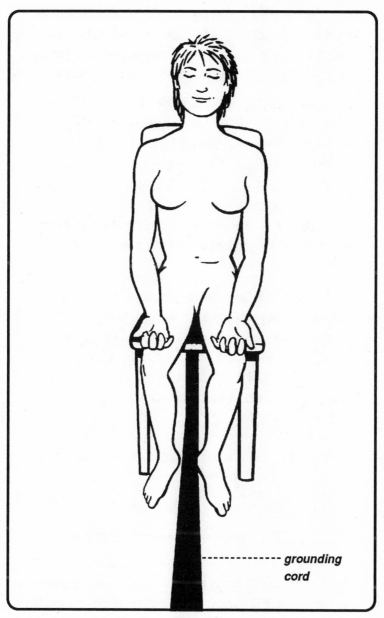

grounding
cord

Grounding

Take a nice deep breath and look at your grounding cord. What kind of grounding cord have you created? Is it thin and wispy like a cord on a balloon or is it big and strong like a redwood tree? What kind of grounding makes you feel real, safe, and functionable?

Take another deep breath and send all of your tension, any effort and any emotions, feelings or thoughts you are holding onto down your grounding cord to the center of the Earth. Feel your body as it is stabilized by your grounding cord. Your grounding will automatically bring your body and your energy into present time, a creative mode of the here and now! It will enable you to channel your own higher spiritual self through and into your body so you can then access information about the planet and the system that balances it.

Grounding can be done anywhere and at any time. An ideal state would be to have your body grounded **all** of the time and have your spiritual self grounded through your body. You do not have to be sitting in a chair to put a grounding cord down from your First Chakra to the center of the Earth. When you wake up in the morning you can put down a grounding cord and use it throughout the day, at work and at play. Your grounding cord will tell your body that it is safe and secure and that it is part of the cellular planetary essence and that it is all right to bring in higher forms of information from your spiritual self and to access the planetary memory banks.

Many people never really bring their spiritual self **into** their bodies. The spiritual being sits on their shoulder, over their head, behind their body, or sometimes off in the distance. The farther away your spiritual self is from your body on a daily basis, the less direct contact and communication you can have with your body and the planet Earth. Grounding enables you to bring the higher sense of your Self—the advanced spiritual side of yourself—directly into your body. It allows you to experience the God Within Yourself, or what some people call the God of Your Heart. It also allows you to experience a sense of being whole or connected to the planet, of being a part of the balanced energy system rather than standing apart from it.

When we stand apart from the system we tend to try to control it. As we are learning, it is not wise to try to control Mother Nature. We do not always have the ability to see the whole picture. As we become a part of the system we will "go with the flow of energy" and learn to channel the energy that needs to move and recharge the system. We will learn to work in accordance with the stream of life instead of believing that we can totally direct it. It is grounding that gives us that direct connection between spirit, mind, body, and the body of the Earth that is the whole system of which we are an integral part.

"I think that it is a great achievement to put a man on the moon, but to put a man on the earth—that is even more."

—*Harrison Salisbury*

8

BEING
CENTERED

Now that you have grounded your body, the next step is to bring your Higher Self, your Spiritual Being, into your body to become "centered." But where do you bring the spiritual being into the body? Do you sit your consciousness in your foot, in your elbow, in your emotions, in your throat, in your mind, or where? Where can you place your spirit that is bilateral, so that you can be centered and neutral, so that you do not have to constantly feel the effects of raging emotions and thoughts?

There is only one neutral space in the body that has no energy channelling through it. It is almost as if Mother Nature purposely created this empty space for your Higher Self to occupy. We call this spot the Center of The Head. If you took an x-ray of your head you would actually see this totally clear empty cavity. Every other space in your body is busy as energy channels through your body and creates your life experiences. In this empty spot, which just happens to be situated bilaterally and in the center of your head, you can access true inner peace and enlightenment.

The following is an easy exercise for finding the Center of Your Head.

  ## EXERCISE – FINDING THE CENTER OF YOUR HEAD

Take your hands and place them at the top of your ears and draw an imaginary line across your head from one hand to the other — from the top of one ear to the other. Now put one hand in front of you at your forehead and place the other hand directly behind you at the back of your head and draw another imaginary line through your head to connect your hands. Where the two lines intersect is the Center of Your Head.

LOOKING FROM ABOVE

Now, be in the Center of Your Head. Yes, just take a deep breath, close your eyes, and place your entire consciousness in the Center of Your Head.

Look around in the Center of Your Head. This should be an empty space! And it should belong entirely to you and you alone! Whoever is in the area we call the Center of Your Head is able to consciously control the entire body. So, turn on all of the lights in the Center of Your Head and view your space. Is there anyone else in there with you? Often you will find a friend, relative, parent, or child sitting in the Center of Your Head. If you do find someone, say hello to them and send them back to their bodies.

From the Center of Your Head you receive all of your spiritual or higher information as it comes down into the body and you also receive all of your body or lower information. As your spiritual self sits in the Center of Your Head you can "feel" your body, as well as "knowing" your intuitive and transformational information.

Bring a large golden sun above you and let it come down into the Center of Your Head. As it fills the Center of Your Head with its radiant energy, own the Center of Your Head and bring it into present time. To own the Center of Your Head is to know and claim this space as yours. It is created for you and only you to live in.

Sitting in the Center of Your Head could be likened to sitting in the cockpit of the plane so that you can **view** your voyage in life clearly. When you are in your body, being in the Center of Your Head puts you in the driver's seat.

When you have placed your consciousness directly in the Center of Your Head you might see a golden bright light. This is sometimes called the state of enlightenment.

When people walk through life grounded and centered, they walk with gracefulness, bearing, and purpose because they are moving from their internal center. As you walk through life grounded and centered, you are bringing your consciousness into your body to be one with your Higher Self, innately in tune with the information of the planet with which you are biologically and spiritually connected.

Some people discover the Center of Their Head quite easily and find being centered very comfortable. Others have never been there before and need time to adjust to having a whole new ability and perspective. Do not confuse the Center of Your Head with your mind! The Center of Your Head is a very neutral space where you place your Higher Being's consciousness and experience peace and spiritual oneness. The analytical mind is your computer that enables you to process information and make rational judgements. The mind enables you to analyze a situation. Being in the Center of Your Head allows you to use all of your higher intuitional ability to know what works for you.

Being in the Center of Your Head gives you focus, inner peace, intuition, higher knowledge, expanded awareness, clear communication and knowledge of spirit, and the ability to communicate with the planet Earth. Whenever you are awake and in your body you can be in the Center of Your Head.

With this basic skill you have the key to inner peace, the ability to see clearly, and the chance to be in touch with the whole picture.

From the Center of Your Head you do not have to think, to look, to listen, to judge, to consider, or feel…you can just be one with yourself, the planet Earth, and the universe.

9

DEVELOPING CLARITY BY CLEARING YOUR ENERGY

One valuable skill for learning to develop clarity and being able to clear your energy field is that of Running Energy. Running Energy is a simple intuitive skill to bring your Higher Self into your body and to help you clear and cleanse your energy field. It can be a meditation for changing the quality of your life. It can also enable you to reduce stress, learn to relax, develop focus, increase your self esteem and self awareness to heal yourself and the planet and, of course, to develop your higher spiritual awareness.

As you learn the process of Running Energy you will develop a simple yet clear and powerful connection between the Earth and your physical body, your personality, your mind, and your Higher Self. This connection between spirit, body, and the planet will enable you to actualize your ability as a planetary healer as well as opening you up to your own higher awareness.

Running Energy is like taking an energy shower. It cleans up the extraneous, old, or stuck energy that you might be acting through and gives you a set of clean energy clothes to wear. As you run your life force energy through your energy field (your Aura) it cleanses it of unnecessary and old concepts and of foreign energy. The energy running through your arms clears your healing and creative energy. The energy running through your legs enables you to put thought into motion and act upon your ideas.

The Running Energy meditation is the process of combining cosmic and earth energies. These neutral energies become your own essence as you allow them to run through your energy field. Running Energy is an altered state of consciousness that produces a light trance state. By Running Energy for twenty to thirty minutes a day you can clean out your entire energy system— your Chakras and your Aura—without any effort.

You will always wish to remain consciously awake and aware when you Run Energy as it is an "in the body" meditation.

MEDITATION –
RUNNING ENERGY

To begin "running energy" sit in a comfortable chair and allow yourself to feel at ease. Loosen any tight clothing. Remove your shoes and put your feet flat on the ground. Now, use your newly-learned techniques and put a grounding cord down from the bottom of your First Chakra, through the chair, through the floor, through the ground, all the way down to the center of the earth and hook it to the center of the earth. Now **be** in the Center of Your Head. Turn on all of the lights in the Center of Your Head and make sure that no one else's consciousness is in there with you. Take a nice, deep breath. Say hello to your body. See who says hello back. If anyone else says hello back send them over to their own body. Now you have started a clear communication between your spirit, your personality-ego-mind, and your body.

In the soles of your feet are energy centers called Foot Chakras. They open and close like the iris of an eye or the lens of a camera. Be aware of your Foot Chakras and open them up to a place that seems comfortable for you. Then conceptualize bringing up about 15% earth energy through your feet, up your legs, through your thighs, into your First Chakra and down your grounding cord. You can visualize the earth energy as being whatever color that is comfortable for you. You have now formed what is called an inverted U. Now, keep this inverted U of earth energy constantly running.

Earth energy is very powerful and you only need enough to give yourself a sense of being grounded so please do not use more than 15%. Your Spiritual Self is able to exactly measure the percentage of energy your request, so if you request 15% you will get 15%.

This earth energy will give you solidity and strength. It will also clean out your leg channels. This is important since when you conceive of a project or activity it is your legs that take the energy and manifest your ideas into reality. As you run energy through your legs you are cleaning the channels so there is a more instant communication between your **will** and your **activity**.

At the top of your head is an energy center called your Crown Chakra. It also opens and closes like the iris of an eye or the lens of a camera. While keeping the earth energy running in the inverted U configuration, be aware of your Crown Chakra (but keep your consciousness in the Center of Your Head) and open it. Imagine your Crown Chakra opening up as a spiral to a place that is comfortable for you and then allow about 85% soft, golden

91

cosmic energy to come down through your Crown Chakra, along the back of your spine, and into your First Chakra. In your First Chakra the soft golden cosmic energy mixes with the earth energy coming up your legs. As the two forms of energy mix together, they create a natural reaction and form a pumping movement which propels the mixture of energy up the front of your spine and back out your head and Crown Chakra where it fountains out into your Aura. Some of the energy branches off and moves across your shoulders and down your arms and out of the palms of your hands. To release the energy through the palms of your hands, open up your Hand Chakras (they open as spirals). Some of the energy goes back down your legs and out your feet. Let any excess energy go down your grounding cord. Now keep this energy constantly running through you.

In the beginning the process of Running Energy may seem difficult or like doing three different things at once. As you practice this method of Clearing you will find that it becomes easier.

When you are just beginning to learn the Running Energy meditation, you should only practice it for five or ten minutes at a time. When you wish to stop the meditation, bend over and stretch and drop your head and arms toward the ground and let any excess energy flow from the top of your head and your shoulders to run out into the ground. This process is called Dumping Energy. Often when you practice the Running Energy meditation, excess energy will collect at the top of your head or on your shoulders. Dumping Energy empties you of excess energy and enables this extra energy to return to the Earth. Now sit back up in the chair, open your eyes, take a good look around yourself, and get your bearings. Since Running Energy is an altered state of consciousness, you want to bring yourself back to "normal" when you have finished before you go on to doing something else.

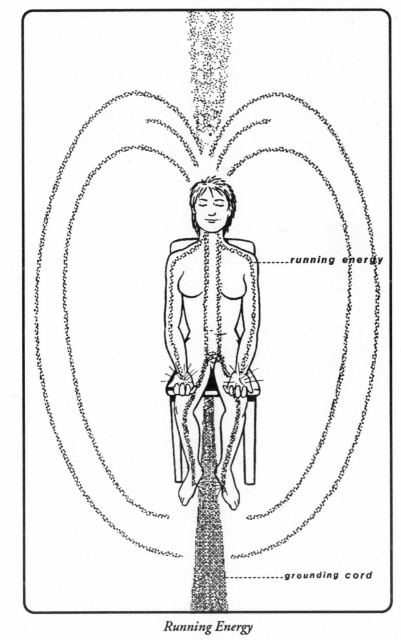

running energy

grounding cord

Running Energy

Running Energy allows you to raise the energy vibration of your body so that your Higher Self can communicate more easily through it. As you learn the meditation of Running Energy you might notice that many things in life seem simpler and easier to accomplish since Running Energy moves out other people's energy, ideas, and concepts. This cleaning and clearing meditation allows you to have more space in your own energy field to use for your own perceptions.

Running Energy will open up your system to a new awareness. It is a very safe method of opening and clearing your energy system as long as you are aware of and use these methods:

1. Always practice the Running Energy meditation in a safe place where you feel comfortable since it "opens" you up.

2. Always practice the Running Energy meditation while you are sitting in a chair with your feet firmly planted on the ground so that you are grounded.

3. Always finish the Running Energy meditation by "dumping" your excess energy flow into the ground. This last task of "dumping energy" is so that you can distinctly come out of the trance state and back to your normal awareness.

If you follow these basic guidelines you will find that Running Energy is a very powerful energizing means of opening up to your internal self, as well as your Higher Self, the planetary energy level, and to the Cosmic Oneness of which we are all a part.

As we learn the Running Energy meditation, how to be grounded and how to be in the Center of The Head, we begin to have to acknowledge the awesome truth...the truth that we have all been avoiding...that we are the spirit of God or the Cosmic Oneness walking on the planet. That each act we do in life has meaning and purpose as we move in harmony with the Higher Self. That our life is a great learning experience in the kindergarten of the earthly plane. That the power of spirit lends the radiant light of life force within us to fulfill not only our personal dreams and expectations but to fill our waking moments on Earth with the ecstasy of purpose and the knowledge that once you walk as one as spirit you are never alone...you are never lost...you are never just a human being. You are more than that. You are spirit eternal and as such you are a shining light in a sea of shining lights whose wholeness makes a gorgeous giant glowing sun as you become the light of life and knowledge for yourself and for everyone else around you.

*"To be awake is to be alive.
I have never yet met a man who
was quite awake."*

—Henry David Thoreau

10

THE EXERCISE
OF THE ROSE

By using the Exercise of the Rose you can learn to use your energy to focus, concentrate, and create visual images to achieve a desired end. The Exercise of the Rose is an invaluable tool for learning how to get in touch with your ability to create and direct energy in the internal archetypal stream of life so that you can move energy to heal the planet. We use the rose because it is a living image and an eternal symbol of love. Christian woodworkers would carve a symbol of the rose into the ceiling of their mystical lodges so that everyone would always meet under the symbol of love. As a living image, the rose can change and grow with you. It is a symbol of the eternal enfolding nature of the spiritual self. As you use this exercise on a daily level you will find that the rose you use can change and grow as you do.

 ## THE EXERCISE OF THE ROSE

Right out in front of you create a big beautiful rosebud. This rosebud is **your** creation. So you can create it as any color that would be pleasing to you. You could create a red rosebud or a lavender rosebud or a purple rosebud with pink polka dots. Make sure that you create a rosebud with a stem. If you like, make your stem with leaves and thorns. Now look at your rose. See if you can make it real for yourself. Can you smell your rose? Can you see any drops of water on it? Really take notice of what it looks like. You want to have your rose be real—so real that you could practically reach your hand out and grab it.

Slowly drink in the color of the rose and the texture of the petals and the strength of the stem. When you have the feeling and sense of it really existing out there in front of you, then ask your rosebud to begin to unfold. Slowly you should see the petals of your flower unfolding in front of you until the rose is a fully blossomed flower. It should be as if you are watching a camera filming a rose in your garden over a period of time as it buds and then blossoms. In full bloom, it is at it's full beauty and glory and at the height of its perfection.

Each thing that we create in life we must also destroy. It is a natural process of energy on the planet. It is built into the form of the ecological system.

So, look at your fully blossomed rose in its radiant glory. See it getting older and beginning to droop and wither. Slowly see your rose withering and wasting away and dropping its petals. As it begins to decay, you can see it disintegrate right in front of you until all of it, the stem, the leaves, and the petals that have dropped, as well as the core of the rose, turn to a fine dust that, too, finally dissolves totally into the air from which it came. This is the natural law of the planet, the law of creation and destruction.

By creating your rose you are using your innate creative ability to create and focus on a living and loving symbol. By seeing your rose you are using your spiritual clairvoyant ability. (Clairvoyancy means "clair" for clear, "voyancy" for seeing; the ability to see colors, pictures, or energy on your internal movie screen.) By smelling and sensing your rose you are tuning in to your ability to use your elemental senses. By destroying your rose you are allowing yourself to "let go" of your creation and to understand that the chain of life on this planet is built on the unalterable sequence of creation and destruction. As you destroy your rose you are allowing yourself to experience the transformation or exchange of energy from one form to another.

On a physical plane, we see the law of creation and destruction when we pop a kernel of corn into popcorn or when we cook scrambled eggs or make ice cubes. On the energy plane, we perceive this when we have an emotional release or when we create a rose and then destroy it, knowing full well that we can always create it again.

The Exercise of the Rose is a technique that you can play with every day. All you need is a few spare moments to view your rose. You will find that if you use this technique regularly you will begin to have a finely tuned sense of focus and you will be able to see, hear, smell, and touch your rose. Once you have developed these elemental abilities you will be able to use them as an energy worker to rebalance the elemental energies around you on the planet.

There is a percentage of people who have difficulty visualizing. If you are one of these people I would recommend that you get a rose and put it in a vase and place that vase where you can view it a few times a day. Each time that you look at that vase create a duplicate of the rose in your mind's eye next to the rose in the vase. Within the week you will have witnessed and practiced the process of the rose unfolding and blossoming. Within the next week you will have seen and practiced the process of the rose withering away and disintegrating back into the life force from whence it came. Each time you look at the rose create your own rose next to it. By doing this, eventually you will find that you can create or "visualize" your rose easily and without effort. I have found that repetitive simple exercises such as the one given here can teach you to visualize easily.

"In every age there is a turning point, a new way of seeing and asserting the coherence of the world."

— Jacob Bronowski

11

SELF TRANSFORMATION

Self transformation is the process of changing energy. This chapter is an exercise in learning how to transform energy to change yourself and the world around you.

EXERCISE –
SELF TRANSFORMATION

First of all, find yourself a comfortable chair to sit in so that you can keep your back fairly straight and have your feet solidly reaching the ground. Take off your shoes, loosen any tight clothing, take a deep breath, and relax. Now close your eyes. Take another deep breath and say hello to yourself. Let yourself be right here, in the here and now, in that wonderful creative space we call present time. Create a grounding cord from your First Chakra down to the center of the earth and hook it on. Now be in the Center of Your Head. That's right, just take all of your conscious energy and put it directly in the Center of Your Head. Now you are ready to begin to allow yourself to transform any stuck patterns, concepts, or emotions that you hold.

We are going to explore the world of creation and destruction, the constant interchange of the energy flow on this planet. First of all, you are going to create something. Right out in front of you, in front of and outside of your Aura (the life force energy around your body), create a big, beautiful, gorgeous rose. Your rose can be any color you choose. It can have a stem, and, if you wish, it can have leaves and thorns. You are using your ability to create on an energy level, so have fun and create the color rose you like and want. Your rose might be completely open or it might be half opened or a nearly formed rosebud.

Now look at your rose. That's right. Really take a good look at the rose you have created with your energy. If you can see your rose, then you are a clairvoyant, a person who can see images and energy. Now, create a stick of dynamite under your rose and blow up your rose into tiny little particles of energy. If, after you blow up your rose, you see it has pieces of someone else's energy then send everyone else's energy back to them. Just give it a push and say "go home" and it will go back to wherever it came from originally. Now bring all of your energy back to you as a giant golden sun above your head and let it come in and fill up your Aura and own it.

Your ability to create something is a wonderful gift. But you also have the ability to destroy that energy because you know that you can use it to create again. And you can probably create something even more beautiful the second time around. Creation and destruction is a natural process on this planet. So, what we create we can destroy because we can create it once more. Transforming the rose and destroying it is like taking a kernel of corn and making popcorn or a glass of water and making ice cubes or a raw egg and making a fried egg. It is using our ability to change or transform energy.

Very often we will find patterns stuck in our energy field, such as old belief systems, old ways of doing things, and old patterns in relationships, that hold us back. These old energy patterns happen when we store our energy in a fixed form. We can release this energy and let go of our old patterns and beliefs by simply allowing ourselves to blow them up. Once we have released the energy in our old patterns and beliefs we can bring the energy of these old patterns back as new life force energy and have more energy with which to explore and create our life experience.

Let's try it again. Take a deep breath. And create a big, beautiful, rose out in front of you, outside of your Aura (your life force energy field). Right now, place everything in your life that does not allow you to be happy, healthy, wealthy, wise, and at peace with yourself into the center of your rose. Put all of these things right into the very center of your rose. Put all of the "mind chatter" that stops you from being able to meditate, focus, or concentrate effectively into your rose also. Make sure that everything you put into your rose is truly in the very center of it. Make your rose as large as you need it to be to contain everything you place in the center of it. It can even be as large as the planet if you need to have a giant rose.

Now, put a stick of dynamite under your rose and blow up your rose into tiny little particles of energy. If you find other people's energy released from the explosion then send everyone else's energy back to them. Just tell it to return to its original energy source and give it a push and it will go back to wherever it came. Now, bring all of your energy back to you as a giant golden sun above your head and let the sun come in and fill in your Aura.

Create another rose in front of you and outside of your Aura and place your mother inside of the rose. This will not harm her—I would never give you a technique that would harm anyone—this actually might help her. By placing a person in the rose you are enabling yourself to let go of any of their energy that might be in your space. As that energy gets sent back to them, they receive more of their own life force energy to use. This is like giving them a healing. Often we find our mother's energy in our space because she was the one who spent the most time teaching and disciplining us to learn the basics of life on a physical body level. Having someone else's energy in your space can be like putting leaded gasoline into a car that only runs on unleaded gasoline. Your mother loved you and meant well, but having her energy in your space left you with an imprint that continually tells you to do things the way she would have done it. Each one of us is unique and different. On this planet variety is the spice of life. What your mother would eat or the clothes she would wear or what type of music she might enjoy works for her, but it might not be what you want or desire in your life.

Each one of us is unique and have our own life path to walk. By putting your mother in a rose and blowing up her image, you allow yourself to transform any of her energy that is in your Aura, your energy centers, or your physical body into neutral life force energy and return it to her. So, blow up your rose with your mother in it and if you find other people's energy released from the explosion send everyone else's energy back to them and return all of your life force energy back to you as a giant sun above your head and let it come in and fill in your Aura, your energy field.

You can put anything into a rose—your argument with your lover, a bad feeling you hold onto, a nostalgic memory that makes you feel sad, something that makes you angry, and any programs or patterns that tell you "You can't have" or "You can't be." Anything that you put into a rose and blow up will be transformed into new and neutral life force energy. This new and neutral energy frees you so that you do not repeat the same old patterns and programs or sit stuck in old beliefs. You can even put a pain that is in your body, a physical pain, into a rose and blow it up. Physical pain in your body is there for a reason. It is there to tell you that there is a problem. Sometimes you need to know this. But other times you do not need to hang on to your pain. Suppose you stub your toe on a chair. Your toe will hurt. Once you acknowledge this hurt and check to see that there is no major damage, you do not need to keep experiencing this pain. You can put your pain into a rose and blow up the rose. By blowing up your rose and de-energizing your pain, you will easily let go of at least 80% of your pain. If you really stubbed your toe pretty hard you might have to blow up your pain five, ten, or twenty times before you can totally de-energize it. There is no reason in life to experience pain once you know the reason for its existence. You can blow it up in a rose and let go of it! You are the person in charge of creating your reality. And if you do not wish to have pain, or an old sadness or emotion or memory running through you, all you have to do is put it in a rose and blow it up.

Blowing up roses can be fun and quite invigorating. You can put anything in a rose and blow it up and transform the stuck energy or pattern that you hold onto into neutral life force energy. Each time you blow up a rose remember to put whatever you are blowing up into the very center of the rose and to blow up the rose into tiny little particles of energy so that you know it is transformed. Also be sure to send everyone else's energy back to them and to bring all of your energy back to you as a golden sun above your head and let it come in and fill in your Aura.

You can blow up a rose and transform your patterned or stuck energy into new life force energy all day long, at work and at play. Whenever someone says something to you that causes you to react, you can put it in a rose and blow it up. As you use this skill on a daily basis you will find that you become more neutral in your dealings with people. As you keep blowing up charged feelings or issues in a rose, you will stop being the reaction of the people and the world around you. Each time you blow up an emotion, feeling, or concept in a rose you are transforming your patterned life force energy into free and neutral energy that you can use to create more of the reality that you would like to have.

Too often we concentrate on the negative, on what we do not want, on what we do not like. Often, if you ask someone what he or she wants in life, he will tell you what he does not want. You get what you put your energy into. If you feed the negative—your doubts, fears and dislikes—then that is what your energy is tied up in and that becomes your reality. If you put these emotions in a rose and blow them up and release them, then you can go on to put the positive reality in front of you and create what you really want in life. You can create a positive reality with free and neutral energy.

"Not til we are Lost, in other words,
Not til we have Lost the world, do we
begin to find ourselves."

— Henry David Thoreau

12

REBALANCING
YOUR SELF

As we become aware that all things on the planet are created out of the elemental building blocks of earth, air, water, and fire, then we can begin to take notice of how we can balance these elements within ourselves and for the planet. Before we begin to work on planetary balancing, we first must begin to understand how these essential elemental forces work. One of the best ways of learning the process of working with elemental forces is to learn to balance the elemental qualities within ourselves.

To heal the planet we will be using the ancient spiritual concept known as the Hermetic principle: "As above, so below." This principle is based on the modern scientific concept of microcosm/macrocosm. For our purposes, the microcosm is the little world of the human being (the physical body, the astral body, the Aura, and soul). The macrocosm is the larger world of the universe and the planet, Mother Earth. The microcosm (the human being) and the macrocosm (the planet and the universe) have similarities and are inter-connected. They each have the ability to resonate with and affect one another. This interconnection is represented by the six-pointed star, called a hexagram, consisting of two triangles interlaced with one another. The six pointed star is used to illustrate all of the elements in harmony and balance.

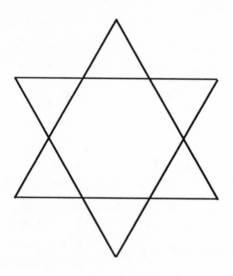

Six-Pointed Star

Energy workers have learned through the centuries that we can affect the macrocosm by changing the microcosm. Or simply put, we can change reality by changing our internal actions. This is not just changing how we think or perceive, but actually changing what we do with our life force energy. This is more than the power of positive thinking in action, it is the power of moving your spirit to be aligned with the way you wish things to be. To the 20th century person this can be a difficult concept to understand and act upon. It is a concept that tells us that what we create internally within our own little world can change the greater world. Though new to us, all of the ancient religions and spiritual practices have believed and employed this principle for centuries using chanting, trances, ritual, dances and movements to enact their belief in the concept. We do not have to use these old methods to enact this belief. We can, from within the confines of our living rooms or our backyards or even in our offices, learn to get in touch with ourselves on an internal level. We can learn to release a power greater than that which can be generated by one person or greater even than the power that can be generated by a group of people. This release of power is the key to healing the planet and it is within each one of us. Engaging that spiritual power is a potent force for change.

With the planet in such dire shape and the prognosticators informing us that our time for turning it around is quickly running out, we need to use all that we have to change the situation! And that includes using the potent power of our spiritual nature. Because our spiritual nature is in tune with the nature of the Earth, all we have to do is allow ourselves to open up and experience it, then we will quickly become Earth nature healers.

Most of what stops people from doing anything to help the planet is a paralyzing fear of inaction. Haven't you ever said to yourself, "Yes, I know there is an ecological problem. But, what can I do?" It is a good question. What **can** you do? There are many things you can do. Besides donating money to your favorite ecological cause, recycling in every conceivable manner, and giving your time and efforts in whatever ways you see fit to help solve the problem, you still have one untapped resource left: your spiritual ability to **rebalance** and **align**, and thereby help to heal the planet.

It may be presumptuous to believe that humankind, which has done its best to unbalance the nature of the planet, could also be a potent force for resolving the problem. Perhaps, in what is definitely an evolving age of the human race, we can now begin to take the responsibility we were originally given as the Keepers of Mother Earth, including taking our position in the proper place in the ecological chain of events.

The macrocosm of our planet is dying and is reflected within us ("As above, so below"). Therefore parts of ourselves—our microcosm—are dying. If we tune into our life force and allow ourselves to broadcast this life force energy we will then be "living" and our planet also will "live" with us. It is similar to the experiments that people enacted with prayer on plants. The plants they spoke lovingly to grew and prospered. The plants that they said hateful nasty words to withered and died away. We have this very potent power locked within us and there are some very simple techniques for beginning to release that power in an easy, usable, and fun manner.

However, before you can balance the planet you have to be able to balance yourself. The rest of this chapter describes steps you can take to enact that balance.

BALANCING YOURSELF ELEMENTALLY

First of all, get yourself a small notebook where you can keep notes and observations about yourself. In this notebook you are going to make an elemental mirror of yourself to see who you are and how you are balanced.

ATTRIBUTES

On a page in your note book make two columns. One is for your bad qualities and faults and one is for your good qualities and positive attributes. List your good and bad qualities under the appropriate headings. Use as many pages as you need to complete your list. Once you have listed your good and bad qualities assign to each one of them an element. (A partial list of personality qualities and the element to which they are assigned is given later in this chapter.) Here are some examples: strength, stability and patience are earth elemental qualities; stubbornness, resistance, and apathy are also earth qualities. Go through your entire list and correlate each good and bad point with an element.

After you have finished correlating your attributes and elements, categorize your list according to how important or serious the attribute is. You might also wish to prioritize your list according to importance, with the most serious or bad points listed together, followed by the less important faults, and then the rare or infrequent faults that crop up. Once your list is reorganized you will be able to see how balanced your internal system is. Perhaps all of your faults deal with one element and your good qualities come from a mixture of all of the elements. By listing your qualities according to their element you are clearly able to see what element you have in excess and what element you lack. Energy workers have called this the creation of an elemental or intuitive mirror. One side of the mirror is the dark side of yourself (negative), and the other side of the mirror is the light side of yourself (positive). As you begin to access your information from your internal elemental mirrors you see quite clearly what you lack elementally.

The following is an example of an elemental list:

BAD QUALITIES or FAULTS		GOOD QUALITIES	
anger	(fire)	optimism	(air)
jealousy	(fire)	lots of energy	(fire)
rudeness	(air)	enthusiasm	(fire)
apathy	(earth)	forgiveness	(water)
lack of commitment	(earth)	responsibility	(earth)
stubbornness	(earth)	a nurturer	(water)
resistance	(earth)	intellectually smart	(air)
indecision	(air)	courage	(fire)
overspending	(air)	determination	(fire)
self-importance	(air)	aggressive	(fire)
thinking too much	(air)	assertive	(fire)
aggressive	(fire)	loving	(water)

Soon you will have a full notebook of the elemental associations of your life and you will begin to understand what your strengths and weaknesses are, what elements you lack, and what you can bring into your life to add to it and thus rebalance yourself. Many of these qualities are also subjective and might switch from one column to another (from the negative to the positive or vice versa) according to the particular situation you are experiencing. Being angry in the proper situation where you need to experience and express yourself might be seen as positive and healthy, while being angry and discordant for long periods of time can be interpreted as negative and destructive behavior. However, honestly admit to yourself how you use your anger and in which column it is most often listed.

Now that you have defined yourself in elemental form, begin to look at the rest of your life and list it according to elemental qualities. For example, list the people with whom you socialize, your relatives, your business associates, and any other people with whom you interact. This should give you a great deal of information. Though all people are a mixture of the elements, we can still generalize a definition such as being a grounded person or a stodgy person (earth), or a person of fiery temperament (fire), or an overly emotional person (water), or a person who lives in his head and is spaced out (air). Then assign to each person the element that correlates to the definition. Now, check your lists. What element dominates? Is there a mixture or do you lean towards people with one particular element? Are your relatives one element and your work companions another?

PEOPLE

No one person has a single elementary makeup. All human beings are a true combination of the four elements. But you will find that you can generally categorize people by specific elements. A person who has too much of one element, your mother who is overly emotional, for example, might appear as a water element and your companion at work who is irritable and quick to anger would be a fire element person, and so on.

113

The following is an example of how you might categorize your friends, co-workers, and family.

FRIENDS		PEOPLE I WORK WITH	
George	(fire)	Gary	(air)
Mabel	(air)	Bill	(water)
Anna	(air & fire)	Jean	(air)
		Marvin	(air)

MY FAMILY			
Mother	(fire)	Uncle	(air)
Father	(air)	Cousin	(earth)
Sister	(water)	Niece	(air)
Brother	(fire)	Grandmother	(fire & air)
Aunt	(fire)	Grandfather	(earth & water)

Once you have created your lists of people, create a list of your activities and your hobbies and interests and define them by element. Then create a list of your clothes and the colors you like to wear. And of course, create a list of the foods you eat. Are you getting the idea yet? From all of these lists you will be able to know which elements you are comfortable with and know innately how to use and which elements you are not familiar with and must struggle to know how to use. The unfamiliar elements are the ones that you need to learn about. This is where growth must take place to bring you back to balance. You could also get your astrological chart done and see what your planets are listed in. Your chart is the blueprint you have created for this life and it might give you a clue as to how you use your elemental consciousness. In order to balance yourself elementally you must know your strengths and weaknesses. If all of your friends are earth and water, try cultivating some fiery people into your life and see what happens.

FOODS

You can divide the foods you eat into specific elements. The system used here is from *The Astrology Diet* by Jon Stevens. You may find other systems, or devise one yourself, that defines the foods into different elements.

Jon Stevens' System

The following list is based on the newest original work done by Jon Stevens. He defines all foods as being composed of the four basic elements. He lists these elements as protein, fat, carbohydrate, and water. Then Stevens states that these four basic elements correspond to the four astrological elements of earth, air, fire, and water.

PROTEIN	=	FIRE
FAT	=	EARTH
CARBOHYDRATE	=	AIR
WATER	=	WATER

Stevens forms this unique correlation for the basis of his Astrology Diet. Following is a partial list of foods by element according to his plan.

PROTEIN = FIRE ELEMENT FOODS

Beans (black, chili, garbanzo, kidney, red or white)
Beef
Caviar
Clams
Cottage Cheese (lowfat)
Crab
Duck
Eggs
Fish
Gelatin
Lentils
Lobster
Mussels
Oysters
Pork
Sardines
Soybeans
Tofu
Tuna
Yeast, Brewers

FAT = EARTH ELEMENT FOODS

Avocado
Bacon
Butter
Cheese
Coffee with Cream
Corn Oil
Cream
Cream Cheese
Milk
Nuts
Olives
Peanuts
Peanut Butter
Peanut Oil
Pork
Safflower Oil
Soy Oil
Sunflower Oil
Wheat Germ

CARBOHYDRATE = AIR ELEMENT FOODS

Apples (cooked)
Apple Juice
Applesauce
Apricot
Bananas
Black-eyed Peas
Blackberries
Blueberries
Boysenberries
Breads
Catsup
Cereals (wholegrain)
Cherries
Cocoa Powder (sweetened)
Coconut
Coffee with Sugar
Corn
Cranberries
Currants
Dates
Figs
Fructose Sugar

Grains
Grapes
Grapefruit
Honey
Lima Beans
Maple Syrup
Milk (lowfat, skim, or dry)
Molasses
Nectarines
Oranges
Pasta
Peaches
Pears
Pineapple (cooked, canned)
Plums
Popcorn
Potatoes
Raisins
Raspberries
Rhubarb
Yams
Yogurt (lowfat, unpasteurized)

WATER = WATER ELEMENT FOODS

Apples (fresh)
Apricots (fresh)
Artichokes
Asparagus
Bamboo Shoots
Beans (green, wax)
Beets (red, sugar)
Blackberries (fresh)
Blueberries (fresh)
Boysenberries (fresh)
Broccoli
Brussel Sprouts
Cabbage
Cantaloupe
Carrots
Casaba Melon (fresh)
Cauliflower
Celery
Cherries (fresh)
Chinese Pea Pods
Chives
Cinnamon
Coconut (fresh or dried)
Coffee (black)
Currants (fresh or dried)
Eggplant
Garlic
Ginger Root

Grapes (fresh)
Honeydew Melon (fresh)
Kale
Leeks
Lemon
Lettuce
Mango (fresh)
Mushrooms
Okra
Onions
Parsley
Peas, Green
Peaches
Peppers, Hot Chili
Peppers, (sweet, green, red)
Prunes
Pumpkin
Radish
Raisins (uncooked)
Squash (hubbard or winter)
Strawberries (fresh)
Summer Squash
Swiss Chard
Tangerines (fresh)
Turnips
Turnip Greens
Vinegar (white or cider)
Watercress
Zucchini

DIFFERENT SYSTEMS

I have many friends with different systems of categorizing foods by elements. Many of these are eclectic and not always complete systems, but they are very interesting. Some people define their food by simply choosing the element it best relates to. They consider any grain or root food to be of the earth and categorize corn, bread of a wholegrain quality, potatoes, and beets to be of the earth. Air elemental foods are foods that are lightweight and filled with air, such as popcorn, parsley, mint, and Chinese snow peas. For the water element they consider all foods that are white or that have a high water content to be "of water," such as broccoli, cabbage, lettuce, cucumber, yogurt, milk, cheese, and so on. Fire element foods are categorized by red or fire color and by how much heat they have, such as hot peppers, red peppers, meat, and cherries.

Another person I know separates the food by categories, with meat and fruit as fire food; dairy, vegetables, and some fruits as water food; grains, roots, and nuts as food of the Earth; and many seasonings, air popped (puffed cereals or popcorn) or air raised (bread or baked items) foods as air elemental foods. Sometimes he also divides the elements more specifically, categorizing not just Earth, Air, Water, and Fire but making the distinctions of: Earth of Earth, Air of Earth, Fire of Earth, and Water of Earth, and so on. For example, juice would be fire of water and yams would be fire of earth. Any of these types of systems will work for you as long as you set up your own system and you are consistent.

PERSONAL SYSTEM

Over the years I have developed my own personal system of categorizing food by element. It is not necessarily a logical or rational system but it works for me and I would like to share it with you. In order to clarify what a food is by element, I have further defined my system by breaking it down into specific elemental qualities, such as Earth of Earth which could be grains, for example, and Air of Earth which I perceive as bread (which is earth with an extra air quality in it) and so on. By breaking the elements further down into specific qualities I can easily categorize the effect of the specific food upon my system. Perhaps the following will give you ideas for creating your own personal system of elemental categorizing.

EARTH OF EARTH

Avocado   Potatoes (white)
Barley   Turnips
Cereals(wholegrain)   Wheat
Corn   Wheat Germ
Nuts

AIR OF EARTH

Bread (wheat or wholegrain)

FIRE OF EARTH

Carrots   Sweet Potatoes
Eggs   Yams
Soybeans

WATER OF EARTH

Bamboo Shoots
Bananas
Beets
Garlic (ground)
Molds

Mushrooms
Pasta
Rice
Tofu
Water Chestnuts

EARTH OF AIR

Alfalfa sprouts
Bean sprouts
Parsley

Peas
Popcorn

AIR OF AIR

Mint
Nutmeg

Sage

FIRE OF AIR

Allspice
Black Pepper
Cayenne

Cinnamon
Garlic (ground)

WATER OF AIR

Coconut

Turnip Greens

EARTH OF FIRE

Bacon
Beans
Butter

Garlic
Red Meat

AIR OF FIRE

Chicken	Honey
Duck	Quail

FIRE OF FIRE

Commercial Candies	Hot Peppers
Crystallized Ginger	Mustard
Currants	Raisins

WATER OF FIRE

Catsup	Ginger Root
Chives	Green Onions
Dates	

EARTH OF WATER

Applesauce	Peaches
Apricots	Pumpkin
Beer	Squash
Cauliflower	Yogurt
Cheese	

AIR OF WATER

Club Soda	Rose Water
Orange Water	Tea (herbal)

FIRE OF WATER

Apples	Oranges
Blackberries	Papaya
Blueberries	Prunes
Boysenberries	Radish
Cantaloupes	Raspberries

Cherries

Coffee

Elderberries

Fruit juices

Leeks

Liquor

Onions

SodaTea (caffeinated)

Tea (caffeinated)

Tea (caffeinated)

Tomatoes

Vanilla Bean

Watermelon

Wine

WATER OF WATER

Asparagus

Brussel Sprouts

Celery

Cucumbers

Lettuce

Milk

Water

123

"We are sinful not merely because we have eaten of the Tree of Knowledge, but also because we have not yet eaten of the Tree of Life."

—*Franz Kafka*

13

WORKING WITH
THE ELEMENTS

Working with the elements is fun and exciting and can give you a tool for healing the planet. Remember how much you enjoyed reading your childhood fairytales? Well, these stories were about the elemental realms. The worlds of childhood fantasy are based on the stories of the fairies and gnomes; the myths of heroic warriors, dragons, and maidens fair; the spirits of rivers, brooks, and lakes; and the interplay of light and dark, good and evil. The elementals, in essence, are the doorway to these fantasy realms. The elementals also offer us another doorway to an ancient pathway that can now be resurrected for healing the planet.

In order to call on the elementals or their leaders, the Keepers of each of their Kingdoms, to help you rebalance the order of the planet, or at least your chosen piece of it, you have to be able to identify with the monospiritual essence of the elemental. You have to be able to experience the elemental as existing in reality on your own internal level of awareness. The following actions provide you with methods you can use to contact and experience the elementals.

THE EARTH ELEMENT

Let us start with the element of the Northern Quarter, the Earth. Sit in a comfortable chair. Loosen any tight clothing, take a deep breath. Allow any tension in your body to drain out through your feet. Let yourself relax. Make sure that you are breathing regularly. Imagine yourself sinking into the earth and becoming a part of it. See yourself as being surrounded by the earth and being stable, secure, and permanent. Feel yourself as no longer having a separate body, but as part of a living, breathing piece of the earth and allow yourself to communicate with it as you would communicate with your arm or your elbow or your big toe. Remember that the earth energy you are experiencing is not the true earth but the elemental essence of the earth. Feel yourself as a true piece of the earth—as a rock or crystal, part of a mountain or desert or as a molecular piece of the earth.

As you do this exercise you are actually allowing yourself to experience the earth aspect of your own nature, the reality that governs your inner sense of stability, security, and permanence. You are also allowing yourself to communicate with the greater or larger earth essence which is the elemental level of the nature of earth on the entire planet.

As you become aware of the larger essence of earth and learn to communicate with it, you will be able to see, hear, and speak with the gnomes and the creatures of the elemental earth realm. These are the easiest elementals for humans to speak with as they seem to be the closest to our own level of reality. It takes some time to refine your ability to create the essence of an element and to become immersed within it. So you may have to practice this exercise quite regularly before you begin to take notice of the elementals and develop a communication link with them. It might also take you a while to come to terms with the sense of becoming one with the element of earth. Once you have absorbed this sense of earth and begin to understand it and intuitively know its essence and power, you will be able to recognize the nature of the earth element wherever you are on the planet. You will also be able to more easily balance the earth within yourself so that you develop the security and stability that you need to function as an eco-spirit planetary healer.

After you have learned to immerse yourself in the element of earth you will wish to move on to the next exercises which show you how to immerse yourself in the elements of air, fire, and water so that you can learn to create the dimensions of these elements to call upon their help in the planetary rebalancing.

 ## THE AIR ELEMENT

Air is the element of the East Quarter. It is the element that, although somewhat invisible and therefore more difficult to see, actually surrounds us and fills us with energy and vitality. You can get in touch with the air element by taking yourself outdoors to a place that puts you in touch with the quality of air, such as a deck where the air blows all around you or a place high up on a hill or mountain where you become immediately aware of the sky and the air. If you cannot take yourself to a natural environment that seems to be governed by the air element, then seat yourself in a comfortable chair, loosen any tight clothing, close your eyes and remember the last time you were in an environment that seemed to be created mostly of the air element. Feel the wind on your face, the air you breathe in deeply, and the power and grandeur of the air medium. Feel yourself growing lighter and lighter so that you could actually lift up and become part of the air and fly into the giant billowy clouds overhead. Let yourself become one with the movement of the air, with the lift of its vibrant gusts that let you fly as a Sylph to the giant clouds above. As you fly you become the air, you become the power to be everywhere, the power to permeate all environments and all bodies to create the great surge of life force that carries life in and out and around the planet. As you ride the air waves of the planet you can actually feel the planet itself breathing and sighing and pulsating with the movement of its breath. You can feel yourself moving in the powder blue universe of the air of life. You become all manner of air. You can be the air of a warm day or the air of a hurricane or the air of an electrically-charged storm or the air of a crisp, autumn evening. Allow yourself to experience being all manner of air so that you truly feel and understand the qualities of air.

In this universe you will see the air elementals, the Sylphs flying on the currents of the air. They are small and delicate, lace-like fairies—tiny angelic energy workers that carry and direct the currents of the air and its energy to all manner of places. Allow yourself to see the Sylphs and to communicate with them in their own manner. When you have learned to ride the currents of the air as the Sylphs do, then gently bring your consciousness back to your body. Feel the air going in and out of your lungs, feel the air that surrounds, caresses, and holds your body. Say hello to yourself as a spiritual being, in a physical body, who has felt the power and grandeur of the spirit of air.

THE FIRE ELEMENT

Fire is the element of the South Quarter. Fire is the highest transformative element. It is quick, all-consuming, and somewhat beyond the control of human beings. Fire can warm us, heat and cook our food, and it can destroy us. You can learn to observe and become one with fire by just sitting in front of your fireplace and observing your fire. The type of fire you have will be determined by the type of fuel you use. Wood gives off the cleanest spiritual or elemental fire and the type of wood you use will determine what type of fire elementals or Salamanders you might view in the fire. I have many friends who have spent their childhood staring into the flames of their fireplace observing the little "fiery lizards" in the flicks of the flames.

If you do not have a fireplace or if you wish to experience the fire kingdom further, then seat yourself in a comfortable chair, loosen any tight clothing, take a deep breath, close your eyes, put your feet solidly on the ground, and imagine yourself staring into your imaginary fireplace. You can see the wood burning brightly, forming different colored flames. You watch the flames leap from log to log. And in the area where the coals are hot and bright and glowing, you can see the brightly moving fire lizards, the Salamanders. For a moment take a deep breath and imagine yourself as the fire element. Imagine yourself as all fire, as a flame of fire burning brightly, as the hot flame of life constantly changing and moving. As you become the flame of life, the ever-moving hot flame, you can converse with the elementals of the flame, the Salamanders, as they too move within the flames of the fire. You are the heat of life, the ability to transform all things, and you can feel yourself as a yellow, orange, red flame in motion. Become the fire in all of its many aspects. Be the fire of heat and nurturing, the fire that cooks your dinner. Be the fire of passion that makes love.

Be the fire of destruction that reclaims an ancient forest. And be the fire of life that helps you to digest your food.

Then return to just being the flame of the fire in the fireplace. Once you have experienced being the flame, then bring yourself back to your body. Bring some of the nurturing heat of fire with you and fill your body with the warmth of the fire and the quick motion of change of the fire and the instant transformational quality of the fire. Feel the heat move throughout your body, filling your feet and your legs and your groin and moving up your spine to fill your chest, your arms, and your head. The fire element is the nurturing heat of action that will enable you to take action and make changes in your world.

 THE WATER ELEMENT

Water is the element of the West Quarter. Water is the great cleanser of our planet. It channels emotions and love for humans and brings life to all. To get in touch with the water element you might wish to travel to a local stream, brook, river, or waterfall. Here you can watch the water move, observe how creatures relate to the water, and notice the ability of this element to be either incredibly nurturing with life or destructive in how it changes the terrain around it. Like all of the elements, water can be "the giver of life," as an oasis in the desert, or the "taker of life," as a flash flood.

If you do not have a brook, pond, river, or waterfall to observe, or if you just wish to immerse yourself further into the element of water, then find yourself a comfortable chair to sit in, loosen any tight clothing, close your eyes, place your feet flat on the ground, take a deep breath and allow yourself to be in any place of water that you know. You can create your own waterfall, swimming hole, river, or brook to be in. See and feel the water around you in your internal intuitive environment and observe the water. Feel yourself being immersed in the water as if you are becoming totally one with it. You are the water and you can feel every pore of your body **be** one with the water. You can feel yourself flow in the water and move with the water. And you can feel yourself move with the currents of the water as the Undines move. You might see the Undines moving near you. If you do, communicate with them and learn to watch, listen, and understand their ways.

Feel the water you are in. Is it calm water? Is it nurturing water or transformative water? Nurturing water would quench the thirst of a tree or plant or animal. Transformative water might be deeply and slowly cutting a path through the rock to form a canyon or it might be the water of a storm or hurricane. Feel the power of the water you are in and experience its many aspects so that you know how to sense the lightness or the heaviness of the water. Water moves things from one place to another. Water can move your emotions away or bring them to you. As you become one with the water you experience the great movement of life that carries you onward. You are suddenly part of the whole of life in movement. You have no wants, desires, or needs—you are just here in the present time of the movement of the water. When you have finished sensing the quality of the water, separate yourself from it and bring your consciousness back to your physical body. As you do so, imagine all of your unwanted emotions and feelings flowing out of you into the water where they will be drained away and cleansed. Now take a deep breath and allow yourself to be once more aware of yourself and your surroundings while retaining the ability to flow with water.

In order to work successfully with the elements, you have to learn to visualize, experience internally, and create the world of each element. Practice the exercises above until you are able to "call" the elemental world to yourself at will so that you can create an inner environment of that element. This will enable you to call upon the angels of creation, the keepers of the elemental kingdoms, who govern the elemental forces and can help you to create a world balanced in its elemental qualities—which of course will be a world balanced in its ecological systems. Once you have learned to immerse yourself in the elements and can create the elementary dimensions at will, you need to know how to create, open, and use elementary windows to move these elementary energies to rebalance any area that you are working on.

CREATING ELEMENTAL WINDOWS

Before you can create elemental windows you must first learn not to be afraid to use your imagination. In our modern 20th century world asking an adult to use his or her imagination is usually asking for trouble! People have been taught since early childhood that to use one's imagination is to stray off the tried and true path of life into illusion, mental madness, and fantasy. Though it is acceptable for poets, musicians, actors, writers, and storytellers to use their imaginations to create worlds for us, we do not allow ourselves, the people of the normal work-a-day world, to get carried away creating new and novel lands with our capacities for imagination.

I co-taught classes with a meditation teacher who used to announce at the beginning of every class that people should use their imaginations. She would state that using your imagination was a healthy and creative way of accessing the inner world of your spiritual, emotional, and mental nature. Most of the class would be shocked and reticent. They would ask whether using the imagination wasn't just "making things up" and "creating illusions." And she would answer that seeing life with your imagination is seeing things in your mind's eye. And seeing things in your mind's eye is seeing life the way your spiritual self perceives things—as visual images and pictures like constantly running colorful movies.

It is these inner movies of life that are the wildly running rampant emotional scenarios of our inner nature. We can channel and use these movies to access information and contact the inner sense of our nature to help us hook into the outer sense of nature as a whole. Children use their imaginations wholeheartedly and with tremendous focus but do know the difference between the real and the imagined. Most adults, however, are afraid to hook into their creative imaginations. It is as if they fear not being able to know the difference between the shared reality of the outer world which we all collectively create and the personal reality of the inner world—the realm of inner symbolism. It is the inner world that enables us to enter into the realm of the collective unconscious, the true symbolism of our higher selves. We are not in fact "playing" with our imaginations but are gaining access to other dimensions which can teach us a good deal about who we are and why we are here. To an energy worker the imagination is a tool to be used just like any other tool at their disposal.

Elementals live in another dimension. You can bring the elementals here by opening a window to their dimension. Each type of elemental comes through the window of its particular direction in relationship to the Earth. For example, the air elementals come through the eastern window while the earth elementals come through the northern window. In order to bring the elementals to a certain area to do earth-healing work you need to create a window to the dimension that they live in. Once you create a window to the world of the elementals you can speak with them and ask them to help you in healing or rebalancing various areas of the Earth.

To create a window to the world of the elements you will need a compass.

CREATING
ELEMENTAL WINDOWS

Let's start with the element of the Earth. Look at your compass and face north, the direction of the Earth. Now imagine having a multi-colored marker in your hand and draw a window as a medium sized yellow box in the air in front of you. This yellow box is the Eastern "Tattva" or symbol for Earth. We are using these symbols because they are the easiest and most direct to use in creating energy windows.

When you draw your yellow box it is best to start in the lower left hand corner and draw the line upwards, then across, down, and back to the corner where you started. In other words, you always draw your symbol clockwise in the direction of the sun moving forwards, and in one continuous line. Symbolically, moving sunwards is moving forward in time and moving in the direction of light, positiveness, and creativity.

Imagine your yellow box as a window through which you can envision and create the element of Earth. It is here you use your creative and imaginative abilities to create the realm of Earth. You must see, hear, sense, and become familiar with the Earth that you see through your yellow window. It must be like the Earth immersion that you have felt and seen in your exercise. It is the essence of Earth, the quintessential experience of what Earth is to you. When you have created the experience of Earth through your window you will have created a window to the realm of the element of Earth. By creating the elemental essence of Earth you are allowing this dimension to exist, so there can be a window between the worlds. You have created a window between the world of human reality, the earthly plane and the dimension of the Earth element. You can now call on the Keeper of the Earth Element, Auriel, to speak with you.

Since all of the elemental realms are governed in a hierarchical fashion, you always want to speak with the governing leader. Auriel, ruler of the Earth Element may appear to you as an angelic being clothed in the colors of the earth: olive, citrine, russet, and black or perhaps as a person covered in green and russet robes with a wrinkled weathered face holding the solidity of the earth within his grasp or just as an energy force that can communicate with you.

Your perceptions of an entity of the elemental realm is entirely up to the manner in which you structure your own internal imagery. It is different for each person. The Keepers or Rulers of the Elements are called Archangels or "spirits of the light." These are energy beings that rule over certain areas of energy, the elements being one of those areas.

Once you have an open window of communication with the Keeper of the Element, you then ask him to channel some elemental energy through your window to the area you are working on. You are asking this elemental ruler to help you rebalance the area you are occupying. As the earth elemental energy comes pouring through your window you can create a channel or direct it to the area which you are balancing. When you have finished working with the earth energy, then thank the Keeper of the Element and move on to the next element which is Air.

I hope you realize that when you are "speaking" with these elementary guardians you are speaking "inside of your head" or subvocally, on a totally internal level. Someone standing right next to you might notice that you are extremely focused with your mind but would not "know" what you were doing or hear anything.

Check your compass and face the direction of the East. Use your imaginary magic marker and draw the Tattva symbol of a blue circle in the air. This is your window to the element of Air. As before, draw your blue circle by starting on the left and drawing it clockwise or sunwards in one continuous line of energy. See your circle as a window to the realm of Air and create the all encom-passing world of air. Call on the Keeper of the Element of Air, Raphael, and ask him to channel some elemental air energy into the area that you wish to balance. Although the Archangel Raphael is not a human being, you might perceive him as such dressed in flowing robes of pastel blue, powder blue, or light bright blues. Thank Raphael for helping you in your task and then move on to the next element, Fire.

Face the direction of South, the home of the element of Fire. Bring out your imaginary magic marker and draw the Tattva symbol of a red equilateral triangle with the apex upwards in the air before you. You could see this as a red triangle or a multi-dimensional pyramid that stands in the air before you. Remember to draw your triangle in one continuous line, starting at the left point and going sunwards towards the apex then to the bottom right point and then back. This triangle is the window to the realm of Fire, the active element and the giver of light and heat. Within your window create the realm of Fire, then call to the Keeper of the Element, the Archangel Michael, and ask him to send some elemental fire

136

energy to help you rebalance the area you are working on. You might perceive Michael in flowing robes of orange, red, bright yellow, and golden sunshine if you see him in a human form, or you might just become aware of a cloud of fiery energy with these colors. Thank the Elemental Guardian and then move on to the last element, Water.

Turn towards the West, the home of the element of Water. Bring out your imaginary magic marker and draw the symbol of a silver crescent with the horns facing upwards. This is your window to the elementary dimension of water. As before, start drawing it in the left hand corner and make one. continuous silver line that goes clockwise and ends where you began. Now see the inside of this crescent as a window that opens up into the realm of water. Here you see a dimension totally conceived of water, every type of water you could think of: lake water, the tumultuous ocean, the babbling brook, the water of a rainfall, and so on. Once you have created the dimension of water so totally that your window to that realm becomes real for you, then ask for the Guardian of the Element of Water, the Archangel Gabriel. You might see Gabriel as a human clothed in the colors of silver, blue, and green or you might just perceive a misty cloud of water droplets appearing at your window. Ask Gabriel to send some elemental water energy to your area to help balance it. And then thank him for his effort.

After you have called upon the elements—earth, air, fire, and water—to rebalance your area with the proper proportions of each, you might want to help further balance your area by calling on an archetype energy or neutral akashic energy. There are many different techniques you can use and energy fields that you can call upon to cleanse and rebalance an area. When you have finished with whatever techniques or processes you use, you will want to close your elemental windows. You will not want to forget to close the windows. If you were to leave the elemental windows open there might be a leak between the dimensions and some of the elemental energy might fill your area or be drained from it. Closing the elemental windows secures your energy balancing so that you get and keep the proper amount of elemental energy that is needed. It completes your energy work.

It is simple and easy to close elemental windows. Start in the North, where you began opening your windows. Your window is there in the air where you left it. Thank the Guardian of the Northern Element, Auriel for helping you in your task and inform him that you are closing your window since your work is finished. Now take the lines of your box and fold them in upon one another to close your window. Then imagine the window and the lines being sucked back into the elemental dimension until, poof! they disappear. I usually hear a popping or gentle sucking air sound as the window closes.

Then face the next direction, the East and thank the Guardian of the Element of the East, Raphael, for helping you in your task and explain that you are finished with your task and are closing the elemental window. Then pull the circle into a tiny dot and imagine the dot being sucked back into the elemental level of air until, poof! it disappears and your window is closed.

Next, face the direction of the South, where you left your triangular window and thank the Guardian of the Fire Elemental dimension, Michael, for aiding you in your work and explain that you are going to close your elemental window since your work is done. Then fold the lines of the triangle in upon themselves and again imagine them being sucked back into the elemental realm until the lines and the window disappear.

Then face the last element, the realm of Water. Thank the Guardian Archangel of the Water Element, Gabriel, for aiding you in your task and explain that you are closing your window since you are finished with your task at hand. Close your window by pulling the lines of the crescent together, seeing them being sucked or pulled back into the realm of the element so that this window is closed.

This process of opening and closing elemental windows might seem difficult or complex, but it is actually quite simple once you have done it a few times. When you open the windows you have to remember to go in the order of the elements: earth (North), air (East), fire (South), and water (West). Close them in the same order. By imagining and immersing yourself in the elemental level of awareness you allow yourself to create this window in the actual elemental realm. You can then channel or direct elemental energy to any place you need it on the planet. If you have too much energy of one type of element, such as too much heat or fire or too much water, you could open that elemental window and send the excess energy back to its elemental realm.

It is possible to open just one elemental window without opening all of the other elemental windows. You just have to always remember to have your trusty compass or your innate natural ability to know which direction to face. Then face the direction for that element and use the Tattva symbol for that element to create your window. And of course, always close your window afterwards. If you are dealing with too much of one element, or too little, you might wish to just open just that one window and discharge the element or re-energize it. If an entire area needs to rebalanced then you need to create windows for all of the four elements.

Speaking With the Elementals

Besides the technique of balancing the four elements, you can also speak with the elementals and ask them to direct their energy or efforts towards healing a certain tree, plant, or area. Although the elemental beings are not commonly known, most people have heard of fairies, elves, gnomes, mermaids, and will o' wisps in children's stories, theatre, classical music, and modern-day movies. Sometimes it is difficult for adults to see and perceive these subtle beings. Children seem to have an easier time of perceiving these nature elementals. It might be due to the fact that children have not been told that elementals do not exist. Or it could be that children do not have to explain or understand or make sense of the existence of an elemental or nature spirit. If the elemental is there, and it is seen or heard or otherwise experienced, then it exists. Whereas adults usually must understand or "explain the presence of" or "decide what action must be taken due to the discovery of." Adults tend to have to use their reaction to a discovery in order to take action, while children just experience what is happening at the time. In training adults to allow themselves to perceive and communicate with the elementals I have learned to allow them to communicate as a child would: in natural awe, in innocence, and without agendas (such as taking pictures, proving something, or rationalizing). Without such agendas we can acknowledge what is truly happening for us in the here and now.

Communicating with the elementals takes time and patience. They are not always easy to communicate with. The Gnomes of the earth are probably the easiest and the fire Salamanders are reputed to be the most difficult to develop communication with.

Each one of us has a different elemental personality makeup. If you remember the elemental list of attributes in the chapter "Rebalancing Your Self," it can clearly show you how balanced you are in proportion to each of the elements. A simple list will show you those elements that you know and understand and, thus, mirror daily and those which you lack and do not project for yourself. The element which you know and understand is the one which you would be most likely able to communicate with easily. So, if you are a fiery person by nature, you would be most aware of the Salamanders and have a good chance at perceiving and communicating with them. If you are an earthy person then you might find the Gnomes more accessible.

Please do not get the idea that the Gnomes or the Salamanders are the only elementals within their respective Kingdoms. Many times I have walked in my garden, and also even in local plant nurseries, to find all sorts of earth and water elementals living with the plants, dancing around the plants, and helping the plants to get their nourishment and food. Some of these beings are but an inch and a half high while others are two feet tall. In my wild and natural back yard in the Santa Monica Mountains I have seen an earth elemental that is twelve feet high. (The twelve foot tall earth elemental frightened me at first, just because of its size, but it was one of the most gentle of creatures I have ever met. It simply was an earth guardian for the general area.)

I am using the term "elementals" very generally here. There are a myriad of creatures that work in the earthly kingdom that makes up the nature of our planet. The elementals are "elemental" by nature. That means that they are made up of only **one** element. We, as human beings, have four elements plus life force

141

spirit (akasha). There are also beings called fairies that are created of a few of the elements. Elementals and fairies are more simplistic than human beings. That is, they are less intellectual, they use much less of their mind but are constantly doing their job, which is emotional and has to do with transferring energy from one place or object to another.

Fairies and elementals are rather joyous beings who sing and dance and frolic as they help to transform the movement of dynamic life force energy from one part of the dimension to another. The fairies tend the plants under their jurisdiction and help them to receive life force from the sun, from the water, from the earth, and from the air. The fairies and the elementals are a very fun-loving group whose sole job is to tend to their little patch or piece of existence.

Elementals and fairies are created of pure energy which makes them appear transparent and seem to glow. They do not have physical bodies. Because they are made up of one or two of the elements they do not have the weight that humans do and they do not have the attachment to the physical realm. Theirs is the realm of pure spirit—the realm of the movement of energy in its pure vibratory form. A fairy tending to its plants is a being of light that is dynamically moving around the life force from one place to another. Whereas humans relish or reminisce about the past, worry and plan about the future, collect physical items to own, control, and care for, the fairies and elementals simply live in the joy of present time and of caring for their charges, the world of nature. For the most part, the fairies and elementals will ignore you unless you purposely choose to communicate with them. Most elementals and fairies do not understand humans and have little or no reason to communicate with them. They might observe our behavior for a moment or two but then they are off to sing and dance and frolic in the garden while they do their work. They are not contemplative creatures and their intellect would be considered below that of humans.

You can communicate with the elementals and fairies and learn a good deal about them and what they do. However, they do not have the type of free will that we experience. When you wish to change something that they work on, you will need to contact their Angel, the guardian that rules the kingdom who actually tells them what to do. The Angel is the motivating force in the dimension to which they are all connected.

NORTH	*EAST*	*SOUTH*	*WEST*
E A R T H	A I R	F I R E	W A T E R
Auriel	*Raphael*	*Michael*	*Gabriel*
Gnomes	Sylphs	Salamanders	Undines

The Elements, The Angels, and The Elementals

"The world is too much with us: late and soon,
Getting and spending, we lay waste our powers:
Little we see in Nature that is ours...

— *Wordworth*

"Miracles happen, not in opposition to Nature,
but in opposition to what we know of Nature."

—*St. Augustine*

14

FINDING YOUR
ARCHETYPE

What is an archetype? How do we find it? And why would we want to do this? An archetype is the essential part of yourself that connects you with the earth, the universe, and expands your consciousness to understand who you are internally and why you are what you are.

The dictionary defines the term archetype as a model or first form; the original pattern after which a thing is made or to which it corresponds. Carl Gustav Jung, the Swiss psychologist, coined the word archetype to mean the "primordial images" which he viewed as elements of the collective unconscious (that part of the psyche that is universal to all peoples, all time periods and ages, and all cultures). We receive these archetypes as part of our nature, apart from our parents or our culture. These archetypes are not the concepts or ideas we have gleaned from the higher part of ourselves or our spiritual inheritance. They are the blueprints for our inner behavior as we act out the information we are born with as energy beings in physical bodies.

To an energy worker an archetype is the original or essential energy form that connects directly to the essential sense of your self. When you want to communicate with the planet, for example, you contact and communicate with the archetype of the planet. In the past, people called this archetype Mother Earth, Mother Nature, Magna Mater, the Goddess, or the internal depths. When you communicate with the planet you communicate with its basic energy structure and its basic archetypal existence that you know how to contact. As we are a part of the basic energy structure of the planet, you will make contact with the part of your self which is a part of the larger picture. You, being the microcosm, will contact that part of your self which is the macrocosm of things.

As an example, let us take a look at an archetype. If we want to contact an energy source that is within, or a part of, or represents the planet, then we must have a method or mode of contacting that source of information. The method of making contact is understanding the primal essence of our own energy field. Each one of us has a unique makeup of our energy, consciousness, and patterning. It is the same as having fingerprints and your own set of genes. Each one of us has our own energy patterns based on experience and the particular configuration of our energy system. When you contact an archetype you are communicating with the energy that mirrors your inner energy pattern. It is similar to a child being able to pick out his or her parents. There is a similar energy pattern that innately tells the child who are his or her parents.

Our archetypal patterning is based on the essential energy of our primal spiritual being. Your archetypal response to something is innate and without conscious awareness—it is uncontrollable. Most people contact their archetypal self without any awareness of what they are doing. So, if you "mother" someone and you have a Great Mother archetypal pattern within your spiritual self, you might trigger that pattern to become charged and begin to interact with the universe, or Great Mother. The Great Mother pattern might cause you to feel responsible for the person you are mothering, to take charge and direct that person, to nurture him, and to care for or mother many things around you. As you "become" the Great Mother you might become more dynamic, more forceful, more nurturing and you might gain weight (as all Great Mothers are perceived as large overencompassing mothers of all). If you stay within the confines of this pattern you might become the "mother" for your group of friends or for your fellow workers. If you get stuck in this pattern you might become the "mother" for everyone you come into contact with. If a specific person triggers this pattern within you then you will just mother that person. If you are aware of this pattern then you can choose when to use it, when you see it as being appropriate, rather than being the effect of it or being used by it.

So an archetype is a powerful storehouse of energy that is formed into a specific pattern. There are some archetypes within the planetary framework that have been created and fed by the energy from masses of people over long periods of time. When you call on an archetype that represents the inner core of your being, you vibrate on the same level and you know it. You know it because suddenly you are charged with the energy that is channeled through that archetype, energy of the thousands of people who have channeled through this form, or the life force energy that has charged this pattern. The archetype is the pattern that your innate inner conscious responds to. To get in touch

147

with that archetype you might, consciously or unconsciously, connect with it as you "mother" someone and tap into the Great Mother archetype. Or you might enjoy a movie with a hero in it, such as Superman, or a heroine, such as Wonder Woman, and unconsciously become aware of the super hero archetypal pattern within yourself. I have found that these patterns can have specific types of identities, such as heroine, mother, martyr or hero, father, warrior or "larger," greater identities such as the mountain, the stream, or the universal cosmic consciousness.

Whenever I enter a place of worship or a place of sacred space—a grove of trees, a majestic mountain range, or a sanctuary people have made their own—I always try to connect with the inner archetype or its inner energy source. In this way I learn and experience the majesty of life and spirit on the planet. And, of course, I have learned a great deal about which churches, temples and sacred spaces are truly holy and which spaces are just showplaces empty of life force or lifegiving energy. I have been in many churches in Europe and in the United States and only a few have what I experienced at a local church one day. I had gone to a local Protestant church for a community meeting. The church had extra rooms it rented to local community groups. We were standing in the hallway waiting for someone to unlock one room when I casually grounded myself and internally spoke to the "powers that be," the energy of the building, the congregation, and whatever they connected with in their worship. By hooking into the archetype of the people who created their church, I could feel a golden pillar of energy flowing into the building and the entire floor begin to vibrate with a soft gentle intensity. The building was charged with their belief and their worship of the spirit of what they call God or Oneness.

You can get in touch with any archetype that exists in the universe. However, you will find that there are specific archetypes, or images, that enable you to get in touch with the oneness, or the power of your essential self. You do not have to believe in an archetypal level to experience it, but the particular archetype that you feel comfortable with is the one that you can work with most easily. I am not a Protestant, but I enjoyed the sense of oneness and life force that they had created in that church.

People often set up archetypes as God forces. An archetype, however, is the essential energy that creates a pattern. Think of the first statue that is the basis for a mold. Later statues are in its image and are of its kin, so to speak. The original image does have a great deal of power in it and because of that, when you connect with it, you are generating your innate ability to become one with everything on the planet that vibrates on that level. This can be a very powerful tool! An archetype can be a God force, such as the mythological gods and goddesses, but it can also be a means of communicating with the very depths of your internal self. The gods and goddesses and your internal self are all a part of the oneness of God or the universal life force. You do not have to believe in God to hook into archetypal energy. You do not have to **believe** in anything. You just have to allow yourself to experience.

By experiencing an archetype you are experiencing yourself on a more intense and internal level. Very often I will speak with the basic earth archetype and it appears to me as a creature—immense, colored sienna brown, made of the earth, brutish and rough. It is female and is always curled up, as if it is a cat sleeping on its favorite rug in front of the fireplace. Before earthquakes she looks uncomfortable and displeased and begins to move and stretch. When I perceive the lady of the earth I act as if I were her and experience what she is feeling and sensing. This allows me to become one with, to share consciousness with, what I am perceiving.

There are many archetypes or energy patterns of the earth. You will find in history, religion, and mythology that the earth archetypes are usually seen as feminine. In the older Shamanistic religions that were numerous and flourished everywhere on the planet, the earth was usually seen as feminine while the sky was seen as masculine. Some Native American Indians named them Mother Earth and Father Sky. Other Indian tribes named them Mother Earth and Father Sun. We generally see the earth, the creative womb, as feminine and that which impregnates, the air which scatters seed, as masculine.

When you work with an archetype you can choose to contact a specific pattern or you can simply contact the energy of that particular location and see what pattern you perceive from your connection. Many older religions based their worship on following or exemplifying a specific archetype. The Greeks and the Romans, for example, used archetypes to represent specific qualities that each person would strive to embody. They had very large pantheons of gods and goddesses that portrayed the perfection of different lifestyles. There was god, the Father, or god, the Mother. There was Hestia, called Goddess of the Hearth or Goddess of the Home, there was the Goddess of Wisdom, representing the old crone or ancient lady, and there was the god Pan, the god of nature and fecundity. Each person could choose the god or goddess of their liking to understand, emulate and observe and become. Please understand, these are not substitutes for God, the one God, the whole or the oneness. These are aspects or parts of the God force that is within everyone and causes us to act out certain patterns or plays in life. As you get in touch with an archetype and learn to become one with it, and to channel it as yourself, you become the essence of that energy force. Ancient hunters sought to become one with whomever was the best hunter of the tribe. Two or three centuries down the road this person became an archetype, a hero whom they could contact, channel this essence, and become one with in order to be the hunter. Shamanistically, this was originally accomplished by becoming one with an animal. So if you were hunting an animal you would become its natural predator and take on the aspects, mannerisms, and actions of the predator. Or you could just become the animal you hunted and seek it as its equal. Like the story where the little boy finds his lost cat and when the father asks how he found it, the boy replies, "I just pretended I was the lost cat and went where he would go...and he was there." As mankind advanced and not everyone had to be a hunter we became aware of other essential archetypes within us and we set up more refined aspects to seek oneness with.

We would like to believe that we do not seek to merge with any aspects of archetypes in our modern-day society. However this is far from the truth. Children first merge with the archetype or pattern of their parents, the hero or heroine, the mother or father, and so on. Then, when they notice that their parents are not infallible, when their parents fall off of their pedestal of truths, the children switch their attention to the archetypes of their generation. These archetypes representations become the heroes and heroines of their childhood and their adolescence. We do this unconsciously now. But Batman, Superman, Wonder Woman, Spider Man, Mickey Mouse, Minnie Mouse, Uncle Scrooge, the Green Hornet, Captain Kirk, the Simpsons, Michael Jackson, Teenage Mutant Ninja Turtles, and many other heroes and heroines are the archetypes of our modern generations. These examples are what we unconsciously choose to represent as our inner truths and patterns, our modern day archetypes. They represent the qualities and images that speak universally to our inner selves. When you go to a movie or a play you usually try to identify with at least one character as your "representative," your hero or heroine, your essential archetype in that situation. The archetype is the essential energy of the hero who was first represented by your father, then perhaps a teacher or athletic star, and then becomes represented by Superman. As you grow older your archetype becomes another image, perhaps a business superstar or a movie star as an ideal or a well-known politician. The actual archetype is the heroic energy. How you create your own personal representations of this stem from the particular beliefs, culture and environment you live within.

I have often watched my friends and family go to a movie and become so entranced and enchanted with a universal archetype that they go home and recreate the entire scenario as their life experience. A movie with a universal archetypal appeal goes on to create many side markets for products that are selling that archetype. *Star Wars* was a good example of a movie that used the archetypes of good and evil; and of youth, impetuousness, and innocence contrasted with age, wisdom, and experience. Those who saw the movie *Star Wars* seven or eight times and created the scenario in their own lives were learning the energy lesson that "the force is with you." They were also learning to incorporate the qualities of their archetypes, of the heroes and heroines, within their own essential beings.

Understanding your archetype is not accomplished by using the mind but by experiencing and becoming that particular energy level being for a moment in time. As you merge and become one with that essence you *know* how it acts and you act as it to channel its energy force. When I become one with the earth archetype I have the strength of the earth, the stability and solidity of the earth, and the ability to channel the energy of the earth as she would. I become the earth for all practical purposes. It is a way of melding your energy with a greater force for a short period of time. This melding then allows you to direct the whole of that energy pattern in a specific direction. When you become the archetype you are the essence of that energy and you can empower it to move into a specific or given direction. I have seen energy workers use these skills to control storms or move them in other directions, or to disperse or drain some of the energy from specific earthquake faults, or to create more of life and nature within a park in the city, or to make an area less hospitable to intruders. Merging with an archetype is using your spiritual ability to become one with a particular energy flow. It is like joining a great river. You can paddle your canoe but you have to go with the flow of water. Sometimes you can influence the path of your canoe and, similarly, working with archetypes you can greatly influence how an energy pattern affects the planet. You are not really in control. You are so enmeshed with the energy that you become a part of it. You can not control it but you do influence it and can direct it to your benefit.

I have always found archetypal work to be fascinating and a tremendous learning experience. By becoming one with a chosen archetype you perceive life and the world around you from another viewpoint or aspect of yourself.

By using archetype interaction you can influence the planet and nature for the better. There are some exercises in this book for learning how to connect with an archetype and how to merge into oneness with it. These exercises also show how to channel the archetype energy. Merging with an archetypal force changes your perceptions of yourself so that you have more of a world view and more of an understanding of the underlying forces with which you are constantly interacting. Archetypal work allows you to consciously understand and experience the energies and forces which most people think of or allow to be unconscious. This work also allows you to experience the interplay of life force energies from the most basic cellular level to the grandiose play of spiritual life forces surrounding the planet.

15

ARCHETYPAL EXCURSIONS

In order to go on an archetypal excursion you have to focus your energy upon how to create your essential archetypes. Sit in a comfortable chair, ground yourself, run energy and meditate. Meditation will relax your body and mind so that you can tune in to both the inner essential you and your higher self—the part that represents the divinity on the planet, the coming of the awareness of the God force within you. It is easier to tune to these higher vibrational levels of awareness when you are in a meditative, relaxed state of consciousness.

Bring yourself into present time, that great timekeeper of the here and now. Allow yourself to breathe deeply and to feel comfortable sitting in your chair. Just as we embody many different aspects of our personalities so, too, can we manifest the ability to become many different archetypes.

THE INNER YOU ARCHETYPE

As you say hello to yourself first ask who you are speaking to. There is the Inner You and the Higher Self. The Inner You is your body personality, that part of yourself that derived its wisdom and knowledge from your life experiences in this lifetime. The Inner You has aspects of your personality that I call body personality archetypes. When you speak to the Inner You, who answers? What type of person speaks back to you. If you could, for a minute, make believe that you were another person speaking to yourself (which is kind of like holding up a mirror to yourself) and you could shake your hand and say hello, who would be the person saying hello back?

We humans, all of us, carry within us the seeds of our destructive behavior as well as the seeds of our highest self realization. As you say hello to yourself who says hello back? Is it the stubborn five-year-old who wants attention? Or the resistant rebel who does not want to be told by the adults or the person in authority what to do? Or the romantic teenager who sees life through strangely colored glasses? Or a person who is just plain angry? Or a person who is confused? Or a person who wants to run away and hide from the chaos of our overdeveloped world? Or the parent who is in charge? Or the adult who has no permission to laugh and have fun. Or the wide-eyed child of innocence and wonderment? Who is the Inner You that you connect with? It could be many different aspects and they do change constantly, but who is the Inner You that you are speaking with **right now**?

As your Higher Self comes into the body to communicate with the world it has to speak through the Inner You. It has to work through the Inner You, which is the vehicle that it has helped to create in this lifetime to further its actions. Each action that you create in the world to shape your reality and your universe is formed by the interplay of the Higher Self, the conscious mind, and the subconscious or Inner You. As you wish to create your reality, to make a beautiful universe for yourself, you have to learn to integrate these three parts of your working energy anatomy. If the Inner You is filled with anger or sadness then you cannot channel the higher part of yourself nor the aspect of your chosen universal archetype onto the material plane.

The Inner You must be clear and unblocked. To do this you must begin to know the Inner You, that internal subconscious part of yourself, the inner persona, that fills your waking life with emotions, feelings, and meaning. Say hello to the Inner You right now and see who says hello back. Or take notice of what part of yourself is running the show right now. Do not be upset if you discover that the Inner You does not live up to your expectations of being the sweet, nice, gentle, loving, caring human being you think you are. We are human and it is the body personality, the human part of ourselves, the inner persona, that is the closest to the natural animal state of awareness.

It is the Inner You that could feel hatred for someone and yet at the same time feel love for that same person. It is the Inner You that produces all of those deep impassioned emotions that tend to obfuscate your issues in a situation and run you around in circles. And yet it is the Inner You that you must contact and know and begin to understand its processes in order to channel the higher archetypes. Otherwise, if you wish to be the universal archetype of Venus, Goddess of Love, and your Inner You is mad and angry, you will not achieve your goal as the love vibration archetype. You will not be able to channel that love archetype through a mad and angry body archetype. So you must begin to understand what is happening to you internally.

The Inner You is the "feeling" message that you give to yourself and others. You can learn to sense it, know it, feel it and change it by putting that feeling or message into a rose and blowing it up (as described in the energy exercises in the Self Transformation Chapter) to release the energy or charge you hold in "feeling" this way. You will know if your rose worked for you because if it works you will actually "feel" differently.

The Inner You is the archetype or pattern you choose to be at this present moment. That could be the child, the parent, the adult, the authoritarian, the innocent, the victim, the martyr, the warrior, the hero/heroine, the miracle worker, and many more. Whatever you are feeling or sensing, you can condense into **one** of the archetypes of experience. Follow your feelings and keep asking yourself **why** you feel "this" or "that" until you reach the essential archetype your body persona is projecting at this moment. You must reach an experiential knowledge of this archetype and then be able to clear by de-energizing it in a rose, in order to get to a higher state of awareness that can then manifest a universal archetype.

For example, if I am on edge and out of sorts and not balanced within myself I keep following those feelings until they lead me to a strong emotion. I then discover that those feelings are of anger and frustration. I follow those emotions until I come to the realization that I am angry at someone. At first I think I am angry at my friend but soon realize that I am angry from when I was six years old and could not get the candy I wanted. I am angry at an authority figure and I am angry at feeling helpless and powerless. When my friend does something that makes me feel powerless in a particular situation then my past history of feeling powerless crops up and I become the angry, frustrated, powerless six year old. This is my archetype, the angry, rebellious six-year-old child. Or, in short terms, **angry rebellious child.** If I do not clear this out I will be channeling my higher archetype through this and I will be stuck in accomplishing all of my goals through anger and rebellion. My world, or my personal universe will mirror my anger and rebelliousness to bring situations that cause or seem to further my anger. If I am doing energy work to reown some land and create it as a local park instead of a development project, I would experience channeling my efforts through anger and rebellion during the entire energy working. This is energy draining and a waste of my resources!

When you incorporate the use of a higher archetype you need to have the "lower" part of yourself, the body personality, clear. In other words, once you have discovered what the essential Inner You archetype is, you begin to clear it by putting the anger and rebellion into a rose and blowing it up. You put the images of your childhood into a rose and blow them up. You place the feelings you have into a rose and blow them up. You transform the "stuck" energy into new life force energy and you clear your personal vehicle of your old patterns. Then, when you have cleared and processed the lower body, the Inner You archetype, you are ready to be the Higher Self universal archetype. You then are ready to go to work, to actually be able to accomplish something with planetary healing.

THE UNIVERSAL ARCHETYPE

The Universal Archetype is a "charged" image that people associate with unconsciously. It bridges culture, race, time, and even belief systems, and becomes an unconscious awareness that people channel through themselves to access the collective unconscious. Ancient peoples used these charged images to create a mass awareness, such as a particular religious holiday, so that everyone could identify with a specific action or emotion and thus lend their energy to it to heal themselves or cultivate their crops or raise energy for their harvest. Some older Universal Archetypes are the mythological gods and goddesses such as Demeter, Kore, Pan, Venus, Thor, Zeus, Isis, Diana, Dagda, Deae Matres, Quan Yin, Ometeotl, and Quetzalcoatl. These archetypes hold a great deal of energy because generations of people have channelled their energy through them and have used them to affect their reality. Whenever you connect with this level of information and awareness, consciousness that has been charged for centuries, you embody the power, knowledge, and ability ascribed to that archetypal being.

To make a connection with a higher or greater aspect of life, choose an archetype you want to become one with. Many people, at first, choose to connect with the archetype that represents the mythology or history of their culture or genealogy. People of Northern European descent might choose to get in touch with Woden or Freya, a Hawaiian might choose to get in touch with Pele, or a Mediterranean European might choose to work with Pan, Diana, Verbius, or Poseidon. There are multitudinous archetypal connections that you can choose to make. For a person of Middle Eastern descent it could be Innana, Ishtar, Ninhursag, Isis, Al-Uzzah, the Virgin Mary and Enki, Utu, Osirus, Jesus, or the Trinity of Christ. In India it might be Visnu (Rama, Krishna), Shiva (Rudra, Nataraja), Ganesha, Parvati, Devi, Kali, or Shakti. An American Indian might choose Shakuru, Paiyatemu, Ataksak, T'ahn, the Sioux Wakan Tanka, Huruing Wuhti, or Iyatiku depending upon tribal ancestry and beliefs. An African might choose to work with Amma Dogon

160

(Sudan), Khonuum (Pygmies), Anansi (Ashanti), Balubaale (Uganda), Nyambe (of the Koko in Nigeria), Obassi Osaw (of the Itausa of the Niger), and so on depending on their tribe, location, and belief system. A Japanese might choose Izanagi, the creator god, or Amaterasu, the Japanese goddess of the sun or Tsuki-Yomi, a god of the moon, or Susanoo, the guardian of the seas, or Kichiyo-Ten, the goddess of good fortune and beauty. And so on around the world. The list could go on for pages.

You may, of course, not choose to connect up with a god or a goddess or a God force but might choose to make a connection with the moon, the sun, the stars, the earth, the wind, an animal or insect, a river, or a mountain. You can also choose to connect with the archetypes of divine or superhuman stature such as the Hero/Heroine, the Warrior, the Magician (one who can transform a situation or make magic), the Martyr, the Innocent or Fool, the Healer, or the three-fold side of human growth the Maiden/ Mother/ Crone (female) or the Initiate/Father/ Elder (male).

When you are making a connection with an essential archetype you are not worshipping or revering this life form or energy essence. You are becoming like it and one with it. You are learning to vibrate as that being would vibrate, as if it were here in the room with you and was a part of you. Please do not misinterpret becoming a god or a goddess as worshipping or revering it. This was the uneducated manner in which people were led to believe they were to connect up with an essential archetype. This led in the past to flagrant abuse of life force and free will.

Becoming an archetype is manifesting the qualities, abilities, and attributes of that essential being. If you become the mountain, you have the strength and solidity of the mountain. If you become the river, you have the strength and freedom and power and movement that the water has, and the life-giving abilities of the river. If you become the archetype of the Great Mother, you have the power to give birth, to protect and nourish, to create and care for all. If you are "being" the archetype of Jesus, you have the attributes of healing, divine wisdom, love, compassion, and being the essence of the martyr—depending on what qualities you choose to take on. And, if you become the archetype of Poseidon, you have the qualities of generosity, a good heart, the ability to direct the rivers and the seas, and to "create" earthquakes because, as Poseidon, you are the father of life, the keeper of horses, bulls, and farms, and the great power of the collective unconscious.

If you work with the essential archetypes of the superhuman experience, such as the Hero/Heroine, Innocent or Fool, the Warrior, the Martyr, the Healer, the Magician, or the Mother or Father, then you will innately begin to see parts of your life mirrored in these essences. You will learn what games or images you play on your stage of life and how you can modify the ones that you use too much and how to initiate strengths from the archetypes you are afraid to manifest or own within yourself. You can learn to use these concepts in daily life to understand your ability to define your own power and consciousness. *The Hero Within* by Carol S. Pearson is a good resource book on this subject that delves into the ability to identify, understand, and realize the archetypes we manifest and how to use them to allow ourselves to change and become "whole."

Whether you choose to or not, you will become the result of the archetypal images that you unconsciously or consciously channel through your awareness. You can work with these on a psychological level to understand what these images are and how you choose to identify or use them. If you work with these images using archetypal creations that are similar to ones you are introduced to in this book, then you will become aware of these essential energies through action and your ability to act them out on your inner stage of life. For example, one archetypal image that exists and is necessary for fulfilling our growth is the Warrior. Men are trained as warriors from childhood while women often ignore this ability, shy away from it, and are generally frightened to own or define it. The Warrior is the person who is in constant battle. It is he or she who stands up for the innocent, the wronged, and the righteous. It is he or she who can speak out or state the truth of a matter. And it is he or she who can take a stand and fight for what is right.

A Warrior is not the end all or the final stage in personality development, but it is a necessary step on the path towards ultimate enlightenment or ownership of a balanced personality and lifestyle. I discovered this for myself when I was doing an archetypal creation with a group of people many years ago. We were communicating with the goddess of the earth, the wise crone or keeper of the winter. At first we had someone lead us through a relaxation process to feel at peace, relaxed in body and mind, and breathing deeply. The speaker then guided us with a visualization into the depths of Mother Earth. Even now I can hear her crystal clear voice leading us to a cave, showing us where to find torches to carry for light, directing us down the long passageway to an underground lake and around it to an even deeper passageway to a large cavernous opening and telling us to find the goddess of the earth. We were to ask for a gift from her that we could bring back with us to our "real" lives. Immediately

I saw a woman, whom I perceived as a goddess because she was larger than life and somewhat translucent. She glowed with light as if a charged energy field surrounded her. She had long grey hair and strong solid facial features and seemed old and wise and all-knowing. I asked her for a gift to take home with me and thanked her for her presence. She smiled this enigmatic smile, which made me wonder a bit, and then, in this melodious voice she stated that there was plenty and that I was welcome to take home a gift—to just help myself. She gestured towards another cave-like chamber opening and I went over and saw a huge stone box, somewhat like the carved stone burial boxes that Roman warriors were buried in. The stone receptacle was filled with swords. Every type of sword that you could possibly imagine was lying in this stone box. My instant reaction was one of horror! This was not what I wanted. I did not want a sword. I was not a warrior. I was a gentle person. And so I walked back into the other room and told the goddess that I could not find a gift and could she possibly give me something else. She smiled in that enigmatic, amused manner once more and then said that I could go over to the other side of the cavern and take anything I liked and that I should take something as a token of her hospitality and love, and that I must learn to be satisfied with what I was given. I walked over to the other cavern and sure enough there was another stone box. But there, too, were only swords. The place seem to be overrun with swords. In disappointment I picked a sword and returned, retracing my steps along the path I had come. The goddess had disappeared, not to be seen again on my path in the cave.

When I returned to the world of reality and to the discussion held afterwards, we shared our stories about the gifts we had received. I explained how I had refused the original gift of the goddess only to be offered the same gift once more. The people in the group pointed out that perhaps there was a lesson I had to learn about being a warrior and standing up with the sword of truth. I was resistant and could not "hear" or acknowledge this at the time.

However, several months later I learned that I had to speak up and say what was really on my mind. Some people had made statements that I felt used racist and demeaning language to my co-workers and myself. At first I did not wish to say anything. I wanted to ignore their comments, which were more out of ignorance than actual racial reaction, but a little voice deep inside of me told me that I had to stand up and speak my mind for I was carrying the sword of truth. If I did not speak my mind I would carry around these feelings of hurt and distrust for many years to come. I noticed that in speaking out that my anger, fear, hurt, and distrust seemed to melt away. Suddenly I was just a person who spoke from her inner self and who said what was her truth. Several people had used negative concepts, insinuating that their co-workers were cheap, tight, and narrow-minded. However, instead of using those words, they used racial slurs and cultural insinuations. As I pointed this out, they began to understand the lack of consciousness in their language. They saw that their opinions could be expressed in a constructive manner instead of name calling.

So I had become the warrior, a stance I had always been frightened of and generally avoided. But in becoming the warrior who stood up and spoke her mind, I also became the heroine for my co-workers because I justly explained the situation. When the goddess gave me the sword, she was simply pointing out that I might need it and that the time had come for me to stand up and speak freely from my inner self. She had pointed out that, no matter how much I avoided becoming the Warrior, all people have to experience and allow this to manifest at some time in their lives and that my time had come.

As I learned from this experience, and as you will learn from your own similar experiences, once you begin to work with essential archetypal qualities on an internal level you begin to rebalance your overall personality to become the best "you" you can be.

PRACTICAL USES OF ARCHETYPAL ENERGIES

You can use your ability to "become" archetypal energy in any given situation. I have some friends who perform in hospitals during the holiday season. One of them will go dressed as a clown and become the archetype of Mickey Mouse as he enters the room. The qualities of Mickey Mouse allow him to perform in a happy pleasing manner to cheer everyone up. When he "is" Mickey Mouse he is not nervous or concerned about his performance. He truly becomes Mickey Mouse, who is the quintessential performer, the absolute happy person, and the friend of all. As Mickey Mouse, nothing is impossible for him to perform and he is the skilled natural people-greeter because Mickey Mouse can always "make magic".

We normally "become" and "are" archetypes unconsciously and without awareness. When you choose to consciously use your mind and active spirit to create your dreams and fill your life with action you have the power and ability to change yourself and your world. Instead of being or feeling powerless you can assume the archetype of a particular essence and use that to change or help your situation. When I am on the street at night alone in a dangerous neighborhood, I do not walk along with fear, misgivings, and insecurity. I call upon my inner reserve to become the archetype that I can use to create a safe situation until I leave the area. Sometimes I assume the archetype of a large cat, like a tiger or panther, which allows me to increase my hearing, my sense of smell, my night vision, and my ability to walk agilely to protect myself. As a cat I am the predator and am in touch with the acute senses of my body to alert me to danger and to protect me. As a cat I am strong and only the foolish would approach me. When you feel that incredible strength within yourself, the strength of the cat, then you are that archetype and you are one with the essential energy of your spirit and the universe.

When you choose to become an archetype it is valuable to know as much about that river, mountain, god or goddess, animal, or insect as you can. You will learn what that archetype is by just being it. To be able to create as powerful an archetype as you need, you should do your research about all of its qualities ahead of time. You want to know what that archetype does and is and whether or not you are in affinity or agreement with it. It is always best to "become" an archetype that is the same sex as the body you have in this life. People who work with archetypes and "become" other sexual identities often experience confusion and sexual identity problems if they work with their archetype for too long a time. You will wish to pick an archetype that you are in affinity with, feel comfortable with, and that reinforces the sexuality and identity of your body. Some archetypes are neutral, such as a river, or the wind, but others have specific sexual identities. It is wise to pay attention to these identities and pick one that is in accordance with you. As you become the archetype of a certain creation, you intuitively learn all of its aspects as you experience it internally.

You do not want to remain in an archetypal mode for too long. It can charge you initially but if you remain in it for too long it can also drain you. When you are that archetype you immediately use it for your specific project and then let go of it and come back to your own essential self. In this manner you do not lose yourself or muddle your personality with another's. If you remain too long in one single archetype you will suppress your personality and lose your own personal development on the planet. This could become a negative situation. Archetype working is enacted for short periods of time, not for days, weeks, or months. Once you have experienced a particular attribute or aspect of a specific archetype you should be able to repeat it within your own personality—if that is your goal. For example, if you become the archetype of Pan or Flora to become sexual, party going, and fun loving, you only need to experience it briefly. Once you have fully experienced this energy, you should be able to integrate it within your own personality and not need to keep becoming the archetype to re-experience it. If you are using an archetype to channel a specific type of energy to the Earth you will, of course, have to re-experience that archetype each time that you need to direct that type of earth energy. But even here, you should never have the archetype channeling last more than a few hours or it will debilitate you and drain the life force from your own essential personality.

Working with universal archetype energy can be enlivening and will give you an extra charge in life. More importantly, it teaches you to internally and intuitively understand the flow of life force energy from another viewpoint. Being the river or the mountain is a different form of consciousness from being the human being in a car on the way to work. When you "become" one of the old mythological gods or goddesses you might notice that they seem to come with a built-in special extra charge of energy. This is from all of the people who have poured their energy into this thought form. However, unlike new age channeling or old style use of mediumistic abilities, "becoming" the archetype allows you to stay here in present time while also allowing you to become **one** with that energy essence. You are still in control, as long as you choose to be. You still run the show and decide what to do and how to do it. You cannot be taken over or controlled as you are never leaving your body to allow another spirit to take over. You are not channeling or being a medium. You are sharing and experiencing a different type of life force energy. This allows you to remain within the framework of your own personal morality, belief system, and religion and yet also explore and experience the world of spirit. As you become the archetype you will, however, experience the intensity of connecting with a source of power that is sometimes not only power-packed but a stream of consciousness that is far beyond our normal understanding of spirit and spirituality.

"BECOMING"

"Becoming" the universal archetype is an easy process to accomplish. It is so easy in fact, that the problems people often have doing it are because they make it more complicated than it actually is!

When you wish to "become" a universal archetype, ground yourself and clear yourself of all imprints or emotions that cloud or fog you up and generally use up your attention. Then clear your mind and concentrate on the particular archetype you wish to become. First concentrate on the archetype, then list its attributes, and next call to it to come and be with you. Yes, you call to it as if it is another person or being or spirit that can share time and life space and attention with you. Traditional energy workers would call to an archetype as if they were announcing a visitor to the Queen or reading poetry describing the archetype in question. They loudly announce their intentions, their desire to become one with a particular archetype, and they invite it to come and visit them. Sometimes they would create surroundings that would mirror the very essence of the archetypal energy they were calling. So if they were calling the goddess Venus, for example, they would burn rose incense, wear pink and rose clothes, burn a pink candle, and have love items (hearts and flowers, for example) in the room. But this is the **old** method of working. It works, but it is time consuming, sometimes un-wieldy and bulky, and often difficult in public situations.

As a modern energy worker you could do this but it is not necessary in order to bring the archetype energy to you. You do not have to become an actor reading a scripted play, or read romantic beautiful poetry, or loudly prescribe your desire to have the presence of "so and so." I have called in archetypal beings while standing in a public park, at a dance, at dinner, and on a bus. In doing so, of course, I did not stand up and suddenly become a Shakespearian actress to call the essence of the arche-type to me. When I call in an archetype I ground myself, bring myself totally into present time, clear my Inner Self and my emotional level, clear my mind of extraneous thoughts, think of the archetype I desire, list the attributes of that archetype, attempt to feel at one with the essence of this archetype, and call to it and invite it to come to me. Sometimes I wax poetically (my own made-up version of poetry which is sheer perfection to my ears alone) but if I am in a public place I do this silently or subvocally. If I am alone in my own yard or home then I can vocally state my intentions. Once you have learned to call in an archetype and have experienced this sense of super consciousness you will always be able to accomplish making this connection. This is a learned skill.

CALLING A UNIVERSAL ARCHETYPE

Gaia

Gaia is the goddess who has become the symbol of the entire planetary biosphere in action. Gaia sprang forth from eternal Chaos and then bore Ouranos, the sky, and Pontus, the sea. She then mated with Ouranos to bring forth the Titans, the Cyclopes, and the Hekatoncheires, the one hundred-armed giants. Here is a section of poetry by Hesiod, the first Greek to describe the goddess Gaia:

> *Earth, the beautiful, rose up,*
> *Broad-bosomed, she that is the steadfast base*
> *Of all things. And fair Earth first bore*
> *The starry Heaven, equal to herself,*
> *To cover her on all sides and to be*
> *A home forever to the blessed gods.*[8]

James Lovelock, the inventor, published a book in 1979 about the biosphere of Earth called, *Gaia: A New Look at Life on Earth*. Its thesis is that the Earth is alive and that all Earth is a biosphere. It challenges us to learn to see ourselves as a part of a whole living organism that is named after the Greek Goddess Gaia, Mother Earth. Lovelock did not imply that Gaia was a conscious or thinking goddess. Often we energy workers have learned that the goddess does not think with the type of conscious mind we humans use. She simply acts and reacts, balances and rebalances the proper proportions to make nature work in equilibrium and to create homeostasis. It is this properly and delicately balanced homeostasis that allows us humans to exist on this planet.

THE GAIA ARCHETYPE

I am she who is the entire earth, the planet as a whole, the biosphere that you stand upon and are a part of. I am Mother Earth who bore your ancestors and who gives you life: the earth to stand upon, the air to breathe, the waters to drink from, the trees to shelter you, the plants to eat and tend, and the seas to bathe in. I am the creatrix of all. You sit in the folds of my skin and I hug you to my bosom and fill you with the warmth and love of all that surrounds you. I nourish you with my plants and animals, my stones and trees, my streams, rivers and oceans. I am always with you as you are also a part of my life force.

The Great Mother

The Great Mother is the nurturer and keeper of all. A good example of the concept of the Great Mother is the small archeological statues of the Venus of Willendorf, a two-inch high carved stone statue from prehistoric Austria of a mother figure. The Venus of Willendorf has been described as the Paleolithic mother and as of having the feeling of purpose and contentment. The Venus of Willendorf has also been described as amply stating the "mother" with its folds of prosperous flesh and rounded contours and the manner in which she holds her arms and hands upon her hips to give you the impression she is the milk giver. You will find these images in books of prehistoric art and anthropology. If you search around the world you will find these small "Great Mother" fecundity figure statues in every culture where prehistoric history has been unearthed. The Great Mother was obviously a strong influence here on the planet.

The Venus represents the fullness, the rounded female who is pregnant with life, she who is the keeper of all life forms. Emotionally, this archetype is a healing one for people who lack a female parent or have been abused or need to have the nurturing and unconditional love that only a mother can give you. As a planetary connection, the Great Mother gives birth to all and is the nurturing caring part of the planet that sustains all life forms.

THE GREAT MOTHER ARCHETYPE

I am she who nurtures all living beings. I am huge and grand in size and deed. I surround you and give birth to you and take care of you. I am the mother of all. I am she who is the earth, who surrounds you with the nurturing soil of life, who births you in spirit and body in the deep dark caves of my soul, who fills your belly with food, and touches your body with love. I am the mother who suckles you at my breast and holds you in my arms. From me all manner of material matter comes and to me all matter must eventually return.

173

The Spirit of the River

A river is a large natural stream of fresh water that flows across land in a definite channel for all or part of the year.[9] Rivers have been seen as holy manifestations of God or oneness since time immemorial. People bath in holy waters, baptize themselves in holy waters, and generally feel blessed to contact the great spirit of a clean running river. Rivers represent the flowing waters of life, the intuitive ability to be cleansed and changed and anointed with love and life, and the ability to transform into the next step of evolutionary awareness.

THE RIVER ARCHETYPE

I am the spirit of the waters of life. I flow downstream, gently and yet powerfully. I have currents, rapids, eddies, and inlets. I slowly but surely carve out a canyon in the earth with my waters. I am the power of moving water. I give life to all who come and drink of my waters and live in my moving body. I am the waters of life, the spirit of transformation and change, the giver of life to the earth that I run through on my path to the sea. I nourish all who come to my banks with my life giving transformative waters for I am the spirit of change and creation.

The Moon

The moon is an interesting archetypal image to work with because it illuminates all that we think is dark and unseeable. The moon gives us light but sometimes this light is different and illusory in its nature, much like the light you see at night that makes distances and objects seem distorted. In most ancient and primitive cultures the moon was seen as female but in other cultures it was seen as male. In most cultures where the moon was seen as female the sun was viewed as male. There are a few references, historically unproven, to older matriarchal cultures that viewed both the moon and sun as female. This, however, is rare. The moon was usually associated with women because of the natural connection between the phases of the moon in its twenty-eight day cycle and a woman's menstrual cycle.

THE MOON ARCHETYPE

I reflect the sun. My light is pale but strong and illumines your path at night. I move in phases from being invisible but existent, to growing to a pale sliver of light, which are the horns of my moon, and soon I grow fuller and fuller. As I grow in each quarter I give the earth more light. As I increase my light from a quarter moon towards the full moon all that is above the ground grows well, and all that is a positive action moves well. At the full moon I raise the sap in the trees, the quickening spirit in humans, and give all manner of creatures light to travel and be merry by. But I am changeable in my nature and soon wane in light until I am a quarter moon once more and the light is less and I begin to grow pale and wane with old age. As my light dims and wanes the plants that are root plants, under the ground grow stronger and fuller. People stay indoors and contemplate the inner side of their selves. Soon I wane away to a pale crescent of my former self and then disappear altogether. Whatever is seen in my light has the nature of illusion for my light is pale, mystical, magical, and casts a spirit of mystery upon all I illumine in the night air. I am the Moon. I govern women's bodies in that they move in their cycles to match mine own. I bring out the internal feelings people hide, the emotions of their hidden natures, the nature of their changes, as they seek to be like me, ever changeable in my disposition.

The Sun

The sun represents life and light and the spark of the divine that gives our planet the ability to be more than just a ball of dirt in the sky. To the sun we attribute all that is golden, light, successful, and healthy. Traditionally the sun represents the individual, the higher powers of light and life, power, money, willpower, confidence, and the desire for self improvement. For us, all of the creatures on this planet Earth, the sun is our charged battery. It is the eternal light of life that fills us with the warmth and glow of a higher consciousness and is the ultimate source of all forms of energy on the Earth. In olden days the sun was always associated with the King, the divine heir, the highest position and representation of human power on earth. The child of the Sun God was the King of the People. Now we have grown out of the superstitious era into a more universal realm of understanding to know that we are all children of the Sun God (the oneness of life, or God as some call it) and that our individuality is a precious gift of life.

THE SUN ARCHETYPE

I am the fire of life. I can also be the fire of death. I am the fire of eternal spirit. I give light and life and warmth and fire to all who need it. I can be strong and unyielding. Yet it is in my power that all who need me are blessed with the spirit of light and life and growth. I am the spark of life force that fills the earth with the ability to change and grow.

Johnny Appleseed

Johnny Appleseed was the name given to the American pioneer turned folk hero, John Chapman. He was born in Leominster, Massachusetts on Sept. 26, 1774, and died in 1845.

John Chapman procured apple seeds from the pomace of cider presses and established a large number of orchards by planting them in the land between the Allegheny River and the Saint Marys River. Mr. Chapman was known for his extreme kindness to wild animals, his great generosity, and his unusual exploits of courage. As Mr. Chapman traveled westwards towards Indiana he planted his seeds and became a symbol of the altruistic orchardist. He soon became known as Johnny Appleseed. John Chapman was a follower of the religious sect known as Swedenborgianism, called by many the "new Christianity" in that it believed in the power of spirit and in "growth from within." Johnny Appleseed is seen by many as being the patron saint of American orcharding, floriculture, and conservation.[10]

JOHNNY APPLESEED ARCHETYPE

I am a planter of trees. I love trees and enjoy helping them to seed the lands they were originally given to forest. I plant apple trees wherever I go in order to spread the trees of abundance who give us their fruit. I carry a bag of seeds with me and wherever I can I plant some seeds to grow a tree. I am happy in my actions and I whistle and I sing as I travel along my path planting apple trees. I am the planter of orchards, the spreader of seeds, the ardent admirer of trees, the lover of wild animals, and an admirer of nature. I see beauty and shelter and food come from the trees I plant as I travel along my path in life.

The Warrior

At one time or another each one of us has had to connect with the warrior within us. Some of us identify with this archetype on a daily level and others of us only allow this into our awareness when we watch a Hollywood movie. The Warrior is the part of us which must fight to survive. The Warrior needs a constant challenge to survive and must find a battle in every situation. The Warrior is the part of us that must stand up and speak the truth; fight for what is right; protect the innocent, wronged, and needy; and stand up for our power and our right to respect ourselves.

THE WARRIOR ARCHETYPE

I am the Warrior. I fight to survive and to win and to care for all that is. I know no other way to exist but to fight. I am skilled in all of the arts of combat, no matter what culture I am in, since I am an exemplary warrior. All life is a battleground, all battles a challenge to action, all actions an act of war, all life a challenge to win. I know only to fight and succeed. I am the champion of causes, the protector of the innocent. I choose to sustain life-giving activities, to fight for what I deem is right, to nourish and care for all who need me. I am strong in my power and quick in my action. I fight to protect myself and to care for the world I live in. I fight for the right of all life force to exist in a loving, nurturing, positive world.

The Healer

The Healer is a person who needs to nourish, care for, and transform all that come into contact with him/her. To be a Healer is a gift of nature but to live as a Healer is a life style.

THE HEALER ARCHETYPE

I help to heal and change all that I come in contact with. By my very nature I cause all who interconnect with me to transform and change. I am the Healer. I do not choose to heal. My very nature is that of change. Since my nature is change, all who meet me transform to their next challenge in life. Because of my nature I can reach deep down into the hidden inner recesses of the mind or the spiritual being or the body and enable a person to release and change his totally unconscious patterns that cause dis-ease or uncomfortable discordant behavior. Almost on a totally unconscious level I can speak to the trees, to the earth, to the winds, to the elements, and to the wee beings, and help them to purge their essences of the toxic poisons that the humans have unconsciously or unknowingly dumped on them. I am a healer because I help others, be they human or earth, spirit or material, animal or mineral, to see their options and act on them to change in a fast, positive manner. As a Healer I give of the very inner core of myself without asking for anything in return. I seek to merge with the very cellular forces of life itself to spin and dance and transform in the music of life. I am the next step in the evolutionary path of this planet.

ARCHETYPAL CREATION

 BEING ONE WITH GAIA

Take a deep breath. You could be standing or sitting in a chair. Ground yourself and bring yourself totally into present time, into that wonderful awesome creative awareness of the here and now.

Say hello to yourself and see who says hello back. What type of answer do you receive? Clear yourself of any extraneous thoughts or feelings, of what you must do tomorrow and what you did yesterday, and just let yourself be in touch with the simple essence of your inner self, the peaceful part of yourself that is just still and knows.

You are still. You are quiet. You are at peace with yourself.

Now, you wish to become the archetype of Gaia, the goddess who is the earth, the sky, and all that surrounds it. She who is the total sphere of life force which gives you the ability to be alive and to be one with the planet Earth.

Imagine, for a moment, a place that represents the spirit of life, the spirit of nature, the whole of nature's totality. Right now you can see yourself in the woods. You can smell the trees, hear the birds, hear animal rustlings in the bushes, feel the wind in your hair, and see the green grove of trees and the wild herbs growing nearby. You lie down on the ground and feel the warm leaves beneath you cushioning your body as it lies on the earth. And you look upwards and see the grove of tall green trees around you and the bright blue sky through the leaves of the trees. You feel comforted and nurtured by the warm earth that seems to hold you in its grasp and surround your body with its warmth. You begin

181

to think of Gaia, the goddess who is the Earth and all that is, in the here and now. She who holds your body and cradles you in her warm leaves. You see the trees as her hair and the sky as her breath. As you lay very still you can hear her breath and feel the warm winds caress you.

Feel your body and the energy around you and imagine yourself as being encased in a big bubble of energy. This sphere of energy is you, your personal universe, your feelings and your energy. Now slowly expand your sphere of energy. You can feel the leaves on the ground become a part of your sphere of energy. You can sense the soil underneath you become a part of your universe. Slowly and gently you can feel the sky above you and you become joined and one with it. As you expand your sphere of energy, your consciousness joins with each thing that you bring into it. And so you become the earth, the leaves, the trees, and the sky as your bubble of energy continues to slowly expand. Soon you are encompassing the woods that you are in, the rolling hills beyond, the land and cities beyond that. And as your bubble expands you become the entire continent, the seas, and soon the entire planet. Feel yourself joined as one with the planet. You can feel it breathe and move, you can sense its reactions and its life force awareness. You can feel or sense that the planet is constantly rebalancing and you might even become aware of hot spots or trouble spots where the earth is having a problem rebalancing its nature. And your bubble of energy keeps moving outward as you encompass the entire planet and move outward and beyond to include space.

When you have gotten your consciousness beyond the planet and a little ways out into space, then stop your bubble sphere from growing any further. Take a deep breath and allow yourself to see the planet Earth, be the planet Earth, and feel the planet Earth. Internally, from your mind's eye you can intuitively sense

182

the internal workings of the planet, as you have become the entire planet and are one with it. Although Gaia, Mother Earth, does not think, somehow you can know and feel her reactions and the interplay of what is happening with her right now. Take the time to feel this as it can give you invaluable information and totally tune you into the very essence of the Earth as a whole biosphere of one living breathing cellular consciousness.

Once you have felt the conscious movement of Gaia and experienced her rhythm and tides, then slowly begin to have your bubble sphere of energy start to diminish and come inwards. You can feel yourself losing a certain amount of consciousness, of your perimeters being narrowed as your bubble shrinks, but you can also feel yourself gaining more specific focus. Keep pulling your sphere inwards towards you until once more you are back in your own body consciousness in the grove of trees, hearing the rustle of the winds through the trees and the leaves crackle as small animals run hither and about. As you bid farewell to the superconsciousness of knowing and feeling Gaia as one entity and come back to the mortal life of diversification, of individual identity, know that you can always speak to the Goddess of the Earth, and join with and internally know the earth nature force we are all a part and piece of as this is our heritage for we are Gaia's children.

Now take a deep breath and bring yourself back from the grove of trees in the woods. Stand up, become totally aware of who you are in present time and how your body feels. Say hello to your body and bring all of your waking consciousness back to wherever you are physically.

We are always one with Gaia, the whole earth, but often because we are lost in our own individual consciousness we forget that this is so. We forget that we can hook into the greater superconsciousness and experience the overview of life force. We forget that we are a part of the whole. Sometimes our egos and our intellectual minds tell us that we are special and apart from nature and above and beyond it. It is wise to connect up with the archetype of Gaia, the wholeness of the Earth, every once in a while to allow your mind and your ego to intuitively understand the subtle but all too real connection between your body and essence and the planet Earth. The more often we make this connection the more we learn to realize our true positions on the planet as caretakers and creative expressions of the earth sphere, Gaia.

"I claim my life, my liberty, my light,
Part of all life that flows eternally.
I am the microcosm of the Whole
Kindred of star and stone and greenwood tree."

— *from an Invocation*
by Doreen Valiente

16

THE DANCE OF
THE TREES

Since 1967, every five seconds one acre of trees in this country is lost to deforestation!

Everyone in life has something that they are attracted or attached to, their own personal fetish or interest. My girlfriend adores cats. My manicurist is fascinated with hands. My neighbor is an inveterate bird watcher. My friends are entranced with the wilderness. And I love and have always been attracted to trees.

From the time when I was a little child, I would gaze up at the trees in my neighborhood and see the strength of the ages in them. And I would wonder how much history the tree had seen pass by it in its long life. In the fall, when the trees dropped their leaves, my friends and I would collect them and press them to last as colorful mementos of the season. In art class we would take the leaves and put them on a clear piece of paper under a mesh screen then get our old toothbrushes filled with watercolor paint and rub them on the mesh screen to leave a splattered modern art decal of our leaves. Trees offered me an endless array of opportunities to view life in action. I would watch the squirrels run up trees, or the birds who landed in the trees, or simply listen to the wind in the trees.

At some point in my early childhood, and I do not remember exactly when, I began to listen to the trees moving in the wind. To me, the breeze shifting the leaves sounded like a reed flute and it seemed that the trees spoke to me. I was a lonely child. Being an only child and living in a town where the greater majority of people were a different religion and had a different culture, led me to playing by myself and creating my own little imaginary universe. I grew to have many imaginary playmates to speak with. But when the trees spoke to me it was different. I knew that my imaginary playmates were an illusion and were not "real." But when the trees spoke to me, it was real. When the wind blew and the trees turned their leaves, I always knew that it would rain. The trees made me feel at peace and a part of a greater whole as they told me stories that seemed to date back to before their actual existence. They spoke of a time when the earth was covered with forests of trees and the little race of wee people lived in harmony with them. They told me of their sadness and pain at the loss of their larger race and at being treated as "sticks of wood" to be trimmed and pruned and cut at the whim of people. I never questioned the stories or information that the trees imparted to me. It was like an unconscious stream of speech that ran through me and just left me with information and a good feeling of belonging to a greater whole. I was no longer just "little me," through the trees I had a sense of belonging to a great giant race of beings whose roots reached down to the very essence of life.

THE GIVERS OF LIFE

Trees have given us many things throughout the ages. They give us their bark, roots, and leaves, which all have medicinal qualities. They purify the air we breathe and give us fruit, nuts, oil, paper, wood, and rubber. But most of all, the trees give to us of their spirit and heal us both physically and psychically. Many trees emit an energy that calms humans which is why people enjoy walking through the forest. Trees are probably the oldest living things on the planet. The redwoods in California are 4,000 years old and still growing!

In primitive cultures trees were held in reverence because they were the homes of the gods. Each tree was a receptacle for a spirit to inhabit. The spirits that lived in the trees lived long and venerable lives and learned to heal and absorb all negative energies that came their way. Before a tree was cut down the spirit of the tree had to be moved to another home and songs and chants and rituals had to be enacted to numb the tree before the chopping began. Blessings to God or the Great Spirit were offered to ask for permission to cut down the tree. And, because once something was taken away from nature its life force must be returned in some other way, the blessings included promises to plant certain crops or care for certain groves of trees in exchange for the tree that was chopped down.

One of the reasons that wood has been such a revered building medium is that the wood holds the imprint of the spirit of the tree. Have you ever built a fire and watched the wood burn? Often, if you pay careful attention, you can see the spirit of the wood or a face in the wood being released as the wood burns. The spirit of the wood lends itself to the object in which you place it. If you have a wooden bureau or a wooden chair or a wooden beam or doorway you can touch the wood and still feel the essence of the spirit of the tree. Early peoples would oil and rub and care for their wooden objects and treat them with reverence as if they were living things because they were considered "alive" with the spirit of the tree within them. This is the true "warmth" of the wood that people often refer to and this is what makes wooden objects seem more special or of a higher quality than plastics and other artificially-created mediums. You might feel this special quality if you take a piece of wood that has been carved into something and hold it in your hand and take the time to be still and "feel" the essence of the wood that you are holding.

Tomas Braverman, a master furniture craftsman who lives and works in Topanga Canyon outside Los Angeles, describes working with wood this way: "Some pieces of wood are magnificent. They are heroic... When you begin to make something of them you must realize that you are working with material that took nature 200 or more years to create. If you are going to cut down a tree like this in order to make something out of it, what you make had better be of value and beauty, and the person who receives the object should understand the gift... I feel sorry for the majority of people today who lead such alienated, compartmentalized lives. They put themselves in ecologically disastrous cars and drive to work in isolation. They spend their days on the phone talking to disembodied someones. They are alienated from the very processes that allow them to live, like farming or building their own shelter, so they have no real respect for the Earth. They buy things, like furniture, that has been mass-produced and that has no lasting value. The things they buy are disposable. Their lives become disposable. They are rootless and adrift… The poorest peasants in Spain used to have a richer life than we do because they lived closer to the land and their clothing and furniture was handmade with love."

There were, of course, "good" trees and "bad" trees, as humans perceive good and bad. The good trees were the trees that liked humans and could absorb the pain of a person and fill an area with light and life. They emitted a soft vibrant feeling that soothed all who came in range of the tree. People in pain would come and hug a tree and release their hurt which the tree spirit would then absorb. Women in labor would embrace the tree to release their pain as they gave birth beneath the tree. In many ancient cultures women would bury the afterbirth of their newborn between the earth and the roots of a tree to ensure that their child would be connected to the life force of the Earth Mother and to reinforce the relationship that exists between Mother Earth and humankind.[11] The "bad" trees were trees that harbored dark and ill thoughts in life and were not friendly towards humans at all. The bad trees would become energy sumps for decaying, nasty, and malevolent energy. They would fill an area with a heaviness and darkness that could drown the joy and light in your soul and fill you with a strange foreboding. Dark foreboding woods are the stories of ancient fairytales. Few people would choose to spend time in such inhospitable woods. These "negative" old growth trees would magnetize dark, dense, malevolent energy and pull it towards them to fill their negative energy vortex.

Each type of tree has a different quality and purpose in life. The pine tree is the symbol of eternal life and immortality. It is seen as the giver of life because its pine needles represent charged energy. The ancients revered pine trees as a symbol of fire since the tree shape resembles a spiral of flame. The peach tree is a symbol of marriage and abundance. The apple tree is a symbol of female fertility. The palm tree is seen as a symbol of rejuvenation since it renews itself and never changes it leaves. It has been used as a symbol of martyrdom and eternal life. The willow and yew trees are trees of death and sorrow and the dark side of life. The olive tree is seen as the giver of life and a protector against lightening. The oak tree is the sacred tree of the Druids and is seen as the father of humankind. It is considered one of the greatest of trees and certainly one of the eldest. The banyan tree is the keeper of eternal life, knowledge, and happiness. The fir tree is seen as a symbol of strength and masculinity, a symbol of the sun—the great source of life. The bo tree, a wild fig, is sacred to the Buddhists because it is said that Buddha sat under this tree for seven weeks in his search for knowledge. Bo trees have been symbols of spirituality for thousands of years and you can find these trees near every Eastern temple and planted at the graves of monks. The ancient Greeks revered the fig tree and considered it the most intelligent tree. They used it as a symbol of peace and abundance.

Very often we humans live our lives in small, closed-up shells, never taking the time to open ourselves to the sights, sounds, and energies of the nature that surrounds us. We close ourselves up in an artificial reality that we think serves us best. But often this artificial reality keeps us away from the most awesome and incredibly simple awareness that gives us meaning and light, and joy in life. If you take the time to open yourself up to feeling and sensing nature and to speaking to a tree, then you will know what being "a part of nature" is really all about. Then you will consciously join the stream of nature of which you are already a part.

COMMUNICATING WITH TREES

Try hugging a tree. Besides being terribly self-conscious, you might discover that the tree, in its own way and manner, hugs you back.

Since I was a little girl I have had this way of meditating with trees that allows me to feel their energies as they feel mine. I have never attempted to verbalize or explain this meditation before. But I will attempt to share it here because I feel it is a way of showing people how to find that lost consciousness of nature awareness that our very ancient ancestors seemed to naturally possess.

When I communicate with a tree I outstretch my hands with palms open facing towards the tree so that I can communicate from my "in" side. Showing our palms to the tree is like shaking hands with another human—you are telling them that you neither conceal nor carry weapons in your hands and that you are open to internal communication (the open palm symbolizes the inner side of your body). I then locate the spirit of the tree. Often I find this spirit in either the bottom part of the trunk or in the far upper part of the trunk. I radiate what I am feeling at the time, which is like "being" that emotion. If possible, of course, I try to radiate or broadcast love and warmth, just as I would smile at another human being. Most people tend to keep shut down to the warmth and love of others unless they are our immediate family or close friends or people we know. As people pass one another on the street of a small town they smile or say hello to one another. In large cities we tend to be defensive and closed in and only relate to those people whom we know. And yet, on some level, we do know the humanness or oneness that we can identify in everyone. You will find in big cities that people will stand in line at a supermarket and not interact, speak, or even smile to one another, but if there is a young child or a baby they will give themselves permission to smile and interact. I have met many people who are defensive with strangers or critical of others who let down their walls and defenses and relate lovingly to dogs, cats, and young children. Of course that is because the dogs, cats, and young children do not pose a threat to their identity or well-being. Trees also do not pose a threat to us. As a matter of fact, we are the ones who pose a threat to them! And so if you are conservative in your actions, afraid to show the inner love you feel outwardly lest it be interpreted wrongly, you can let it shine through when you "speak to a tree."

Just as with people interaction, if you smile or radiate love to a tree you will probably get love back. There have been quite a few books published in the last ten years documenting studies that prove plants respond to human emotions.[12] The plants seem to respond to loving thoughts as well as to negative thoughts. So, if you walk into a room and think of harming the plant or another human being, the plant will respond to your thought in one way. Conversely, if you think of loving the plant or loving some other person, the plant responds in a different way. For example, in one experiment a group came into the room of plants and told the plants not to grow. These plants withered away and died. Another group came into a second room of plants and prayed over the plants, emoting love and telling them to grow big and strong. These plants grew healthy and large.[13]

At our meditation center in Northern California we used to hold abundance ceremonies periodically throughout the year at harvest times. We would ask everyone to bring a piece of fruit and a quart of milk. We would gather the fruit together to represent the abundance of the harvest of life. The milk was used to represent the womb of life from which pours the overflowing fertility of life. We would get a large round bowl to represent fertility and a small rounded cup, like a chalice. Then we would form a circle with the bowl and the fruit in the center. One person would open the quart of milk and pour it into the small cup being held by another person. The milk would overflow from the cup into the bowl below. As we each took turns pouring the milk and experiencing having our cups overflowing we would chant and sing and hum and charge the milk with the blessings of the fertility of "may your cup runneth over with the good things of life." We would "raise" our energy for all of the abundance of good things to come into our lives and generally have a rousing good time as we celebrated our abundance. We would then pour the milk onto a scrawny tree in the garden as we radiated warm and loving thoughts of abundance. In one year our scrawny little tree grew by eight feet to be strong and mighty.

When I plant a tree I like to take a moment to meditate over it. If I plant it with someone, we hold hands over the tree and think loving thoughts of it growing to be a big, elderly, giant, healthy tree. I have spoken to many people who have trees in pots in their homes. Most of them have named their trees and speak to them as if they were a member of the family. They tell me that the trees not only make them feel good but communicate to them. It is as if the spirit of the tree shares their life space with them.

Trees, like people and small towns, can represent a continuity in your life. If you have planted a tree and seen it grow to maturity in your lifetime, it fills you with a different awareness and respect for that tree than if you just buy a house and the tree is there. I have two pine trees at the end of my driveway that have always seemed to be covered with the energy of love. One day, a few months after moving into our house, we became acquainted with an older couple who hiked up the hill every morning to go past our house and up the dirt road that enters into the Santa Monica National Park. As they hiked each early morning, meandering along the road with their three dogs, we came to know them and hear their stories of the area. They had built their own house and lived in the area for twenty years or so, raising their children and eventually retiring. They had watched a small community of vacation homes become a thriving rural, semi-suburban hideaway. They had lived in the area before the large power lines were put in, when the main highway was a single lane road through town, and when the road to their home got washed out every year as the local spring-fed lake overflowed. One day, 18 years ago, they had planted two small pine trees on the side of the road. These were the pine trees at the end of our driveway. Every morning as they walk past the pine trees they think of how they have grown and lovingly gaze upon them. They do not outwardly define themselves as "spiritual" people, however their loving energy extends outward to fill a very palpable space in the universe of living things.

Dancing With The Trees

The ancient cultures used to celebrate the turn of the wheel of the year seasonally at the Winter Solstice by going into the woods and dancing in a circle around an evergreen tree. This symbolized their desire to see life renewed, to see the cycle of life survive through the winter months to once again come back to bud and sprout in the springtime. The evergreen held energy as a tree that remained green throughout the winter months and it produced the pine cone. The closed pine cone is a symbol of the pituitary gland and the third eye (known as the Sixth Chakra in the Western system of spirituality), the energy center associated with clairvoyance and the ability to visualize or see spiritually.

Each tree has its own energy pattern or wave length on which it broadcasts. So when I commune with a tree I attempt to understand and get in tune with the actual energy pattern of the tree. Many pine trees have their energy and their branches go in a spiral. Pines hold a great deal of energy and the spiral is one of the most common energy raising forces on the planet (like chakras, cones of energy, tornadoes, water spouts, water draining, mixing in your blender, and so on). Some trees have their energy shoot straight upwards and outwards, like poplars. And other types of trees, like weeping willows, reach up and bend over towards the earth like a skirt.

I observe the tree and its pattern of movement. Then I take my energy and form it into that same pattern in my own energy field. It is difficult to describe this as it is a nonverbal and a somewhat innate intuitive action that I have done since I was a child when it came to me naturally. It is sort of like just being the tree. I do not, however, place my consciousness in the tree! I keep my consciousness and my energy in my own field. Essentially I do what intuitive people call "matching energy"—becoming the same wave length vibration or the same type of energy as the tree. Then I take the time to just be quiet and internally experience the tree's energy. I call this "dancing with the trees" because it always fills me with energy and a feeling as if I am dancing as my energy keeps moving in the pattern of the tree.

When I am dancing with the trees I am experiencing the life of nature, the essence of the tree, and I feel extra alive and exhilarated. So often in life people tend to see any object that does not move as lifeless. The trees do not move as we do but they exude a tremendous amount of life force energy that anchors the soil, cleans our air, fills the atmosphere with energy, and gives a resting place to birds, insects, and small animals. When I am dancing with the trees, I find that the trees communicate with me and dance with me in spirit.

To be still and know, to speak as one with nature, is a quality that we humans are just beginning to recapture within our realm of skills. The nature tracker, the bird watcher, the intuitive ecologist, the shamans, the spiritually adept, many farmers, and the Native American Indians of the 18th century and before, knew and understood this quiet skill of just being still and knowing. Perhaps we, the people of the advanced urban technological society, have to relearn this simple basic sense of awareness to allow ourselves the power and pleasure of being in touch with nature.

Many ancient cultures revered trees and worshipped them as living entities. In some cultures a bride and groom would have a ritual marriage with a tree first before their own ceremony to reinforce the lasting quality of their marriage. Afterwards the tree would be blessed and wine and flowers and gifts would be showered on the tree. We no longer worship or enshrine trees with our attentions and love in this manner. Tree worship is seen as a relic of the ancient past. In leaving behind this part of our pagan past we have lost some of our intuitive natural ability to communicate with and be receptive to the great powers of nature and the wonderful beings that are trees. Perhaps as we begin to rebalance our ability as human beings to combine our advanced technological culture with the simple spiritual essence of natural awareness, we will once again learn to communicate, be receptive, and enjoy the presence of these marvelous entities that have given us so much to improve the qualities of our lives. Perhaps we will once again allow ourselves to dance with the trees.

"*I was seeing in a sacred manner the shapes of all things in the spirit, and the shape of all things as they must live together, like one being. And I saw that the sacred hoop of my people was one of many hoops that made one circle, wide as daylight and as starlight, and in the center grew one mighty flowering tree to shelter all the children of one mother and one father.*"

—*Black Elk Speaks*

17

PERSONAL POWER AND PLANETARY TRANSFORMATION

It is not how much power you have but how you use it. The science of physics has taught us that a small amount of leverage can go a long way in tipping the scales. It is not your actual power as a separate human being on the planet that allows you to make a contribution to ecological energy change but your ability to hook into the greater power source and direct it to a desired end. It is your ability to "go with the flow" and have the flow change direction when needed. This means that you have to subjugate your ego or sense of Self and allow yourself to **be** at one with the universal energy source with no thought of personal gain or reward. You do gain personally, though, because as you learn to merge and become one with the elements of nature, you become more in touch with your own nature and who you came here to be in the first place.

With the Eco-Spirit techniques, you are using the most modern up-to-date methods of channelling (moving energy around). These techniques give you the ability to have free will and be self-defined while you still work with the greater Oneness or Power of the Universe. These techniques enable you to be unaffected by the energy that you channel because you are not the vehicle through which it is channeled.

Whether you work with a group or by yourself, at some point you will have to channel or call in a great deal of energy. Perhaps you are working on an area of land that has been logged or "cleared" and is now devoid of a good deal of the life spirit it once so abundantly had. You would want to use the basic techniques of grounding the area, cleaning it, and calling in the elementary guardians to rebalance the elements of earth, air, fire, and water. You might also wish to call the archetypal energy that governs the area. But, after all is said and done, you will probably wish to channel (move) some higher life force energy into the area to give it a big charge to start it off on its way. If you work with a specific spiritual group or belief system, such as Christ force energy, Avatars, or Deities, you might be calling that higher life force energy from an Avatar or spiritually-advanced being or you might just channel the energy of the sun, the moon, or other higher planetary energy, or you might channel just good old simple love energy.

When you move energy onto this plane of awareness you want to move it in the most neutral and direct way possible. Usually people channel energy by calling it in from above them and then channeling it down in front of them into the desired object or area. They direct it with their hands, their mind, and their will power. The old methods of channeling taught everyone to bring it in through their own system through the energy channels in their body. While this method gives the channeler a tremendous rush and ego boost and makes the channeler feel powerful and invincible, it does not always accomplish the desired end. Sometimes the channeler's system does not create a clear channel. When this happens, which is often the case, then the channeler's system gets fritzed and backs up and the energy never really gets where it is being directed. Even worse, the channeler may find himself charged and blocked at the same time. (Some energy workers translate this as a condition of being charged up at 2:00 a.m. with no one to speak with, no where to go, nothing to do, and needing sleep before it's time to get up at 6:00 a.m. to go to work—a condition of being charged up but blocked from action.) The new methods show you how to channel the energy around you instead of through you. In this way you can remain a clear system while you move tremendous energy forces to their destination.

Your body has energy channels throughout it that carry any energy that comes in all the way through them. Some of these channels carry the energy through all of the major energy centers (called chakras) in your body located along your spine. If you are involved or preoccupied with something in one of these energy centers, the energy that comes through your channels and into your chakras could easily get blocked or stopped by whatever you are personally working on. If you are working on your relationship for example, and you channel energy directly through your body, it could get stuck in your 2nd chakra, the energy center in your abdomen where you process your emotional feelings. The energy could either cleanse and rebalance itself or your confusion and unconscious troubles could unbalance and burden the energy in the area you are working on. If you are dealing with your self-image and your inner picture of your identity, the energy could get blocked in your 4th chakra, the Heart Chakra, which is the center of your self identity, your ability to love yourself and others, the chakra governor of your breath, and your

201

ability to be at one with yourself and the universe. Because your Heart Chakra is the "doorway" to your body that governs how you define yourself as a personality in "this" lifetime. If you process too much energy through it you could get stuck in your own personal growth process. From my standpoint as an energy worker this is too big a risk. How many of us can say we are truly clear, at peace, and at one with the world, our friends and lovers, and our work? And for how long can we say this? Because, in order to work channeling energy **through** the body, you must be able to say this constantly! It is easier and simply more neutral to move the energy directly into the matter on which you are working.

Some people direct the energy from above them then channel it from the back through to the front of their Hand Chakras (the back of your Hand Chakra is the back of your hand behind the palm and the front of the Hand Chakra is the palm) to go directly to the "problem" area. Eco-energy workers direct it from above them directly into the "trouble" spot. In this manner you leave none of your own personal imprint, as described in the examples in the previous paragraph, upon the area you are working on. When you channel the energy directly or neutrally through just your Hand Chakras, you can have unsaid and unresolved feelings with no worry of transferring them to your desired area.

When you channel energy, such as cosmic love, cosmic healing energy or higher level sun or moon energy, or the energy of the divine, you are not using your own personal power to heal the planet. You are using a bit of your will or intention to direct a power that is larger and greater than that of one human being or one human spirit. You are no longer Joe Blow or Jane Doe the energy worker. You are not "involved." You are not the "cause" of the planetary healing but simply the director of events. You do not have any personal "power" involved in healing the planet but because you are working on your neighborhood park or an area in which developers wish to level Mother Nature and "concretize" three acres of land down the block around the corner from where you live, you are personally directing "power" and therefore involved. And when you work to change the energy you are working to benefit yourself and give yourself more personal power to have a more beautiful living environment. But that is a different type of personal power.

While you are working on healing or affecting the environment you must not have your **ego** involved. It is not **you** that causes a change, but the energy that your will or intention moves into or out of an area. It is not **you** that makes the entire choice or decision, as the higher powers that exist must be in accord with what you ask for. As you learn to heal areas and spend time interacting as an Eco-Spirit energy worker, you will find that certain areas are fun and easy to affect. The energy flows into them, the negative or degenerative energy flows out of them, and they become either the archetypal situation you picture or something else that is equally wonderful, beautiful, and acceptable.

There are some areas that you will work on, however, that will not acquiesce to your will. You will feel as if you are walking uphill or through a muddy river because the energy will not take hold or move in the direction you suggest. These areas may innately be set by nature to hold a different vibration. If you go into the woods you will find that there are trees and groves and areas that fill your mind, body, and sensibilities with an uplifting feeling of light, wonderment and joy like the dawning of a new and wondrous day. There are also trees and groves and areas in which you will feel a heaviness, a depressive stagnancy that makes you feel burdened or fearful or apprehensive or old with the burdens of the world. You can find these uplifting and depressive areas in the forests, in the mountains, in the cities, in your homes, and in your hearts. Usually if you find a negative energy sump in the city or in your home or your heart, you can do something to cleanse or transform or change the energy. But sometimes when you find these quagmires in nature, you have found the energy level balance that nature created. We are a planet of dichotomies. We have light and so we must also have darkness. Therefore these dark power spots exist to balance out the light ones. For the high places Nature created a low place. For the light places Nature created a dark spot. You cannot always cleanse these areas, nor should you wish to.

These dark, depressive areas are not usually the areas you would encounter in your Eco-Spirit adventures as these are usually areas that have held this deepness or darkness since the beginning of time on the planet and have drawn only more of their like to them. You usually can spot these areas miles before you reach them. They suck the light out of you if you remain there. These, of course, are **not** areas to clean but areas to leave as you found them. If you attempt to clean them because you believe yourself endowed with the "personal power" to rule or change the world, then you will have deceived yourself and be at the mercy of the negative side of the universe.

I speak of these "negative" energy sumps only to make you aware of the dangers of identifying personal power with planetary transformational power. The power of the spirit is far and beyond the personal power of your body personality in this life. It is the power of your spirit to be one with the universe and this planetary level of consciousness that allows you to know when you are in an area to be healed from an imbalance of human energy or an area that is a planetary "dark spot." Please do not be paranoid or frightened of the dark spots of the planet. They are few and far between and are usually so obvious that you do not have to bother with them. It is rare that in any of your healings as a planetary energy worker you would encounter them. Because they are negative, people do not usually place buildings on them or attempt to utilize these areas. They are usually isolated and left alone.

As a planetary healer you will be seeking to cleanse areas that were unbalanced by the human aspect of nature or to rebalance natural areas that have somehow lost connection with the whole or larger aspect of Mother Nature. You cannot and would not wish to attempt to rework or remap the energy lines of the planet or create the planet in your own ideal. These types of grandiose projects would be the work of the God force, and any human who would attempt such a project would be a fool or a madperson. We humans are somewhat limited in seeing the entire picture of what is happening on the planet. We have intelligent minds and are bright spiritual beings, but usually our energy is not light or high enough to grasp the entire picture. It is like being down in the valley and knowing that you want to change the flow of the water by damming a stream. If you get up on the mountain or fly over the valley you can see the whole picture and get some general idea of what you need to do and where to build the dam. As an energy being we humans are not ready to get up on the mountain to see the whole picture and therefore we cannot and should not set ourselves up to be the gods of nature who can reorganize the very structure of the planet.

Even having the ability to see the valley from the mountain top does not always give us the ability to understand the true ramifications of the complex intricacies of cause and effect. We can see how to build the dam but we often do not see how many ecosystems it will destroy or affect. As of yet, as an energy race, we are just not that advanced. We are capable of calling on the spirits of nature to come and rebalance their kingdom and we are certainly capable of learning how we unbalance that kingdom with our misuse of technology and the carelessness of our presence, but we are not capable of "running" the kingdom of nature at this time. As a race, we are young in the scale of the evolution of energy beings. And in our youth we have committed many follies that have caused the planet to pay for our indiscretions. We can only hope and work toward our higher development as a race of energy beings.

True personal power comes from getting in touch with your Higher Self and your intuitive inner self, and acting from those parts of yourself to do what you were meant to do in this life. It is the inner radiance that shines from within when you are acting on the inner truth for yourself. It enables you to do what you as a spiritual being came here to enact in this particular body personality. True personal power is finding the God of your heart or the God-like being within yourself and learning to act upon it. And when you do this, you find yourself in the right job, learning from healthy relationships, and acting out your personal story on this planet. It rings true for you with a certain comfort or a sense of being at peace within yourself. Some people call this being at one with yourself or being balanced. Do not confuse this with the concept of remaining perfect or static. We are all here to learn and grow and experience and so we are always balancing and rebalancing the inner concepts of our personality, our feelings, and our identity. But when you are "on your path" doing what you essentially came here to do in this life, you feel in tune with life. You feel at home with yourself and able to handle even the most stressful of growth situations.

We need to have many people become "in tune" with themselves in this day and age because the planet itself, as well as the human societies upon it, is going through stressful times. The planet is evolving. And in its evolution many of the ecosystems we have cherished and loved and taken for granted are being lost. Some of this is intentional evolution and some of it is in reaction to the restructuring of planetary systems based on a rebalancing of ecological resources.

We humans are evolving as a group also. We are learning about our concepts of peace and accord. We are moving from being small tribes dedicated to our own personal survival to the larger picture of a world nation dedicated to the good of all people and planetary nature. What we take with us as individual human beings to the "peace table" is what we mirror to the whole. If we develop ourselves as conscious, balanced human beings who own their personal power, then we bring this to each action that we accomplish. To develop personal power we merely have to learn to be the God within ourselves, to be the gods we have always searched for in our dreams. For we are the godforce we have spent so much time praying to and searching for. We are the divine radiance of light that transforms ourselves and one another if we allow ourselves to be the highest and the best of what we are. We are the light of God on the face of the planet. Each one of us is a piece of God within a physical form. This piece of God can shine through to enact the highest good within all of us. Acting from this God force is what I call personal power. And if you are completely acting from this God force, then you have the truest and highest knowledge of how to create peace and balance the planet.

The path to personal power is fraught with many side tracks and branches that can mislead you to get lost and out of touch. Our race of human beings is not yet ready to truly become the gods within and act that out through our actions. So, personal power is still "personal" power. Personal power for most people is getting the right job, buying the best car, owning a nice house, and holding their own in a relationship. To energy workers this is the kindergarten ideal of personal power. When we, as a human race, grow up enough to understand intuitively, not with the mind but with the soul, we will know that personal power is the ability to be as God. We will then be the true Keepers of the Planet as well as the great peacekeepers of the universe. To the rest of the galaxy (those alien nations about which we are not supposed to know exist but with which many spiritual people have communicated), we are babies who have not yet grown up to take our rightful place. We are the race that is the "children of promise" that holds the seeds of a new world. We are the children of the experiment of "free will." It is expected that we will be the ones to enlighten others in how to develop a free and creative universe. But first, we must develop and enlighten ourselves which can be quite an arduous and long road.

As you work with your own spiritual energy and channel it to become one with the greater whole, you will develop your ability to have "personal" power. You will create situations in which you have more "control" over your life and in which you seem to "go with the flow." Life is then easy and in tune with you. After a period of working with the basic skills of Grounding,

Running Your Own Life Force Energy through you, and De-Energizing Concepts, you will find that you are more conscious of your actions and their cause and effect in life's situations. You will begin to understand and know why you create your particular life situation and how you can change or correct it to be what you really want and need. When you have gotten to this point you will be able to also know and understand the difference between your own "personal" power and true personal power. Perhaps you will begin to develop your inner true personal power as a planetary healer and guardian. This is the gift of life that we all are given when we incarnate on this planet.

Up to now so few of us have taken the time or had the incentive to develop our "true" natures. As you develop your true nature, the energy of your inner and outer self will merge with your higher power and you will be instrumental in developing yourself as a forerunner in the race of super conscious beings that all of us are moving towards. As super conscious beings we will begin to fit into the role we were originally given on this planet—to be Keepers of the Planet. If we do not achieve this super consciousness, we will just be "fruitful and multiply" until we self-destruct by our own ignorance. The end to our existence will be Mother Nature's way of saying that she made a mistake or that we outlived our usefulness as a piece of the planetary ecological life force cycle.

So now we have a choice to make. We can self-destruct by our own ignorance, or with super conscious knowledge and awareness we can begin to take our rightful place as the Keepers of the Planet.

"This is the true joy in life: being used for a purpose recognized by yourself as a mighty one, and being a force of nature instead of a feverish, selfish little clod of ailments and grievances, complaining that the world will not devote itself to making you happy."

—*George Bernard Shaw*

18

LEARNING TO
HEAL THE PLANET

Anyone who wishes to take the time to focus themselves and learn to use a few simple skills can learn how to direct their energy towards healing the planet.

Have you got an empty lot in your neighborhood or an old unseemly unkempt building near your home or place of business? Maybe you are witness to an ecological disaster, such as an oil spill, or trees dying of unknown causes, or a body of water being polluted by waste in your part of the world. Or maybe the air, water, or food in your area contains dangerous levels of toxicity. If you are experiencing these conditions, then you have a real reason to take the time to teach yourself to heal the planet with your energy. By just exercising the simple skills described in this book and focusing your energy you can make a difference!

Let us take a look at the most common situations that you might encounter where you would want to use Eco–Spirit tools to heal the environment.

Suppose that you have an empty lot in your neighborhood that is overgrown and used as a trash dump. What would you like that lot to be? What could it be realistically, given the market value of your neighborhood and the needs of your community? Keep these questions in mind as you explore the lot and come to an understanding of what is going on with its energy. In order to change the condition of the lot you must first envision it in an idealized state—this idealized state is your goal. As you work on this land you are going to be raising its energy vibration to attract new ways it can be used by your community. You must have an idea envisioned of what you want the lot to become or some other person might move in and create their envisioned reality of the lot.

I, along with groups of people, have experimented in raising the energy in a lot full of rubbish. Sure enough, as soon as the energy on that piece of land was raised, real estate developers showed up and erected a condominium. If an office building or condominium is your goal for the lot, that is fine. But you must take into consideration, from the very beginning, what the actual options for this piece of land could be. Otherwise you might succeed in your endeavor but be quite disappointed in the outcome.

If you raise the energy vibration in an area you will see a result. Something will happen! No, it is not the same as if you actually purchased the piece of land and decided what to do with it. You are affecting the environment indirectly, on a subtle but very real level, by changing the energy within the framework of the land. Once you do this, the "real" world will respond to the change in energy since it is truly the energy that causes what happens in the first place. So, as you change the energy structure

212

of this plot of land you must have some idea of what you would like to happen to it. You can not trust on the goodness of the world and people at large to necessarily create something ecological or beautiful with that piece of land, you have to build that into your energy working construct.

A working energy construct is your concept of what you want to accomplish. You are "constructing" a new reality for the area that you are working on. To start on your construct you map out the exact area you are dealing with—your empty lot. Next you decide what you would conceive of as being the end goal. Perhaps you would like to see that lot as a small neighborhood park. Or maybe it would be fine if someone built a one-family residence there that matches the rest of the residences in the neighborhood. You have to know exactly what you want to see happen in your area and you also have to be clear on what you do not want to happen. If you do not want to see a condominium, multiple family residences, or small office or professional building, then you must acknowledge this. Visually, you will be creating an image of what you want and you have to be able to be completely clear about not creating any doorways or openings for someone to create the reality you do not want.

To start on your construct, map out the exact area you are dealing with. Some people take a piece of paper and make a small map of their construct. You can do this on paper or just in your head on a visual level—do whatever works for you! On the paper you can map out your area and then place anything that you wish to keep in it. Perhaps there are some big old trees on your land and you would like to see them preserved as part of whatever happens on the land. You can make a drawing of the area with the trees on it. On the map place everything you want on the land. If it were a park you would place your walkways, your play area, your greenery and any benches. You probably would also draw in your birds, squirrels or any wild life you would expect to see in that park. Create a beautiful scene with everything you could envision for your park. If you want a home, draw in a house that is in affinity with the rest of the homes in the area. Fill in the landscaping and add in the wild life and greenery.

When I am working with a piece of land, I usually do two constructs. The first one is the ideal goal for that piece of land. The second one is an alternative just in case something happens that prevents my ideal plan from taking shape.

Once you have your constructed reality envisioned you can begin actually working on the energy of the area. If you can do it, physically go to the spot you are working on and get in the center of the area and just stand there and experience the energy and what you see and what you feel. If you cannot get to the area then try to get close to it. Perhaps your lot is fenced in and you cannot physically walk onto the property. You could stand outside of the fence however and this would also work. Now close your eyes and hook into the archetype of the area. You want to speak to the governing overall force of that particular area. Actually, you want to find out what the governing force of that area is. All of the tools that you will be using to work on the energy in the area are covered in previous chapters of this book.

Attempt to locate the archetype and communicate with it. In this manner you can find out exactly what the problem is with your area. Besides speaking with the archetype, which often is like speaking with a being or an energy person since it usually has character and personality, you will also wish to speak with the land or earth itself. The answers you might get here will be more intuitive or of the feeling type. You might "feel" that the earth is tired or worn out or that it is fighting some sort of pollution or imbalance. By speaking with the essential archetype of the area and the earth itself you are collecting information about the reason for the problem. At this point you are being a detective. When you understand a little about what is unbalanced and why or how it became unbalanced it is then easier and more straightforward to begin healing or changing it.

Speaking with the essential archetype or speaking with the earth is gleaning information. It is passive action. With this information you can move into a more active phase of energy working. You can now begin to affect or change the immediate environment.

Usually the best starting place for changing the energy in an area is to clean it of everything that has collected there. This way you are starting with a clean slate. So put a grounding cord down from the center of the area and drain out all of the energy that has collected in the area. You can even put multiple grounding cords down from all four corners of the area to give it some extra grounding and cleansing. When you drain energy from the area you are mostly removing people's energy and the energy of pollution. Regardless of what is removed a certain amount of the raw energy of the earth will always remain. After you have drained out any negative, excess, unneeded, or unwanted energy from the area, then conceptualize bringing the entire area into present time, that wonderful creative essence of the here and now. Often when you clean out land or buildings you will find that there are time warps in which the area is locked in past time which causes it to sink in energy. Now bring in some beautiful golden cosmic sun energy and fill up the entire area. This is the

215

equivalent of filling up the area with sunshine. Right now you are bringing the energy of the area up to a higher vibration so that you can work to create the area into a new form.

Once you have grounded the area and brought it into present time and filled it with golden light, you are ready to rebalance it according to the elements. Here is where you pull out your compass and take note of where the directions lay. Starting in the northern part of your area, and facing north, draw the Tattva of the north, a yellow square or cube in the air. Now see this cube as being a window to the element of the North. As you draw this window look through it and visualize and create the earth element. Then speak to the keeper of the Earth Element, the Archangel Auriel, and ask for and direct the earth elemental energy to come through your window and fill up your area.

When you have filled your area with earth energy then move on to the next direction, the East. Face the east and trace the Tattva symbol of a blue circle or sphere in the air. Imagine this as a window to the world of the air element and see the air element through your window. Call on the Keeper of the Kingdom of Elemental Air, the Archangel Raphael, and explain what you need and then direct the elemental energy of air to come through your window into your area.

Next, face the direction of the south and trace the Tattva symbol of a red equilateral triangle with the apex facing upwards. This is your window to the world of elemental fire. See the elemental fire through your window and call on the Keeper of the Kingdom of Elemental Fire, the Archangel Michael, and explain what you need and then direct the elemental energy of fire to come through your window into your area.

Then turn towards the west, the direction of water, and trace in the air your Tattva symbol of a silver crescent with the points facing upwards. This is the window to the elemental world of water. See the elemental world of water through your window and call on the Keeper of the Kingdom of Elemental Water, the Archangel Gabriel, and explain what you need and then direct the elemental energy of water to come through your window into your area.

The moment that you have a balance of the elements in your area you should begin to notice an electricity in the air, a sense of life force that fills the space you have worked on. This is a good time to contact the archetype you have found for the area and enact your construct for the area. Your construct is your positive vision for what you want this area to be. Remember, when you contact an archetype you are not just "speaking" with it but actually becoming one with it for a moment and then directing it to gather the elements and create your constructed pattern. In this manner you work as one with the planetary energy flow. You become it and thus are able to turn it to a different direction. If it is in accordance with the natural flow of things nature will then continue to create and build in that new direction. By enacting the archetype within your area you are putting a piece of oneness or God force within that area. You are connecting the area up with the "whole" of creation.

Now that you have balanced the area and created your construct, you can finish or you can go on to be more creative within that area. You could call on the elemental beings of earth to come and help the plants and trees to grow and flourish in the area, or the elemental beings of water to come and bring the waters of life, love, and compassion to that area and all within it, and so on. Some people like to fill an area with a particular energy, such as love or raw power. I prefer to leave an area filled with a balance of nature and as neutral as possible. I have found that areas filled with very specific sorts of energy will attract both the positive and negative reactions to that energy level and thus need to be monitored or else the area can easily get unbalanced. Energy workers of old have an ancient saying called "like to like." That is, you will attract towards you what you are. If you charge an area with all one very strong vibration you will attract more of a similar vibration, as like to like. But also, sometimes, because it is such a strong vibration, and because this planet is built or based in modern times upon the attraction of opposites and use of dichotomies, you might also attract the exact opposite to your charged energy field. Sometimes this can cause a problem with a very strong interplay of forces with you having to constantly try to readjust the energy. It is easier to leave no imprint upon the area and just rebalance nature and let nature take its course.

After cleaning your area, calling in elemental energy, and calling the archetype to action, you might wish to call in the fifth element—akashic energy, called Ether by the ancient Greeks or Spirit by modern day energy workers. This is the neutral life force spirit that can fill an area with charge and purpose. To do this you imagine the highest form of energy, God the Supreme Being, cosmic life force energy, or whatever works for you in your own belief system or cosmology, and create a ladder or stream of energy going from this cosmic life force energy or God force directly into the Earth in the center of your area. I usually create this as a golden stream of sunlight that is made up of akashic energy, the spiritual life force of the planet. When I use the term Akasha here I am referring to the actual spiritual essence or soul force that fills us with life. In the old cosmologies people were created from the four elements of the earthly plane and then breathed to life with the soul of Akashic energy, the sense of spirit that activates the elements. It is this sense of spirit or soul that you wish to use to activate your area with life force.

Once you have finished balancing the area and creating your construct, you must close the elemental windows that you have opened. This is done simply by starting in the North where you began and facing each direction and closing the energy window by folding in the lines of your figure one on another, then imagining it being sucked back into its own vortex. Continue closing the elemental windows following this same technique. Whenever you open a window to the elemental realm you must remember to always close it.

You have now completed the basics of energy work in cleansing an area and creating a construct. You have cleaned the area and grounded it, checked in with the archetypal energy and perhaps found the underlying problem, have rebalanced the elements and used the archetype to create your basic construct, and have filled the area with spiritual life force akashic energy. Now you can go home and, if you wish to, take all of the "normal" actions that activists do like sending letters to the local newspaper, contacting local ecological action groups concerned with this problem, or developing a community support group.

Working with the energy of the area causes a change in the outcome. If you are a disbeliever, but would really like to believe that energy working can cause a change in the environment, then give yourself and the environment a chance by practicing a few of these energy working constructs and discovering the power of pure spirit for yourself.

One person can cause a positive change in the environment. More than one person working with these skills can cause an even larger change in the immediate environment. It is easy and possible for one person to cause a change to an empty lot, a run-down building, or a piece of land that has lost its life force. When we consider the larger picture or the bigger issues, such as an oil spill, a body of water that has been or is being polluted, or a mountain with dying or sick trees, it is better to work with group energy because a large jolt of energy is needed to bend nature towards another direction of focus.

When you work with a degenerative problem, such as a polluted body of water, you would wish to contact the elementals of the area. For the polluted body of water you would contact the undines, the water elementals. These elemental beings have the job of cleansing the water and balancing it on a daily level. When there is an imbalance or problem, these beings sometimes get overloaded and actually leave the area. Or they become so worn out under the pressure of too much pollution they are unable to transform it in any cohesive fashion. If the Undines or the elementals of your particular area are leaving because they are overloaded you might be able to speak with them and entice them back. You might also be able to open the elemental window and call to the Keeper of the Elements to send more elementals to the area in trouble. This is like calling in the elemental army to help you cleanse and recharge a troubled area.

One of the joys of working with elemental energy to cleanse an area is that you can do it almost anywhere. Other than needing a compass or knowledge of where the directions lay, you do not need any special tools or paraphernalia to begin to cleanse an area. You can work your Eco-Spirit "magic" anywhere and everywhere that needs help. I have friends who have worked cleansing their local city and state and national parks. They have rebalanced and recharged areas that have been traumatized by people who have committed kidnappings, committed acts of violence against joggers, or collected in groups and gangs to terrorize or molest people and the environment, and to create a hangout for youths to drink and do drugs. They have worked their "magic" on the environment to change the energy where picnickers have left voluminous amounts of trash and food wrappings, where people have carved their initials on the trees, and in areas where dirt bikes have cut into the terrain of the natural hillside. Once you change the energy in an area, your amazing "magic" takes over and people do not leave their garbage anymore but clean up after themselves and bikers choose to go somewhere else and people do not carve their initials on the trees anymore or do anything to destroy the environment. Once you create a clear energy field the area rebalances and the actual site takes on a radiant glow of light that recharges it and draws to it only people who love, care, and protect it.

When the energy of a natural area sinks and manifests to a lower vibration the result is an ecological imbalance of its system. It then attracts lower vibration people who commit all sorts of mayhem. An ecological system out of balance creates destructive elementals, the elementals of the nature of decay and wasting, who break everything down into its baser particles. This destruction energy is a lower vibration level and attracts people with a baser or lower nature. Remember the saying, "like to like"? Well, we have found that a mountain with an imbalanced system where the trees are dying of unknown causes will also attract psychotic people who have an imbalance in their own psychological or physical makeup. Natural areas that are experiencing an ecological disaster or powerful imbalance and are within traveling distance of large city areas will attract more than their normal share of murders, crimes, and discordant behavior. If you have such an area near where you live you can document it for yourself if you are willing to take the time to do a little bit of research. You will most likely find that over the period of time since the area became unbalanced and started showing signs of an ecological problem (trees dying, water being severely polluted, land eroding, and so on), the incidence of local crime, minor and severe, has increased.

Conversely, of course, you will also notice that an area which people abuse and mismanage and commit crimes in also can cause an ecological imbalance. A murder or kidnapping or even a drunken party in a natural park land does affect the environment. Nature spirits shy away from the excesses and brutal acts of humankind. The energy imprint of what happens in a particular area stays there and it attracts more of the same kind of activity unless someone comes along to change or clean the environment. Many of the older spiritual religions knew this and would send their postulants through the town or main street of a city singing chants and ringing bells. Much of the time they were not calling to a deity but just attempting to break down the pattern of thought forms and energy left lying around on the street of life. They were dispelling or getting rid of the negative thought forms that, when allowed to collect, form a sump and fester into nasty vortexes of dark malignancy. It works equally in both directions. Thus the environment can become unbalanced and attract to itself more unbalanced acts and unbalanced people. This can progressively change the energy in an area and create its destruction or further its imbalance. Being an energy worker you can go into both of these types of areas and transform their very nature by using simple elemental balancing techniques.

You do not have to be public or noticeable. You do not have to bring any special tools with you or dress in any special fashion. You do not have to wave your arms or act in any strange manner. You can stand in an area and do your energy work in pure outward silence. I have seen friends who are energy workers go into a local park where there are families picnicking and proceed to do group energy work to clear the space of past negative energy fields without ever disturbing a single person and without drawing any attention to themselves. There are people who enjoy singing and dancing and chanting and announcing themselves as they use energy techniques to clean the planet. And this can be great fun and very uplifting, especially if done with a group of people. It can even become a spiritually uplifting experience as the natural setting of the environment becomes the church or holy setting for finding the light of the God force within and around you as nature so often presents without any pomp or fanfare. But you do not have to sing, dance, and chant for the energy techniques described in Eco-Spirit to work and be useful. For many people it is possible to take a half an hour or forty-five extra minutes on the way to work to cleanse an empty lot near their home or to work on a small city park near their office building. The possibilities of what you can work on and what you can do are endless and totally up to you!

"Destiny, or karma, depends upon what the soul has done about what it has become aware of."

—*Edgar Cayce*

"Ideas have to be wedded to action; If there is no sex, no vitality in them, there is no action. Ideas cannot exist alone in the vacuum of the mind. Ideas are related to living."

—*Henry Miller*

19

THE PLANET AS A SPIRITUAL ENTITY

Too often we tend to take our wonderful planet for granted. We think of it as something that is just there—the land we walk on, the air we breathe, the panoramas we view just exist without thought of how they got to be as they are. Sometimes when a person spends too much time in the city atmosphere, encumbered by cement, by block after block of towering buildings, by the noise of traffic, and by the throngs of people, he will begin to wish for the quiet of nature, the majesty of the tall trees, the space of the plains or the desert. For many people the forests, mountains, deserts, and plains of our world become the open outdoor spiritual sanctuaries of our planet. The camping trip to a wilderness area is not just to rest and relax, but a spiritual revelation of the life force on the planet, or what some people call God.

This uplifting ability to perceive the God force as a natural experience can put you more in touch with the basic concept of a "living planet." A living planet is an ancient concept and belief that ecologically-aware people are now beginning to popularize and re-insert into the mainstream thinking of our society. People are beginning to understand the concept of a "whole" living breathing entity, a combination of cells, a conglomeration of parts that fit together and interact as a whole being. This concept can not only be applied to a dog or a cat or a lion or a tiger or a human being or an ecosystem of lakes or mountains, but to the whole planet. For some modern-day people this is a relative jump of light years in consciousness. But if you spoke with some of the more primitive cultures you would find that to them this belief is commonplace. They protect the Earth as she is their mother. And if you study anthropology and archaeology, you will find that the older cultures dating back to the matrilinear way of life felt protected in the bosom of the Great Mother of the Earth.

At the present time I, too, see the planet as one whole spiritual entity, as one entire living creature. I believe this and interact with the planet as an entity probably from having been trained in an earth-nature spiritual tradition. Twenty-two years ago I studied in an oath-bound spiritual "mystery" tradition that taught people how to communicate with the planet, as an entity, and how to be a Keeper of the Planet—a person whose job it is to oversee the balance and healing process of the planet. We would go to nearby wilderness areas where groves of trees stood in their majesty and learn to communicate with the spirit of Mother Nature. Earth was seen as a goddess, an aspect of the divine, and we performed guided meditations to communicate with the side of Her that would instruct us in the workings of her mysterious ways. The trees were seen as her hair, the rolling rounded mountains as her breasts, the caves were her womb, and she was always being reborn from the sea of primordial matter. Fruit, vegetables, animals, humans, and all that grew upon and in her surface were her children. All life had a purpose and we were only to "take" life from necessity, after blessing the creature or plant and sending its spirit on to another job. Everything we did had cause and effect. We were taught that if you cut down a tree in Wisconsin it affected some aspect of the Goddess Mother Earth somewhere, whether it be Wisconsin or California!

This Shamanistic, earth-nature "mystery" tradition was simplistic in its attitudes and yet held a basic similarity to what we know of ancient pagan nature cults. It held each person responsible for their actions. Because the Earth was seen as a living entity she was communicated with and asked permission of rather than taken for granted. As a goddess of nature, she was asked to bless the crops and create a good harvest and also to reveal the secrets of the workings of the planet. From these meditative communications with the divine workings of the planetary essence, I learned a little of working and divining the weather, working with the fairies and the elementals to create bountiful harvests and gracious wild spots of friendly nature, and how to flow with the cycles of nature, the phases of the moon, and the natural procession of the seasons.

Much of what I learned, at the time seemed archaic since I was an urban person who had little need of working with the fairies to create healthy large harvests or of calling the clouds to bring rain for my fields. I learned it from an almost inner love that called me to practice these skills as my lifestyle. And I learned it from experiencing an incredible sense of oneness and from the sense that everything I encountered in nature was a part of the God force from which we are created. Through many years of urban, and now rural living, this sense of wonderment and connected oneness in all living things—earth, animal, plant, sea, sky, and so forth—has never left me. It has been a guide for how I perceive myself in relationship to the world and everyone else in it. Now that these simple skills I learned as an urban youth may prove useful in enabling us to heal and change the planet, I would like to share them with you.

I write here in this book only that which is not bound by oath. Early shamanistic and mystery spiritual groups always made their members agree to secrecy and the sharing of certain sworn oaths to protect their power, their "magick", and their beliefs from strangers. Those things about which I swore never to reveal, which are of little relevance to anyone who was not involved at the time, I would never reveal and are not contained here. But information I personally gleaned from my many "meditations" with the goddess of Mother Earth I share whole-heartedly and freely in this book. Most of what I find important to share are the simple early concepts of the planet as a whole eco-system, as an entity whose simple breath covers the length and width of the planet, as a being who, having been kicked or pinched in one place reacts by moving or stretching or rumbling in another place, of the power of communicating with the spirit of a live being that cares for us as we should care for it.

There is an old mythological story. It is about how, at the beginning of the creation of the planet when God had finished the seven days of forming the planet, there seemed to be some quandary about where to put the secrets of the planet and the universe. This job had been given to the gods and goddesses, the aspects of God that were nature and awareness. The gods and goddesses stood about and discussed where to put this valuable information. They debated it for a while. One god wished to place this information at the top of a mountain for it was basically seen that human beings would never get there to grab it and the information would stay hidden and safe. But the gods and goddesses shot this idea down saying that humans were too enterprising and would sooner or later climb up to the tops of the mountains. Another goddess spoke of placing the secrets of the universe at the bottoms of the seas but all of the gathering present believed that if humankind could reach the tops of the mountains they could surely also reach the bottoms of the seas. For a while they all stood around being perplexed and then one rather jolly goddess interjected the idea of putting the secrets of humankind within the humans themselves. "They will never look there and all will be safe for quite a while," she said. The gods and goddesses cheered her on and declared for all that this be done. Then one god also added that the secrets of nature be stored within the planet, Gaia, the Goddess of Nature, in full view where none would see except those of conscious awareness and spiritual stature who could use the information wisely. And so it was done. Humankind was given its own enlightenment to use if they could find it. The Earth was given the secrets of nature, built into herbs, grasses and trees that could be used as medicines; into symbols built into the plants, the land, the rocks and the seas; into the cycles of nature through the moving of life force in reaction to the moon and the sun, the sexuality of nature, and the winds and tides of reproductive life; and into the early races of spirit: the elementals, the fairies, the giants (who later disappeared), and the angel guardians—all Keepers of the Planet.

As we begin to view the planet as a living entity we have to learn to understand the cycles and systems by which this entity is ruled. Just as we in our human bodies have cycles (the female menstrual cycle, the diurnal 24 hour cycle, the child bearing cycle, puberty, youth, middle age, old age, and so on), we are ruled by and must take into account that the planet too has its cycles and seasons. These cycles and seasons are mirrored in nature. If you were to shut yourself off from the procession of the seasons, as if locked in a dark cave, and suddenly emerged onto the face of the planet, you could tell what season it was from the position of the stars, sun, and moon, and also from communicating with the fairies, elementals, and nature spirits. These creatures are totally ruled by their seasons and take on the aspect of the current season. In each season they perform different services for the planet and so their image appears differently to an observer. Sometimes different spiritual nature beings appear at different seasons but often they actually change their appearance to correspond with their work and the energy that they channel.

In springtime, late April or May, I have seen crude primitive and extremely sexual nature beings in the mountains. They are asserting the part of nature that reproduces. Towards summer they become fuller, more rounded, and happier. Many of the fairies seem even more jovial in their singing and their dancing and the mountain spirits seem fuller and more at peace with their bountifulness. Towards the fall they turn into darker colors, greens and russets are more predominant, they seem thinner and more concerned with their work. And in the winter they seem cool and aloof. If you are in a winter climate where there is snow and cold temperatures, the nature beings seem to take on the images of winter and the old man and old woman of the mountain with aged, wrinkled faces, strong stone cool aloofness bespeaking of strength and endurance and the wisdom of the ages. If you are in a Mediterranean-type winter where instead of snow and cold you have rain and greenery, then the nature beings take on the aspect of green growth, of amused and constant growth.

Within the kingdoms of the nature spirits there are many different beings. Many of them have their own coloring and appearance. Some seem pale yellow and incredibly transparent while others in the dark forests seem deep green and brown and more substantial. In my experience, however, all of these do change and react to the seasons and the cycles of nature just as we do. For example our bodies react to the increase of light in Summer, of the need for preparation in Fall, the need for more food in the cold months of Winter, and the uneasy and somewhat sexual feeling of Spring fever. We seem to mirror these cycles according to our genes and ethnic backgrounds even if we move to another climate where the procession of the seasons is different.

As we begin to understand the movement of the seasons in regard to the movement of the energy flow of the planet as a whole, we can learn to work with the flow of energy. We can begin to understand the actual tidal ebb and flow of energy within our own bodies and that we are as affected by these energy cycles as the nature spirits and the planet itself. If we allow ourselves to see the planet as a living entity (Gaia, the Goddess of Mother Nature) we must also allow ourselves to become aware of the fact that we are not separate or apart from Her but a part of the entity upon which we live and interact with. To see ourselves as separate and apart from the planet is to situate ourselves once again as the "rulers and controllers" of the planet whereas in actuality we are just a piece of the puzzle of life, a reflection of the creative life force on the planet. We might decide that we are the "intelligent" piece of that life force that can "think" for the planet. And once we learn to balance this "intelligence" with our true inner intuitive capabilities, we may accomplish what Mother Nature set us here to do. Right now we seem to be the "limited" intelligence of the planet, with wonderful free will capabilities but too much capacity to destroy when we "think" we are creating.

The cycles of the planet are based on the seasons. This is shown to us through the procession of the stars and the sun and the movements of the animals. Ancient cultures were very aware of these seasonal changes, and they measured them precisely since they were spiritual holy days that marked the turn of the year. The old cultures built observatories such as Stonehenge and the Pyramids to mark these special times, such as the solstices and the equinoxes, to make people aware of the passage of the power of the sun and the planets. Often in modern urban societies we have gotten out of touch with the movement of the sun and the moon and the seasons, measuring the seasons only by the return to school, Hanukkah, Christmas, New Year, Ground Hog Day, the Easter egg hunt, the May Day Festival, the Summer Solstice vacation, the Fall Harvest, Halloween, and so on. We hear these time markers announced on television and radio and change our wardrobe and take vacations to mark them and celebrate the holy religious holidays of our belief system. But we have forgotten what they make us feel like or what they really mean as a change in the consciousness of the planet. Just as the planet goes through its yearly cycle of birth, puberty, the fullness of creation, harvest, old age, and death (to be reborn again), we too experience the changes brought about by the cycles, although on a much more subtle level of feelings with unconscious awareness of the changes of life force energy, the ebb and flow of the energy web of our planet. To learn these "life change markers" of the planetary movement is to learn about ourselves internally as well as to learn how to communicate with the planet at the proper times so we can efficiently utilize our energy to heal and change a planetary ecological situation.

In the planetary cycle of the year there are four turns of the seasons or energy points that are marked by the change of the sun and by the change of how much light we are exposed to on the planet. These four times fall equilaterally on our calendar and form what is called the Cross of Matter. All ancient cultures related to the simple Cross of Matter, such as the cross of the four elements that the American Indians use to denote the four directions (North, East, South, and West) and the four turns of the seasons. These are the special times that are marked by ancient astronomies and by the cosmic knowledge of planetary movement. There are four other times during the year that also mark the change of energy movement upon the planet. Some people say these other four times of the turn of the year are the oldest and most powerful markers of the tide of energy changes upon the planet. They represent the movement and fertility actions of herds of animals and swarms of insects.

Described on the following pages are the eight energy markers of the planet listed in chronological order with their appropriate correspondences. The first four energy markers represent the tide of the seasons and are the solstices and the equinoxes as they measure the movement of light. The second four energy markers represent the culmination or high points of the rise of the change of the tide of energy within the planet. All of the energy doorways or energy celebrations or actual energy marker times are the night before the actual date set here. The actual energy time for being in touch with December 21st, the Winter Solstice, would be the night of December 20th which would be the longest night and the next day, December 21st, would be the shortest day.

ENERGY MARKER DATES

December 21st – The Winter Solstice

A planetary birth of light. A celebration of the birth of the sun. This is the longest night and the shortest day on the planet. With the "birth" of light the sun grows brighter with each passing day until the fullness of the Summer Solstice when the sun "peaks" and the days begin to grow shorter.

The Winter Solstice has long been a celebration time for the major religions on this planet. Christians moved the birth of Jesus from the springtime to December to coincide with the birth of the sun since to them Jesus was the bringer of light, the son of God. Jews celebrate Hanukkah, the festival of lights, when the oil of the temple lasted for eight days and eight nights when it should only have lasted for one night. Whether this is a true story or a symbolic one, it is interesting that the festival of light falls at the time of the birth of the sun—a light awareness celebration. Many of the old pagan and nature religions celebrated the Winter Solstice and Saturnalia as a time to celebrate the birth of the child of God, the birth of enlightenment, the celebration of light in the winter, the return of the Sun. The ancient European nature cults drank wine and danced around the evergreen trees of winter to celebrate lifeforce and the coming of the sun. They also gave one another small tributes of summer (herbals, dream pillows, pressed flowers, etc.) to remind one another of the coming of the summer and warm times.

February 1st – The Feast of the Waxing Light

This is one of the oldest herding markers on the planet. To many ancient religions it represented old fire festivals, a time of beginnings and initiations. In Europe, February 1st was dedicated to the Brigid, goddess of childbirth, smithing, and poetry. To the Catholic Church it became dedicated as Candlemass, or the Feast of the Assumption to Saint Brigit. To mark these times people sang and danced, recited poetry, shared stories, and rolled fiery wagon wheels down the mountain.

In the ancient calendar, February was the month of ritual purification. In northern European countries, such as Sweden, Norway, and Denmark, the youngest female virgin of the household would don a crown of candles and march throughout the house to "cleanse" it of the impurities of the old year. Often they would throw out all old bread and old salt, and douse the fire. Then the village elder (a female who represented the Earth Mother) would start a fire by hand and pass that one hot coal from house to house to start an entirely "new" fire that would be the initiator of a new and bright year.

Within the perspective of nature, February 1st represents the first green shoots of the baby trees and the small plants rising up and breaking ground to announce the beginning of a new cycle, the very first stirrings of spring. February 2nd, Ground Hog Day, was later initiated as the predictor of the weather. If the ground hog, who lived in the caverns that represented hibernation, the underground, and winter, came up and stuck his head out then people saw that as a prediction of a short or mild winter (longer springtime). Some people just predicted their vision of the coming spring from the actual weather on the day of February 1st or February 2nd. If it was mild weather they predicted a mild spring. If it was blustery they predicted a longer winter.

February 1st is also the time when the animals come together and couple to insure a new offspring for the summer times.

MARCH 21st – The Spring Equinox

Equinox is a word that means equal day and equal night. As the sun grows in its intensity it finally gets to the time when the days and nights are equal. While the tides of energy that flow at the Summer and Winter Solstices are gentle, the energy movement at the Spring and Fall Equinoxes are strong and more forceful—like a rapidly moving stream. This is a very good time to initiate projects of healing and rebalancing the eco-system of an area.

The Spring Equinox is seen as a time of celebration, of death energy moving to life energy, and of the fertility of animals, crops, and humankind. To the Christian Church springtime is the resurrection of Christ. To the ancient pagan world it was seen as the resurrection of all God force energy. To the Jewish community this is the time of Passover, a holiday of freedom that celebrates the resurrection of the spirit of humankind.

Easter, the Christian world's celebration of resurrection, derives its name from the Teutonic goddess Eostre. The celebration of Easter as a child's holiday of "finding the eggs" and eating the chocolate bunny rabbits derives directly from the pre-Christian influence of the original celebration of March 21st—a strongly fertility-based celebration. The eggs represented the world as a whole and the renewal and fertility of that world. The rabbits represented fertility and bountiful reproduction.

MAY 1st – May Day

May Day is the ancient fertility festival of the entire year. By March 21st the fields had been planted and growth had begun. In May the people would encourage the crops to grow by dancing nakedly in the fields of young plants and calling to the fairie folk to come and help the plants grow and multiply. Of course, some of the "naked" dancing in the fields led to in-the-flesh fertility rituals which the Christian Church ended when it became more widespread and powerful.

May Day is one of the strongest of the old celebrations of fertility for it is at May Eve (the night before the day) when the doors to the astral worlds are wide open and it is easy to accomplish energy work of any type. Perhaps it is the strong innate fertility drive within plants, animals, and humankind, but May Day is an excellent time to do energy work.

JUNE 21st – The Summer Solstice

The Summer Solstice is the time of abundance, the height of the power of the summer sun, the longest day and the shortest night. To the ancients midsummer was the strongest time of the God of the Sun. It was represented by the pregnant Goddess of Life, she who is sensuous and also represents the waters of life, the giver of life.

For most people midsummer is the celebration of warmth, sun, and good times. It is a time to gather the gifts of nature and to travel and see the sights of the land. It is a time to see old friends for it is easy to travel in the warmth of the sun.

AUGUST 1st – The Early Harvest Festival

Traditionally August 1st was the first harvest and in the New World and Europe that first harvest was of the corn. It was a time to work for an increase in material supply and to begin to plan for winter. In some ancient religions, August 1st is seen as the forerunner of the dark times, the beginning of the wane of the sun energy, and when the dark side of the time begins to rule. To these people who would scry and foretell the future on the night before August 1st, all predictions held a lot of weight. August 1st was seen by them as a time to protect themselves and prepare their harvests and homes for the long winter months.

SEPTEMBER 21st –The Autumn Equinox

As mentioned previously, equinox means equal day and equal night. On the evening of September 20th there is a complete balance of light and the tides of energy on the planet flow smoothly. While the Spring Equinox is the pushing off point to begin the ascent of action and fecundity towards Midsummer, the Autumn Equinox is a winding down of energy that gently leads us into a time of rest and internal retrospection. As we move onward in the year into the period of rest and repose, we open ourselves to introspection, to the time of the year when the veils between the world of matter and spirit are thinnest, when people have communications from their loved ones who have passed on, and visions that give them a spark of intuitive life. September is the season when most people move into a new phase, whether it be a new school, a new job, or just a new perspective. It seems that most people rewrite their priorities and goals around the month of September, which can cause a good deal of emotional and inner turmoil.

The Autumn Equinox marks the completion of the harvest and the thanksgiving for its bounty, as well as a farewell to the spirit of the sun, the god of the sun. The Autumn Equinox is the movement from life energy to death (death in the ancient world was seen as release, renewal, and rebirth). Therefore at this time people would band together to share the fruits of their harvest and to acknowledge the cycle of the year as it begins to die off and move to be reincarnated later. This is a time of letting go of old concepts. In the ancient world, death was seen as a transformation of the soul. (And in present times this "death" or change of consciousness is known as transformation in the New Age concepts of psychology, metaphysics, and release.) The Jewish religion celebrates Yom Kippur, the day of atonement, their holiest holiday at the end of September. Yom Kippur is a time for atoning for sins and being purified by fasting for a day and praying for release. Sometimes it is amazing how all of the major religions have holidays that parallel these old energy markers on the planet.

OCTOBER 31st – Halloween, The Feast of Souls

Halloween is the celebration of transition, of death energy. It got its current name from the Christian Church as All Hallows Eve. This is the time when the veils between the world of humans and the world of spirit is the thinnest. For the ancients, this was the time to speak with your dearly departed, to speak with the guides or spirits in your life, and to acknowledge the end of the year. For many of the ancient cultures the time of Halloween was known as the New Year and many things had to be completed by this date to be ready and prepared for winter. The harvests had to be gathered and stored. Since a limited amount of food could be kept on hand to feed the cattle, if there were too many animals they would decide how many were needed to last through the winter and to repopulate the herds then kill and salt the rest. This decision was a weighty affair, since killing the wrong number of animals could cause hunger in the future months.

In olden times, All Hallows Eve was the time to set the table with a good feast of symbolic foods: nuts and seeds for fertility and the rebirth of the seasons to come; apples for life force and to represent the cosmos (the apple when cut straight through shows a five-pointed star which in metaphysical terms means four points representing the four elements, earth, air, fire and water and the fifth point representing akashic or spiritual energy, the God force); bread and cake to represent the grains of the harvests and the body of the planet, goddess, god and therefore God force; wine to celebrate the blood of the earth and the goddess; and saltwater and incense to purify the area that your dead departed guests would be invited to.

All Hallows Eve was also a good time to make your peace and amends with all who had departed or left their physical body that year. People would set the table and call their departed loved ones to speak with them and clear their "karma."

Halloween was seen as an eerie frightening time of the year and the remnants of these fears and beliefs have been handed down to us as superstitions that form our present time holiday celebrations. Because the veil between the world of the humans and the spirits was thin, people were afraid of ghosts, goblins, and all manner of spirits they believed to walk upon the earth at this time. The goddess of the season was the wise old crone. Sometimes, because she was the oldest of the archetypes of the earth she was seen as the bringer of death. She came to be represented as an old wicked witch who has come to be the bearer of ill tidings. Halloween occurs when the year is old, the light is less, and a chill is in the air, so people ventured out only in groups. The uneducated and unenlightened feared what they could not see or understand. The wise or learned people spoke to the archetypes of the earth as the bearers of death with little or no fear as they understood that this was a part of the cycle of life, and they intuitively understood when it was or was not their time to depart. They also understood that although their body might die their spirit would live on and that gave them courage to face the mask of death represented by the old crone.

Nowadays, we cover our fears with parties, costumes, and make-believe. To the ancient and not-so-ancient (200 to 300 years ago) peoples of the earth, Halloween was a time to reassess relationships with all who had passed on, to face death head-on so as to be reborn for the new year, to be introspective and divine and foretell what could come ahead since the veil between the worlds was the thinnest, and to reinforce the life force held so dearly at this dark time of the year with drinking, dancing, and merrymaking.

The period of time between the end of September and the middle of December, when the veil between the worlds of spirit and matter is the thinnest, is when many people have psychic and precognitive dreams, experience visions, and often see disincarnated spirits or "ghosts." This is a very good time of the year for making peace with the internal side of yourself by doing meditations to get in touch with your spiritual side of awareness. For it is at this time of the year when people most sense the "other worldliness" of spirit and must deal with their visions and their fears. As you conquer your fears you allow yourself to be "reborn" in a newer image of yourself, owning the essence of your spiritual self.

Throughout the year the Earth is seen as making changes to represent the cycle it is going through. In December, at the Winter Solstice, the goddess is seen as giving birth to the young

241

sun (or young son). In some cultures she is also seen as the child being born. As the year progresses, she is seen as the young child being initiated into the mysteries of life and growth in February then the young adolescent daughter growing up in March, then the ripe, sensual young woman in May then the full, pregnant, bountiful young mother in midsummer then the older mother in August then the more mature woman and mother in September at the fall harvest; then finally the wise old mature crone at Halloween (who transforms between Halloween and the Winter Solstice to once again repeat the cycle). The earth mother goddess does not die, she just repeats the cycle of life. This incredibly simplistic description is only one way to view the cycles of the planet, there are many other systems of describing the movement of gods and goddesses, the nature aspects of God upon the planet, and their intertwined dependencies and interactions as representations of life force, seasonal changes, and human attributes.

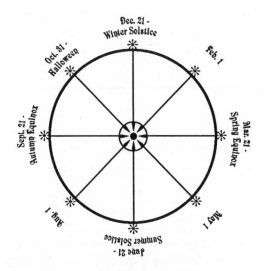

Wheel of the Year

LUNAR CYCLES

Besides being influenced by the energy marker dates of the cycle of the sun and seasons we are also rather intensely affected by the phases and cycles of the moon.

There are thirteen moon cycles in a year. Each moon cycle starts with the new moon, which really means that there is no moon in the sky, and lasts approximately twenty-eight days. The new moon is the dark of the moon time. Before the advent of electricity, people did not travel during the dark time of the new moon. As the moon "grows" each night there is more and more of a crescent reflecting light in the sky.

The Druids called moonlight the "Lamp of the Fairies." During the first quarter of the moon people initiated new projects, new concepts, and began to direct their activities outwardly. During the second phase of the moon people worked on projects that they had begun and continued to further the growth of their concepts. The crescent moon lasts for two weeks and it is called a waxing moon as it grows larger.

Traditionally, it was during the waxing moon that people did energy work to build and create anything of a positive growing nature. For example, all of the old planters' guides and almanacs advise planting above-ground crops in the time of the waxing moon. As the moon grows fuller and fuller, people have more light and with it more energy. At the time of the full round moon people have the most energy and it is a time for parties and travel. Many religions, such as Buddhism and Judaism, follow lunar calendars and time their holidays to coincide with the full moon.

Many studies have been done to document the effects of light and the correlations between plants, animals, humans, and the phases of the moon. They have discovered many interesting facts. The full moon pulls on the earth's gravitational field (which most scientists discount) causing the tides, the sap to rise in the trees (which affects the cutting time of trees so they will not rot), and people to bleed more freely (which certainly is not the best time for an operation). For women the moon generates the cycle followed by the inner workings of their bodies. The word "lunatic" stems from the word lunar. Full moon "madness" creates great parties, the mating of quite a few insects and fish, and also more traffic accidents. The effects of the full moon can unbalance some minds, although the effect is very subtle.

As the moon begins to shrink in light (wanes) it forms a reverse crescent—a mirror image of the waxing moon. The waning moon was seen by early societies as the time to release energy, to banish evil thoughts and deeds, and to cut their hair (it grows back slower during the period of the waning moon). Towards the end of the waning moon, people pulled in their energy to rest and reflect upon their actions.

As an energy worker, you must be aware of the three phases of the moon: New Moon/Waxing Moon, Full Moon, and Waning Moon. For example, when you want to clear an area to build some new structure or new project, you should work during the New/Waxing Moon phase. If you are working on sustaining a previously begun project and filling it with energy, you should do this during the Full Moon phase. If you are working on draining the energy from a destructive project (such as trying to rid the area of a proposed development), you would work more on it during the Waning Moon. Though you can work at any phase of the moon, you will find that the previous guidelines allow you to go with the flow of energy, making any energy work easier and more rewarding.

NEW MOON CREATION

The New Moon is traditionally a time for rest and inner reflection. But it is also a time for new beginnings and planting the seeds that will grow with the waxing moon.

The following exercise, which I have termed a Creation, is based on old energy workings. When I first studied energy working the elders, or more learned energy workers, initiated me into new ways of thought and action by helping me to go through my fears and doubts. They had many "tests" to help new energy workers pass the barriers of the limitations the new energy workers had accepted for themselves. Many of these tests are similar to the tribal initiations that young boys and girls are given to enter the adult world or the world of spirit. One of these tests was to take a new energy worker on the night of the New Moon to a cave and to leave him/her there. The cave represented the womb of Mother Earth, the rebirth of consciousness, and the connection with the oneness of all life. Each initiate followed their guide into a cave, led by the light of a candle or torch, and was given a place to sit. The guides then left the initiates, taking the light with them. Each initiate was left in the dark to contemplate their inner self. Sometimes initiates were left in the cave for a few minutes and at other times they were left for hours before the guides returned.

Darkness, or the lack of light, ties into many of the most primal fears of the human race. Without light people seem to lose their sense of time and space. Sometimes five minutes can seem like five hours and five hours can seem like just a few moments. Left alone in the dark many people face their own innermost fears that quickly rise up to plague them. From this confrontation of their fears in the dark people often seem to lose their identity and their sense of self from which they regain a new connection with themselves when they are led out into the light. Even our language speaks of "light" as good and "dark" as bad. But light and dark are part of the whole—we cannot have one without the other! Returning to the dark cave of Mother Earth forces people to return to their inner soul and to their connection with their inner strength. It forces them to reassess and find out who they truly are. Once people have faced their fears and chased out their "demons" they can begin to create a loving world and to walk into the light.

The following exercise will accomplish the same result without you having to be placed in a cave. This guided meditation allows you to face your inner self, find it, speak with it, and draw from its strength. Once you can do this, then your strength will always be there for you to draw upon.

EXERCISE –
NEW MOON CREATION

Find yourself a comfortable chair and sit in it. Close your eyes. Take a nice, deep breath and open your imagination to see things in your mind's eye. So...tune up your imagination...sit back...and allow yourself to become a participant in your own movie.

Allow yourself to relax. Attach a grounding cord to the bottom of your First Chakra and send it down to the center of the earth. Let all of the energy from your tense muscles drain down your grounding cord. Let all of the tension in your body drain down your grounding cord. It will go down your grounding cord, be released, and come back to you as new life force energy. Allow yourself to feel at peace, to breath deeply, to just be.

In front of you create a big doorway. This door will allow you to step onto the energy plane of the world of imagination, that wonderful magickal place where everything that happens is created by your will in your mind's eye. So, take a deep breath. Now open your doorway and step through to the other side. Then close the door behind you.

Right now you are in a beautiful meadow. The sky above is dark, there is no moon but there are many, many stars splendidly glowing in the night sky. You smell the grass and the flowers of the meadow, hear the wind in the trees at the edge of the meadow, and hear an owl hoot in the night. Instinctively you know to move towards the cliff at the western edge of the meadow. It is dark but as your eyes adjust you can see a little. You have been here before and know your way towards the cliff and so you follow the path where the grass has been trampled down by many feet. Once you reach the cliff on the side of the meadow you see a light softly glowing out of a crevice. Follow the cliff until you reach the light.

The light comes from some torches that are set in the entrance way of a cave. Take a torch from its holder and begin your trek into the mouth of the cave and into the tunnel. The tunnel winds around and it is high enough for you to stand in as you walk. The torch gives you plenty of light to see by and you walk firmly, feeling the cool damp air of the cave surround you. Soon you come to an underground lake before you with a path around it. You turn towards the right and follow the path around the lake until you come to a tunnel that leads you into a smaller, rounded cave room.

It is comfortable in this smaller cave, almost cozy and inviting. You see that the floor has been covered with a fine sand that seems to have been raked in patterns. Here you sit down and survey your surroundings and make yourself familiar with your rounded cave room, its walls, its ceiling, and the ground you sit on. And then you take your torch and you rub it out in the sand so that the light goes out. Suddenly you are sitting alone in the dark, alone in the cave, alone with yourself.

You are not afraid although you sense a sudden innate fear of the black inky, darkness. Take a deep breath. You are holding onto your extinguished torch. And you can suddenly hear your own heart beat and your own breath. As you become aware of your breathing mechanism, of every little sound and action of your internal body, you are suddenly forced to say hello to the life within you. Perhaps you feel your fears of the dark: of the unknown, of things that go bump in the night, of the childhood fears of creatures who will attack you, of the primal fears that surface when you are alone in the dark and so you breath deeply and use your skills of putting these in a rose and blowing them up to take the charge out of your fears so that you may begin to communicate with the unconscious inner part of you. You are coming to terms with your fears, the irrational part of you that surfaces in the dark, that sets the stage for you to allow yourself to act out your wishes and your commands. Here, in this cave-womb of Mother Earth you can release the old you and bring in a new sense of life and wonderment, and experience a rebirth. And it is here you must wait until you are at peace, unafraid, repeating no pattern of life experience or thought, living no old loop of consciousness, but simply just being at peace in the internal strength of your own pool of consciousness.

When you have reached this state of being bring your torch between both hands and imagine the bright sun that the moon reflects, that bright orb in the sky. Here, in the land of energy and imagination you can create anything, you can create miracles. So create the beautiful bright golden sun sending a bolt of golden liquid fire sunlight down to your torch and lighting it for you. As the torch is lit with this golden sunlight so you, too, are energized with new ideas, new concepts, and the belief that you can accomplish all that you need to do. The fire of the torch is the spirit to accomplish, to light your way on new paths, and to give you energy to create new projects. If you have a special ecological project that you are working on you can see the torch as representing the project and bring the golden fire sunlight into the torch to illuminate your work.

With the lit torch in your hand stand and once more find your way to the opening of this small rounded cavity that has given birth to you as a person of strength, of patience, and of peace and knowingness. Move from the small rounded cavity to the path around the lake. Veer left and follow the path until you come to the main tunnel. Continue following the path until you find the opening where the torches sit in the wall. Replace your torch in its holder and step out into the cool night air to look at the stars and the sky and the wonderment that is nature in the night. Then walk down the grass path to the center of the meadow where you find your energy doorway, take a deep breath, and say good-bye to the meadow of your imagination, knowing full well that you can always return. Then open your door, step through, and close it behind you. Once back in the reality of the outward physical plane, take a deep breath, say hello to your body, bring yourself into present time—into the wonderful reality of the here and now—and open your eyes.

CELEBRATING THE PULSE OF THE PLANET

By taking note of the energy markers of the planetary cycles you can learn to understand and intuitively experience the subtle lifecycle of our living planet. Ancient peoples celebrated these energy markers as the turning point of the seasons. They gathered together to sing and dance, share their gleaned knowledge, and work with the energy flow to insure that the cycle of life and death, the wheel of the year, continued on its course.

One way of learning about the natural cycle of the living planet is to celebrate and experience these special times and work with the living energy that is generated as the astral energy doors open wide on these occasions. The eight energy marker celebrations of the year are held in the nighttime hours between the hours of 11:00 p.m. and 3:00 a.m. It is at this time that a good balance between the moon and sun energy exists and the ability to pass through the astral doorways of initiation is open. Many people and cultures celebrate these holidays during the day after or on the weekend nearest to the date, but traditionally they were officiated on the evening before the day. If you decide to work with this energy, to experience it, and feel the power coursing through Mother Earth, work on the evening of the date or after the astral energy doorways have opened. You will feel more power and energy.

As you work with these astral energy doorways you will learn how to consciously walk through them and down the pathways that lead to a raised energy vibration. You will become initiated into the God force groups that work with the planetary guardians to heal the planet. As you experience the energy fields of the astral plane you will awaken the energy fields within your own astral and body systems and experience an amount of enlighten-

250

ment and raised consciousness that will lead you to understand how to communicate with the higher powers, the ascended Masters of this planet, the messengers of God, and the planetary guardians. Then you will be "initiated" into the light force, as you are raised to a higher vibration, in order to aid in the rebalancing of the planetary structure. As this process happens over a period of time (and it could be weeks, months or years— depending on your own personal development and background), you will notice changes in yourself. Your self esteem will grow and you will become consciously aware of much that you thought was hidden or nonexistent. You might open up to seeing auras (the energy life force of a person's system that surrounds their body) or begin to "know" who is calling you on the phone before you answer it or what is going to happen **before** it does actually happen or hear messages from your own Higher Self telling you the "easy" way to accomplish your tasks in life or begin to see and hear and speak with the wee ones, the fairies, nature spirits, and elementals. In other words, you will begin to experience a measure of enlightenment as your energy vibration raises to hear and acknowledge and act out the call of the God force that vibrates around and within this planet and all upon it.

You could call this God force, a oneness, or a cosmic unity, or life spirit or whatever term works for you. How you perceive the God force is entirely up to you. The unity of energy that makes up and creates the physical, material, mental, and spiritual nature of our planet, of ourselves, and of our universe can be perceived in a myriad of ways. Your cultural conditioning may cause you to perceive the God force as a small frail man with a long white beard or a giant goddess ten feet tall with a shimmering flowing gown or a pulsating sparkling gas-flame blue cloud of light or a soft golden emanation of light or any number of other perceptions. The oneness and how you perceive it, is how you learn to translate your inner perceptions. It is like looking at an ink blot test. Some people see it from an overview, some from one side, some from the front and others from the inside. It, however, is the same inkblot, no matter from what angle or perspective or cultural conclusion you view it.

The ancient acknowledgments to the turn of the power of the wheel of the seasons gave people the ability to archetypally hook into the greater life force power of the planet. Usually these people would create large celebrations to thank the life force powers for the harvest that would last them until the next turn of the season to call the powers of the goddess, the god, the Supreme Being, and the planetary guardians to be with them and share their bountiful harvest, and to do energy work to heal the planet and keep the harmonic balance of light and dark. Some of these traditional ceremonies have been handed down but they are veiled in the cloak of symbolic words and imagery dedicated to the particular archetypal deity aspect of the part of the world from which they originated. Often the few "traditional" ceremonies are either wordy and stilted, like an old play, or filled with symbolic movement and intuitive gestures handed down from one generation to another that "outsiders" do not fully understand.

If you wish to celebrate, work with the energy, experience the turn of the planetary cycle, or help to heal the planet at the most powerful energy marker times, you might do better by creating your own mythos and movement. To do this you must first understand, to the best of your intellectual and intuitive ability, the actual symbolism of the particular energy marker with which you are going to interact. The Winter Solstice, for example, is the birth of the sun, the birth of the child of the goddess, a celebration of beginnings of the growth of light coming into the year. To celebrate the Winter Solstice you would create an area or sacred space that is a connection between the world of the ordinary and the world of the spirit or the immortal. Though all land upon this planet is a sacred or special space, to work with the energy forces at the turn of the planet or energy marker times, you should always work in a "special", balanced place.

The traditional method of creating a "sacred space" was to bless the area with the four elements and invoke the power of the God or unity force. First, salt and water, the symbols of earth and water, were blessed and mixed together to form salt water to purify and bless the entire area and everything in it. Then incense or vapors of the air were burned to clear the area. Lastly, a candle was lit as the symbol of fire and the flame of life. Each of these four elements is symbolic but each one was also used to create a special space in which all who came were spiritually purified and prepared to experience the site as sacred. These are the same basic concepts that the religious facilitators of any church, synagogue, temple, sacred grove, or holy gathering place would enact. Salt water, the ocean of life from which we all came, is seen as the original purification medium. And as a purification medium it was used to rid an area of negative, strange, or different energies. Incense was used to purify the air, the medium of communication, and to allow the lesser trained spiritual people to perceive spirits in the smoke. A candle gave light to charge an area with the fire of spirit and the unity of a single flame.

If you are going to create a sacred space to work in you do not have to use the old methods. If your sacred space is an area in the woods, at the top of a hill or small mountainside, a sheltered valley, or any place of the land in the greater wilderness then it already is a sacred space. The reason that people purify and attempt to "create" a sacred space is that they are working with an area that is used for "ordinary" events. A glen or small area in a park that children play in and where people drink their beer and have their picnics and barbecues will carry the jetsam and flotsam of the chaotic energy of humankind. In order to make this space sacred, you would have to reconnect it with the greater powers that be. And the easiest way to recreate the land would be to bless and sanctify it—to clean it. You could clean it using the new modern Eco-Spirit techniques of grounding and cleaning out with solar force energy or you could use the ancient shamanistic and church style techniques of salt, water, incense, and candle. Both work well. It is, of course, easier to create a sacred space in the wild, in the land of nature. But perhaps you wish to celebrate or create the experience of the Winter Solstice in your living room. When you are creating a sacred space in a place that is usually used for "ordinary" life events, you have to take more time and cleanse the room or space of the trivial, emotional chaos people leave lying around willy-nilly. You have to purify it so that you are not walking through the daily happenings of that room but are instead experiencing the atmosphere of the divine and sacred.

In order for me to create a sacred space I first have to explore and know the sacredness and purification of the senses within myself. I would probably take a bath and wash away the day's events, imagining my emotional attachments to people and situations being washed away down the drain. Then I would dress in something that is loose, comfortable, and preferably natural, such as cotton. (Natural fabrics allow your body to breathe and enable you to work with energy because they do not form any barriers to it. Synthetic materials, such as polyester, hold in your energy making you sweat and forcing an unnatural division between you and the energy of the rest of the world around you.) To celebrate the turn of the energy of the planet you have to feel comfortable and be at ease with yourself. Next, I would take the time to meditate, to ground and run energy, and to clear myself by de-energizing everything that prevents me from being in present time. In present time all things are possible and it is easy to create a sacred space.

So, how do you see and create a sacred or special place? When I create a sacred space in an area as an energy marker of the year, I meditate carefully on what that time of the year implies and what type of atmosphere or area I would wish to be in if I could close my eyes and just transport myself to the most wonderful pristine place on Earth that would represent the energy marker. For the Winter Solstice I would see myself in a grove of evergreen trees on a hillside. The air would be clean and crisp, there would be soft pine needles underfoot forming a gentle bed on the earth, and I would be able to smell the resin of the needles and the trees. While there, I would take the time to hear the trees and the earth speaking to me, to the tongues of the winter winds blow through the trees and hoots of an owl in the distance. I take my cues from this inner vision and create my sacred place. First I get pine or evergreen incense to burn in my room to remind my of my internal image. Then I build a large fire in the fireplace to symbolize the reawakening of the sun which is going to get stronger from this night on. I might place a soft green rug on the floor to symbolize the color of nature, the life in the winter.

What makes an area just okay and what makes it sacred? To make an area into a "sacred" space you have to be able to connect it to the greater powers that be. You have to reconnect it to the whole of oneness, to God or the life force or the essence of life. You are essentially creating a connection between the microcosm, your sacred space, and the macrocosm, the greater universe at large. You are creating a connection between the physical world based in space and time and the spiritual universe that has no boundaries. I do this by creating my sacred space as a cone of energy. The ground is the bottom of my cone and as the cone of energy spins, the energy travels up and down. In the center of my sacred space I create a small pinpoint of golden light. This light stretches upwards and downwards, like the trunk of a very tall tree, to reach to the God force or oneness of the universe. And when this golden shaft of light reaches its goal, it channels into it and brings back an even more golden shimmering light right back down its trunk that fills and enlightens my sacred circle. My circle becomes a lens of power and fills up with golden light that bathes me in the light of the spiritual power of my own will which is combined with the power of the universe at large. My sacred circle becomes a mirror between the worlds of humans and the worlds of the spiritual dimensions. It is a safe space in which I can now create archetypal visualizations to affect reality on the physical plane. My sacred space holds life and form based on my ability to will it to visually and spiritually exist. In order to charge my area with life force I call to that which is sacred to me, my personal concept of the oneness of the universe, to the God force in which I believe and ask it to come and fill my circle with its light and life. The tools presented here are universal but it is up to you which archetypal forms or images you use to create your own sacred space. You can be very creative as long as you are true to your inner self.

My Sacred Space – A Cone of Energy

Once I have created and can visualize my sacred space, I am ready to move on to doing something within it. If I am working with a group of people I might pass a kiss or hug around so that I can announce that all actions in the microcosm are done in the name of love. There are many things you can do in a sacred space. It is up to you and your ability to use your creativity to create a better world. For example, to celebrate the cycle of the year, you could initiate an archetypal play to reenact the dying of the sun and the rebirth of the new sun of the year. All persons in the group would take parts—one person being the night, another the old sun, another the goddess, and yet another the new sun. Each would act out their parts and then all would call to the new sun to be born and to grow and nurture everyone in its warmth. Through this play you would be calling to the New Sun of the Year to come and grow and nurture the planet and all upon it. Archetypal plays are fun. You can sing and chant and wear costumes and dance and move and lose yourself in celebration. Working in a sacred space can seem like "playing," but it is not the playing of a child but the playing of the adult who uses his/her will or intention to create a connection with the cosmic unity. Each movement, each sound, each action created in a sacred place is created with a will, intention, and purpose. This bonds the power of the mind, body, and spirit to become molded as one with the earth, spirit, and cosmos. You are not "acting" in a play or "saying lines" but **being** the essence of the part you play in the cycle of life.

Besides re-enacting an archetypal play, you can also plan and accomplish an eco-action in your sacred space. Suppose you have a piece of land that you are working on to transform it into a small local park. Bring into your sacred space a bucket of earth from this area and place it in the center. This small mound of earth represents the park you are working on to bring into reality. Now take cardboard or colored art paper and make stand-up cut outs of trees, plants, and anything else you want in your park. Smooth the earth and shape it into your park, then place your trees, shrubs, benches, trash barrels, and whatever else you want placed in your park. This is your willed creation in your microcosm that you are working on to have mirrored in the macrocosm.

When you have created your park in miniature, have everyone sit in a circle and place their hands on the soil of the park. Have everyone take the time to feel the soil and to imagine the park as you wish it to be. Have them visualize this three-dimensional picture of a park in their mind's eye. Have them smell it, hear it, and sense it existing around them. Now have everyone chant to fill the park with life and channel the golden light of the sacred space through their hands (as described in the chapter "'Personal Power And Planetary Transformation") and into the center of the sacred circle. By these actions you are using the unifying force of the universal medium of light and life (some people call this God force) to create your park. When you have finished, place the soil back into your bucket. On the next day return this charged land to the actual spot from where it came and your park will soon exist.

Archetypal enactments and eco-action enactments such as described above are very powerful on energy marker dates because on those dates the astral energy doorways are open. It is easier to put in your request for something to the universe at the right time. Energy marker times are those times when there is space for new creations and the flow of energy is turning and therefore it is easier to bring something in on a new path.

Once you have performed your archetypal play or your eco-spirit action you now have the time to delve into your inner space to meditate on where your own actions in life have led you and what this particular time of the year brings to you, as well as what you bring to it. It is here that I meditate and take the space and time to reassess my own personal situation in life. I take account of who I am now, how my personality has changed, and what I have developed into since the last change of season.

Religion is a code of rules that people live by in order to practice their inner spirituality according to the ideas we humans inherit from the world of spirit. Spirituality is the enactment of making a connection between the essence of the physical plane and the higher or spiritual plane. Early on, people practiced their spirituality by constantly making the connection between their inner selves and the physical world of nature. Every action was an acknowledgment of the divine nature of life. Nowadays, we often relegate this practice to having a holy book or Bible on the shelf to refer to in time of need or question. Our ancestors had a living connection with the realm of spirit and the realm of nature. If we seek to heal ourselves—and, in turn, create a new balance of life force upon the earth—we, too, must begin to create a living, viable connection between our inner world of thoughts, fantasies, and wishes and the outer world of nature, material objects, and the existent earth. We must learn to become the ever-moving eternal spirit of life itself. We must not seek the words on the printed page, but seek instead the words in action that are imprinted in our hearts and our minds and our spirit.

ECLIPSES OF THE MOON AND SUN

When the moon or the sun is eclipsed by the other, its energy is canceled out, so to speak. Ancient cultures were awed by this statement of the gods and would perform a ceremony or raise energy to call back the moon or sun. Even today, in our modern world, people travel to see full eclipses of the moon or the sun. They describe it as awe-inspiring to experience cosmic nature in its rawest form. Some scientists even forget to pay attention to their measurements and instruments as their intuitive nature hooks into the greater cosmic flow of energy—energy that causes the hair to raise on their bodies and their souls to stand in awe.

Usually the energy of an eclipse builds up for two to three days before the event and releases for two to three days afterwards. Unlike the arbitrarily scheduled events that humans create to happen at a specific instant in time, nature's cosmic events span from the build-up to the release of energy. Nature and cosmic time is like a wave in the ocean that takes time to build and recede. If you intend to perform a ceremony or action using eclipse energy, you can time it for the moment of the eclipse or for after the eclipse (when the energy is the strongest). If the eclipse happens on a Friday and you work with a group that can only meet on Saturday, the energy will still be there for you to use.

An eclipse of the moon, when the moon is no longer visible, results in a stockpile of Sun energy. Sun energy is the energy of light, spirit, health, fame, success, power, riches, prosperity, illumination, individuality, mental power, will power, determination, confidence, inner self, self-improvement, vitality, social prestige, superiority, employment, and integration.

An eclipse of the sun results in the opposite effect, an abundance of Moon energy. The moon represents reflected light, the personality, the subconscious mind, emotions, feelings, moods, sensitivity, illusion, deception, all that is hidden or secret, instinctual behavior, imagination, receptivity, intuition, imagination, memory; and it rules the tides and oceans, rhythms of the human body, and all things of a watery nature.

When working during an eclipse you need to know what astrological sign the moon is positioned in. Every three days the moon changes its emphasis by moving from one astrological sign to the next. The twelve monthly astrological signs each generate a different type of influence to the over-abundance of Moon energy generated during a solar eclipse. The following sections describe this influence generated by each astrological sign.

To understand the astrological signs and their influence upon the moon's movements through the astrological heavens you will need to get an astrological handbook and an astrological calendar. You do not need to be an astrologer to do energy work, but it can aid you to know the simple basics of astrology to understand the influence of the moon and the planets upon the earth and the people with which you might be working.

When the moon is in Aries (the sign of the Ram), which is ruled by Mars, you are working with strong, forceful, and impulsive energetic activity. People tend towards emotional outbursts and selfishness. The Aries moon is a good time for starting new groups or activities, for high energy to incite people to action.

As the moon passes into Taurus, the influence of the bull (symbol of Taurus), you are working with stubborn unchanging emotional cautiousness. There is a need for material and financial security. Taurus is ruled by the planet Venus which gives people the ability to appreciate earthly beauty. The Taurus moon presents a good time for holding your ground in a difficult situation and pushing forward with all you've got.

While the moon is located in the double sign of Gemini, whose symbol is the Twins and is ruled by Mercury, people are more adaptable, communicative and changeable. Mercury is the ruler of communication. Sometimes people have a difficult time making decisions while the moon, their emotional nature, is in Gemini, which allows you to see all sides of an issue. A Gemini moon is a good time for news releases, public relations, and communication to the world at large to make your ideas work.

As the moon moves through Cancer you are ruled by the subconscious, the emotions, and instinctual behavior. Cancer is the ruler of the moon and while the moon is in Cancer it is at its strongest and most intense, a time of sensitivity, passivity, sentimentality, and mother-love. Cancer is a fertile and nurturing sign and is a good sign in which to plant and to create projects that need nurturing, life force, and growth.

If you read the *Farmer's Almanac* it will explain to you the times of the moon for planting as each phase of the moon influences a certain type of energy that is conducive to particular plants. Farmers who follow these simple astrological instructions have marvelous results (as you can see in the pictures of giant squashes and other healthy vegetables they send in to the almanac publishers and moon calendar every year.) A Cancer moon provides a good time for starting a project and nurturing it along.

Next the moon moves into the planet Leo, ruled by the Sun. A Leo moon expresses the dramatic in behavior and a time when people refuse to acknowledge their limitations. It is a moon of independent behavior, of ambition, of leadership, of great heart, and the warmth of human kindness and generosity since Leo rules the heart and the upper spine. A Leo moon is a good time for raising pure high energy to heal, love, or help the planet. It is also a good time for facing your adversaries headon since Leo energy is the warmth of the heart, like using the heart of the lion to win your way.

When the moon moves into Virgo it is ruled by Mercury (which also rules Gemini) and it is a good time to take note of the mind as Virgo is the critical intellectual sign of the Zodiac. This is the time to pay attention to details, to critique your project, and to pay attention to your health and your diet. A Virgo moon tends to make people want to "clean house" as they express their shy, internal self melded with the critical, fussy discriminating mind. Virgo is also the sign of the harvest mother, the eternal virgin. The Virgo "virgin" here is seen as the eternal virgin in the same sense that the Amazon warriors perceived themselves as virgins until the day they gave birth to a child. The aspect of Virgo as the "earth mother goddess" is that of an archetype holding the wheat sheaf or an archetype goddess of the first corn harvest. A Virgo moon is a good time for bringing all of the details of your project together, for using your mind to analyze the project, and for pulling it all together into a plan of action.

As the moon passes into Libra it brings people together as they search for the harmony and balance that the sign of Libra represents. Libra, governed by the planet Venus, leads people to beautify their surroundings and to be of an easy-going, flowing, tolerant nature. Libra is the sign of balance—of understanding how to bring together the opposites: day and night, yin and yang, light and dark, summer and winter, male and female. A Libra moon is a good time for working on harmony, beauty, and creativity in an area you wish to clean or work.

When the moon moves into Scorpio, ruled by Mars and Pluto, it brings out the strong passions in people. This is the influence of the critical nature mixed with aggression, and strong feelings of impatience, moodiness, and desires. Scorpio rules the organs of reproduction which includes the lower spine where Kundalini, the fire energy, is stored. A Scorpio moon is a good time to raise emotional energy to charge a project and it is a good time for learning to do breath work to release old emotional attitudes.

As the moon goes into Sagittarius it is ruled by Jupiter, the expansive planet that tends to make people feel spontaneous, intuitive, visionary, and enthusiastic. A Sagittarius moon is one of restlessness, adventure, travel, excitement, and movement. It is a good time to put forth concepts, ideas, printed matter, letters, classes, and all matters of the philosophically visionary-minded intellect. A Sagittarius moon is a good time for visiting a new area that you would like to work on. The expansiveness of a Sagittarian moon might give you visions or inner concepts of how you can put your ideas into motion or how you might be working toward achieving results in a given situation.

When the moon moves into Capricorn people are pulled more into themselves, with an increased need to make contracts in the material world, to create practical methods of accomplishment, and to fulfill commitments and responsibilities. Capricorn is ruled by Saturn, the planet of contraction, security, and task making. This is a time for accomplishing down-to-earth tasks and cleaning up old agreements, responsibilities, and karmic dues. The energy in a Capricorn moon can be slow and sometimes lead to negative and pessimistic thoughts. Accomplishing tasks can overcome these aspects of the Saturnian nature. A Capricornian moon is a good time for dealing with group finances, movement, or actions; for pulling together agreements to act on a certain condition; and for doing practical down-to-earth things.

The moon of Aquarius is ruled by Uranus. Uranus is the planet that provides us with eccentric unique views of life and people. It is the planet of innovative ideas, concepts dealing with freedom and free will, and all that is unconventional. Aquarian influence causes people to deal with the public, work towards the welfare of humanity, and make sudden changes in all that they encounter. The Aquarian moon is a good time for doing action involving a humanitarian cause, the saving of a piece of land from developers, or the brainstorming of a group to come up with new and creative ideas to deal with a situation.

The Pisces moon is ruled by Neptune, God of the Sea and keeper of psychic intuitive information. The Pisces moon is a moon of the intuitive, sensitive individual who is emotional, spiritual, and open to impressions from the world around him or her. During a Pisces moon people lose their sense of the dimension of time, become sentimental, spiritual, gentle, and in touch with the "other-worldly" information line. People with a strong Piscean influence can easily become addicted, develop negative habits to run away from reality, and be righteous, self-sacrificing martyrs. They can also be incredibly intuitive, psychic, and have natural healing abilities. During a Pisces moon the astral doorways to other dimensions that affect the energy flow of the planet are open and alive for all who can learn to use them.

If you have never worked with Moon energy or astrological concepts you might want to start to learn to understand these concepts on a basic beginning level. One method of learning moon energy is to keep a small journal. The moon moves into a different sign every three days. Each day make a list of your emotional responses to actions in the environment around you. You might find that there is a subtle connection between your emotional responses, internal feelings and patterns, and the movement and change of the planetary sign that the moon is going through. As you read past entries from your journal you will begin to notice and understand these subtle energy connections. You should also note the phases of the moon and record them in your journal. You might discover that certain types of behavior occur mostly at the full moon or at the new moon. You might find that the best parties and the most crowded gatherings happen at the full moon and that your incredible inner revelations of awareness occur at the new moon. You might find that certain business deals are easier to enact near or toward the full moon and that it is by far easier to end relationships or let go of old bad feelings during a waning moon. Women understand the relationship of the moon to their menstrual cycle and if you are female you might wish to sleep under the moon or with the moonlight streaming through your window. Scientific university studies have shown that when women sleep in moonlight they tend to naturally regulate their menstruation cycle to match the full or new moon.

To learn about the planetary signs and basic astrology I recommend a basic astrological workbook, such as *Secrets of a Stargazer's Notebook* by Debby Kempton-Smith.

"There are times when the power-tides of the Unseen flow strongly down upon our earth, and there are also places upon her surface where the channels are open and they come through in their fullness of power. This was known to them of old time, who had much wisdom that we have forgotten, and they availed themselves of both times and places when they sought to awaken the higher consciousness."

> — *Dion Fortune in*
> *Avalon of the Heart*

20

ECOLOGICAL SPIRITUAL
GROUP POWER

It only takes one spiritually conscious person who is willing
to use his or her spiritual nature in an active manner to actually
create change in the ecological energy nature of the planet.
However, if you had more than one person working on the same
problem or situation then you would have more than double the
energy of the people involved. Energy workers have long known
that when you have three people working together raising or
channeling their conscious energy for a project, you actually have
triple the energy. So, three people working towards healing a
specific area actually produce the energy of nine people, nine
people working on a project produce the energy of twenty-seven
people, and so on, exponentially, as the numbers in the group
increases. The more people that work on a given project the more
clear, focused, usable energy is being directed into that project.
This is not to say that the power of one single person involved in
raising, or changing the area where there is an imbalance is not
useful, powerful or appreciated. One person can make a difference. It is, however, obvious that nine people working on the
very same project generating the power of twenty to twenty-

seven people would have a greater effect. This exponential effect is something to take notice of because the more raw power you have to change a situation, the quicker and more easily it can be accomplished.

Working in ecological energy groups can be fun and a learning experience. However, there are some basic guidelines you should follow when you are working in a group.

These basic guidelines are:

1. Choose friends or people with whom you have a common bond.

2. Work only with people you naturally trust.

3. Work with people who have the same goals that you do.

4. Never try to influence or convince someone to work with you in a group. People who join groups should do so because they are unalterably drawn and magnetized to do this type of energy work not because a friend convinced them.

Of these, the most important is to always choose to work with people that you innately trust and feel good about. When you are raising or channeling elemental, spiritual, or planetary energy you always want to be in touch with the inner side of yourself. The inner side of yourself reflects your feelings about who you are and what you are doing. If you do not feel good then the energy you work with will be affected by your negative emotion. Working to raise or channel energy is a delicate operation that requires you to check in with the inner side of yourself constantly so that you are manifesting the greater good towards the object you are focusing upon. When you choose to work with other people you want to feel a common bond, to experience similar emotional reactions to the situation you are working in, and have mutual respect. If you do not feel good about someone then do not work with them because it will come out later in the results of your actions.

Once you have the people for your group, you are ready for the next leg of your journey towards ecological spiritual group power: creating a group that can work together and play together and generally function as a unit.

Group work is an art form. Finding people of similar motives and emotional natures and learning to channel these motives and emotions is no easy feat. If you think this is easy, take notice of the many musical bands which have broken up over the years. It takes conscious work to create a group bond that allows total free will and still functions as a unit to accomplish its purpose. Creating a quality group of ecologically and spiritually minded people is a challenge but well worth the effort.

At Advanced Eco-Spirit workshops we teach people how to learn to interact together on an energy level. But before you get to this stage of the game you have to put your time in towards just learning about the people you are working with.

The following are basic suggestions for learning how to form a group that can sustain itself:

1. Start out with preliminary discussions. Discuss every-thing. Why are you interested in doing Eco-Spirit work? What would you do or work on to heal the planet? What are your general interests and what type of lifestyle do you follow?

The best working groups I have ever seen are made up of close friends who share their lives together and might get together on a Saturday night anyway to just **be** with one another, and who innately, almost telepathically, understand one another's emotional natures.

2. Find out who the "leader" is and see if the leadership pattern can be changed or shifted so that each person, at some point, gets the chance to lead the group.

3. Watch for whether you are a listener or a speaker. Try to draw out the listeners and teach the speakers to listen.

4. As you begin to do the exercises described later in this chapter, allow yourself and others to take risks.

   You cannot work well with energy if you are self-conscious about your appearance, uptight about your image, or on your best behavior (as you would be with strangers or at a social gathering). You must be "at home" with yourself and the others in your group. If you are not relaxed with yourself try to find out why and change it. Take small risks, such as looking foolish doing a charade or an improvisational exercise. As they say in some dance classes, "Let your stomach hang loose."

5. Learn to recognize and face your ego. Some people, when placed in group situations, begin to compete with another person in the group. This shifts the focus of the group from their goal to the competing individuals. What makes a group work is when the goal is more important than the ego of any of the individuals in the group.

GROUP EXERCISES

Before your group actually begins doing movement and sound exercises take time to talk for a while and make sure that everyone gets to know one another. Acquainted people work together better than strangers! Take the time to discuss your goals, your aspirations, and your fears about doing energy work to heal the environment.

Then stand up and form a circle. Symbolically the circle represents the whole picture, the whole of creation (the cell, the egg, the planet, the universe, the Oneness of space and time). Forming a circle is also an excellent way of creating equal peer communication in a group space.

Have everyone take a deep breath and, as they breathe out, release all of their fears, old emotions, and anything else they wish to let go of from the day or the week. Have them shake out their arms, legs, and body and see it as shaking out the energy that they are letting go: the energy from the drive to the meeting, the energy from the day at work, the energy from a fight with a friend, or the energy from internal feelings. Now have everyone stretch up and "touch the ceiling" and stretch down and touch the floor, then generally move their bodies to get their blood circulating and air in their body. Have everyone ground themselves with a grounding cord from the bottom of their First Chakra down to the center of the Earth. Have them send all of their excess energy or anything they wish to let go of down their grounding cord to the center of the Earth where it will be released and return to its original life force energy. Then have everyone be in the Center of Their Head and take a nice deep breath. Now everyone in the group is ready to work on exploring themselves within the group.

CREATION

Form a circle and sit down on the ground. Then take an apple and pass it around the circle. Each person should feel, touch, and get acquainted with the apple. Now put the apple away. Starting at the beginning of the circle have the first person create an imaginary apple, which he/she describes to the group and then passes it around. Feel the imaginary apple. How much does it weigh? What does it look like? What color is it? Does it have any bruises? Is there a stem? Are there any leaves on the stem? Is the apple shiny? Does it look good enough to eat? Is it ripe? Only the first person has to verbalize his creative thoughts about the apple. The rest of the people just have to hold, touch, experience, and reinforce the creation of the imaginary apple as it moves around the circle.

This exercise is to teach people how to use their imaginations and how to let go of their shyness about expressing their creativity with others. It is an ancient exercise. Children play like this all the time. But adults stifle any type of creative expression because it is "make-believe." Energy work is not "make-believe." It is real.

By learning to create with energy you are learning to allow yourself to do several things:

1. To use your imagination. Your imagination is what allows you to add 2 plus 2 and get 5. This is called intuition.

2. To take a risk with other people. People who take risks together stay bonded together longer and learn to trust one another.

3. To channel your creative energy onto the energy plane. Healing with the spirit is just that, using your spiritual nature to create a difference on the physical plane.

    Most people doubt themselves when they first begin to work with pure energy. As you practice and experience being an energy worker and allow yourself to work "publicly" with a group of people who "validate" you, you will begin to believe in yourself and your abilities. The results from energy working will happen whether you "believe" in it or not. However, the more you do believe that your actions are real and will cause change the more power you will put behind them and the greater your effect upon the environment will be.

4. To have fun playing like a child while you are also performing an exercise that creates something "real" in the world. When we work to change something in our "world" or in our environment we tend to be serious and "down to earth." Moving energy around works best when you are having fun and in good humor. Humor is one of the highest energy levels on the planet. People in good humor can heal themselves without any effort. What is happening to our planetary environment is a very serious matter, but if we work in love and joy and with good humor while we move energy around, we will have better results.

Many of the exercises used to create a group sense of power and action are very hard to describe. They are of an experiential nature which is best left to workshops where you can learn by doing. However, in the interests of all of the people who would like to start a group or work with your friends helping to heal the environment, I will describe some exercises for working with people.

BEING THE ELEMENTS

Form a circle. Start with the element of Earth. Have everyone feel themselves as being entirely made up of the earth element. Now express this by moving around, having the circle move around in a clockwise fashion—and physically portray your experience of earth. Feel your body as earth. Now walk as if you are totally made up of the earth element. Feel the earth energy in your body. Sense the earth energy in your body. Move as though you are one with the earth. Have the circle make at least three full turns as people act out the Earth element.

You may find that your whole sense of yourself and your body as your vehicle changes. You may feel heavy or dense or weighted down or glued to the ground. Some people naturally have more "earth" energy within them than others. We each have a makeup of the four elements but they are rarely in equal balance (as you can tell from looking at your astrological chart and checking how many planets you have in each element).

Now sit down for a moment and have each person explain what being the element of Earth felt like to him or her. Many people learn to validate their experiences and understand them intuitively by having other people express the same feelings verbally.

Next, have the circle move around and express the element of Air. Use your body. You can use sound but make sure that your physical body expresses your sense of being entirely made up of the element of Air. As you move around the circle at least three times you will find that some people are naturally at home in the Air element. Others will feel lost or uncomfortable. When you have finished expressing Air sit down in a circle and discuss your experiences with one another.

276

Now progress to moving around the circle as the element of Fire. Using Fire should add some movement, action, and excitement to your circle. The most important aspect to these exercises is to "feel" and physically "express" the element you are working with. You do not have to move dramatically. Some people simply walk around the circle but as they walk they are truly feeling from deep within, that they are totally made up of Fire. Others will make sounds and move dramatically as if on stage. It is up to the individual how he or she wishes to express his/her experience. When you have finished your movement sit down in a circle and discuss your experiences.

Now move to express the element of Water. Water is the element of love, compassion, feelings, and the flowing of movement. Be sure that you give everyone in the circle permission to express themselves. You might not want to make a sound or move dramatically but make sure that if anyone does want to do that he or she can feel comfortable in expressing himself. Once you have finished moving as Water then sit down in a circle and discuss your findings.

Sometimes it is enlightening to "become" the raw element and express it through your physical body. You can find how balanced you are elementally as well as letting go of your physical body shyness of expressing yourself in a group. The element that you feel the most comfortable "being" is probably the element that you have the most of in your makeup, are the most in touch with, and can communicate with the most easily. If you examine the people in your group you will learn how well your group is balanced elementally. If two people are "water" people, three are "fire" people, and one is an "earth" person, you will want to do a lot of exercises with air and earth to try and balance the group. You will also want each person to work on themselves to balance their elemental makeup.

I have found that people learn most in a group when they are "doing" something as opposed to just discussing it. You could have everyone do an elemental chart and state what their make-up of elements is, but doing these exercises with movement illustrates it graphically and gives more cohesiveness to the group. Whatever you do, don't just be a **talk** group. Use action, movement, sound, and interaction whenever you can. Talking leads you nowhere but action enables you to create change in your environment.

ARCHETYPAL EXERCISES

 BEING THE TREE

Form a circle and hold hands. Take a nice deep breath and use pore breathing to see yourself as accumulating life force energy within your body. Have one person be the starting spokesperson but everyone can join in as they feel comfortable.

Your spokesperson says, "I am the tree of life. My roots run deep into the planet and bring nourishment to my trunk where I give people and animals shelter. My branches stretch into the sky stretching towards the infinite. My leaves color the environment and cushion the earth when they fall. I am a home for birds and squirrels; a roof for other plants, animals, and insects; my bark is used for medicines by humankind; my fruits and nuts for food; I purify the air with my presence; and I soothe and heal all who come into close contact with me. I am the tree.

278

"I spread my branches and shelter all who come within my domain. My spirit fills the land with love and joy. I share the profound knowledge of life eternal."

As the spokesperson speaks aloud the group moves (still holding hands) and acts out the life and movements of the tree. The group runs into the center with arms raised upwards to be the tree of life and then stretches their arms outwards to be the tree stretching out to reach out to the world and then moves and writhes with energy as the tree communicates to all who can hear.

Each person in the group can add to the litany of sayings of the spokesperson. Perhaps another person in the group says, "I am the spirit of the tree. I speak love and joy to all who come within my radiance and I transmute life force from the planet within to the sky without. I bless those who love life as I do and help those who are lost along their path."

Anyone in the group can speak and say anything that speaks of the tree. There is no set script, just spontaneous statements of how the tree seems to you at the time. Set words, standardized litanies, and scripts, cause people to "act" a part. Here, we want to **be** the tree in all of its manifestations in a spontaneous manner and as unrehearsed as possible.

Groups with people who are "free" to speak have fun and flow with words, movement, and actions with one another to **be** the tree. People might say, "I am the apple tree who is known for bringing its fertile powers to woman. I am the ash who has special guardians that reside in my trunk and help in absorbing the sicknesses of humankind. I am the palm tree, the very essence of life that is always renewing and shedding its skin in rebirth. I am the olive tree. I am sacred and ancient and a great protector against lightning. I am the peach tree. I am sacred to marriage and symbolize abundance. I am the willow tree who takes up the sorrow of loss and death and transmutes it in time. I am the pine tree, known for my energy and great powers of immortality that I bestow upon all who come to me in life and light and love."

"I am all trees who breathe upon the planet and give our sacred spirit to the task of the renewal of life."

"I am the tree who shades in the mid-day sun, and the tree who shelters in the rainstorm. I am the tree who sparkles in the moonlight as a perch for the wise owl. I am the symbol of life eternal."

As the person is speaking and creating a word image the group acts it out as the tree would. For example, as the person describes the palm tree shedding and being reborn, the group moves creating a shedding motion and physically enacts the rebirth of the tree and its spirit.

During the entire Archetypal Tree exercise you always hold hands and stay in a circle. This causes the group to learn to act as a unit and to interact with one another in a cohesive fashion. At the end everyone kneels on the ground and bows their head down and puts the tree to sleep. Then they unclasp one another's hands.

In Shamanistic circles people considered themselves to be the tree and to be the keepers of the spirit of the tree. Whatever they thought or acted out at that time became an actual happening on the planet. They kept their thoughts on the growth and blossoming of the tree lest they create something unwanted or negative. Ancient peoples on the planet venerated trees as the keeper of spirits that could help to heal and transform mankind and also as powerful beings in their own right who protected all who came within their field.

"Becoming The Tree" exercise is a letting go of personal power ego to experience a power greater and beyond the realm of an ordinary man or woman. It is greater than the group that creates it. It is the essence of life itself and as such is a very powerful exercise even though it is so simple.

I hope you will learn to cast aside your shyness, misgivings, and natural reticence to experience "Being The Tree" with your group.

Archetype

Archetypal creations can be done for any number of things. You can explore being the Sun; being the Moon; being the elements of Earth, Air, Fire, and Water; being Mother Nature; and so on.

As you become versed in this method of energy working you will learn how to be something and therefore work with its energy to change its path of action. For example, you could be the volcano and then work with its energy to change its path. You could be the flood and slowly change the course of the flooding waters. You could be the earthquake and release your powerful energy in tiny small amounts instead of all at once.

Once you learn to work together as a group you will come to understand one another's movements and be able to create whole scenarios that function on an internal energy level. With the agreement to use powerful visual images you can proceed to move or change the energy of an existing power around to your advantage. It is not always easy, but it is possible. The only special power it takes is to be grounded, in synch with the whole group, and to give it your entire attention and focus.

281

Being in synch with the whole group is learning to be attuned to each individual and also to the group's movements and actions. It is also learning to be in harmony or affinity with the elements or archetypes that you are working with. As you are working with a tree you are in harmony with that tree. Once you develop a line of communication with an object that you normally consider separate and apart from yourself, you will open yourself up to the world of nature and to a changing landscape of eternal experience. You will experience the reality of your creations which will lead you towards a whole new world of internal revelations.

Archetypal movement creations are just the beginning of learning to work with nature and the environment. They open you up to learning how to communicate as being a piece or part of the natural play of life. Once you have mastered this technique you can go on to then direct or move this play of life towards a necessary goal—like redirecting the flow of the volcano or the path of the floodwaters.

Archetypal Plays

Once you have mastered the method of archetypally **being** a natural object you will want to learn how to combine this into the bigger picture as shown in the following learning exercise.

 PLAY OF LIFE

Form a circle. Create a scene in nature that everyone will enjoy. Now assign a **being** to each person in the circle. Let's use an example. Let's take a volcano on a mountain. If you have seven people assign each person a part or "role" in the play. One person is a tree, another is the sun. The third person is **being** the earth of the mountain, and the fourth is **being** the air, and the fifth person is **being** the animals of the mountain. The sixth person is the fiery earth, the lava. The seventh person is the volcano.

If it makes it easier for people in the group to remember and understand their roles, give each person a prop to carry and use. The use of creative props can be fun in enactments. However, they can also distract from the interaction and business at hand. Your group should experiment to find what works best.

Now create your story line.

Start off by having each person announce who they are and say a little story about themselves.

The Tree: "I am the tree and I live on the mountain. I am a big strong oak tree with a giant span of branches. I am home to many birds and I shelter hikers who come to see the view at the top of the mountain. I have lived for many, many years and am of great strength."

The Sun: "I am the sun. I shine down upon the earth in all of its many aspects. I give warmth and nourishment to the trees and light to the creatures of the mountain. I help all to grow and prosper."

The Earth of the Mountain: "I am the earth of the mountain. I sustain and hold up all that is upon me. I am warm in the sun and have the red glow of iron in my veins. I am home to many animals, plants, and trees. I am strong and give support to all who stand upon me."

The Air: "I am the air which all breathe and surrounds all. I move the clouds around to shade the plants and rain upon the mountain and give it moisture to grow new plants and trees. I give gentle encouragement to the plants to help them pollinate and grow as I blow their seeds about. I cover the people, animals, and plants in their nakedness with the cloth of my weaving, the air. I help the people communicate their thoughts by blowing and moving them about and I help the birds to fly high by giving them crosswinds and a medium to hold their wings. I am gentle and yet I can be strong, boisterous, and powerful too."

The Animals: "I am the spirits of the animals who inhabit the wild mountain. There are many of us. There are the deer, the bobcat, the mountain lion, the skunk, the possum, the raccoon, the porcupine, the gopher, the squirrel, the rabbit, the coyote, the grey fox, and the wolf. I am wild and I am fast. Most of my time is spent feeding myself."

The Fiery Earth, the Lava: "I am the fiery earth, the lava. I flow and spread upon the ground and set all to fire as I move. I cover the earth and when I cool I become new earth. I am the inner heat of the earth that releases as I move about. I cause all to move and flee as I flow down the mountainside for I am the spirit of the fire of Kundalini, the fiery Mother Earth."

The Volcano: "I am the volcano. I am quiet and still for many, many moons but when I awaken I cause all to shake and move. I erupt with ash and rocks and spew forth giant boulders. Tongues of fiery lava flow from me onto the mountainside below. I am the great transformer, the voice of the fiery nature of inner Mother Earth."

Once each performer in the play has announced his or her character you are ready to start the enactment.

Start with a normal day on the mountain and have each person **be** his or her persona. As the day goes on have the volcano erupt and all react to this giant transformation. Use words, movement, action, sound, and general interaction to create your tableau. Remember, you are not "acting" the part but internally **being** the actual persona of your part in nature. Actors make believe or act. Energy workers **be** or experience. If you learn the process of **being** you will always be able to actually affect change upon the planet. If you do not you will just be "reading lines" in the play of life. As everyone speaks encourage them to improvise on the spot, making up their lines as they go. This makes people become involved in their persona. You must allow yourself to be fluid, open, reactive, and verbal as your play continues on. By enjoying and participating in the Play of Life you can allow yourself to learn to work with group interaction in a light-hearted yet educational way. The play ends when the sun sets.

You can use any archetypal nature scene to create your "Play of Life." If this was a genuine emergency in which a neighboring volcano was erupting you would convene your group and everyone would take the "part" of the volcano. As the volcano you would direct the fiery tongues of lava down specific channels or sides of the mountain to avoid any homes, structures, or inhabited areas. How well this would work would depend on many variables. I have always felt that it is better to make an attempt and try than to sit by and do nothing. At worst, nothing happens. At best you achieve some of your desired effect.

Pulling a bunch of people together to form a solid unit or group to work in changing the ecological environment can be a lot of work but it can also be a fun, sharing experience, especially if you are using some of the above-mentioned meditations. Learning to share life's experiences is what a group is all about.

GROUP WORK

Group work has its pluses and minuses. The more people you have to work with, the more that your power increases exponentially so that you have a greater effect upon the environment. But group work is not for everyone. Some people feel more comfortable and generate more of their natural power when they are alone. Groups tend to have a life of their own. Working with a group, whether it is a group of close friends or an alliance with other people of like mind, should not become the equivalent of joining or creating a cult. A group is created for two basic reasons: to generate more power and to validate the individual. It is basic human nature that when you work with a group of people of like mind you will feel more secure about your own beliefs. This is not a necessity, but it does make people feel more substantial. The group itself should not become more important than the individuals who are its constituents. If this occurs the free will of the individual gets diminished, the people feel badly, and the energy work suffers. This assumes that people must learn to respect one another, both for their similarities and their differences.

If you form a group it should not rely on one person to be "the leader." Groups with leaders who set the tone, regulations, and belief systems for everyone else automatically become non-free-will cults. Leadership should always be shared and rotated. Free will is a very fine line to walk on. Very often groups subjugate their individuals rights to the "cause," to getting something done on the grander scale. In the short run this works but in the long run the group either dissolves or becomes statically fixed in a power-cult-one-person-leadership stance. If you are forming a small group try to be aware of the power dynamics of the people involved and try to compensate from the very beginning by moving the leadership around the group. It can be exciting, while working with a group of people, to find each person's innate skill or ability and to use that.

For some unknown reason people seem to relate to and respect group action. If you say, "so-and-so is going to demonstrate for a particular cause," most people say, "so what!" But if you say, "this group (some name of import) is going to demonstrate for this cause" people perk up their ears and listen and most often actually unconsciously lend their energy towards the cause. I call this "the herd effect." Everyone always unconsciously wants to be part of a group and join the bandwagon. A group that has "a name" or is well known can sway many people to action or just create an internal pool of energy that can be used by just announcing their intention to back a particular cause. Regardless of whether these actions are good or bad, group action is the manner in which energy seems to work with human consciousness. You can choose to be aware of it and use it or to ignore it, but it does have an affect upon you, whether you admit it or not.

On the minus side, a small group of people is always subject to the person in the group with the lowest energy level or the most problems. It is very easy to be pulled down to the lowest common denominator. To work with this you must be clear about what are the aims of your group. If your group is formed to work with the environment and one person constantly needs reinforcement and counseling about his or her job or emotional relationships you might send him or her to a therapy or consciousness-raising group instead. Everyone in the group must be there to accomplish specific goals. Side tracks are fine but they are often dealt with best in other groups where those specific issues can be addressed. You must acknowledge what you **can** deal with in your limited time and what is not the **true** subject matter of your group.

When you are dealing with your **true** subject, try to start by picking local issues or areas to work on. A cause that hits close to home is one in which everyone wants to be involved and each person feels connected enough with it to spend their spare time and energy to remedy the situation. Keep notes and a journal of your actions and activities, and their results. As you develop a modicum of success on the home front you will feel more secure in tackling larger problems that are farther away. It is best for a group to work together for a while to learn about itself as "the group" before you tackle some immense project like an oil spill or a dying forest. As you learn about your interaction as a social and working group you will begin to understand your strengths and weaknesses and adjust them to work for you. You will also build group self-esteem as you begin to have some small successes.

A good deal of group interaction is built upon group trust. Group trust is built on the individual members of the group learning to interact and depend on one another. A group that spends one weekend camping in the wilderness where they wish to access an ecologically blighted area will either come together as working companions or fall apart as disenfranchised strangers. Your group will work best after you have created the "working companions" situation. This might engage you in weekend group activities or a special evening or two dedicated to learning about how you work as a unit. It is amazing how once you isolate people and force them to function as a unit, which becomes your small tribe or village, they very quickly learn how to band together and use their group power.

I have a meditation student who goes on wilderness trips every year. One year she joined a wilderness tour and went with a small group of people to the Amazon rainforest for two weeks. They went up river by boat and then hiked in to their camp. The trip had a profound affect upon her understanding of social mores and human consciousness. She explained to me that as they got further and further away from "civilization" and all of those luxurious conveniences to which we humans are so attached, the people began to drop their "social" manners. She said, "It was as if they let down the walls and barriers that made up their personalities for living in the cities and dealing with strangers and social situations." There were leeches they had to pull off of their skin and very large mosquitoes that bit them constantly no matter what type of insect protection they used. They had to band together to survive in their environment, to help one another carry their load, and to keep everyone safe, sound, secure, and healthy. She told me that people who were "removed" and had shy, closed personalities thought nothing of walking around semi-naked in the humid heat and shared their thoughts, emotions, and lives. Conversely, when they came out of the jungle, she noticed that everyone began to build up their personality shields as they got closer and closer to "civilization."

You do not have to take your group to the Amazon rainforest to experience a sense of group bonding. But you do want to create some sort of working situation that will force everyone in the group to create a group interaction and bonding. Learning to function as a group is the key to making group energy channeling work. Performing any action that isolates the group and enables it to develop a sense of group spirit, group camaraderie, and group accomplishment enforces the skill of group bonding. Sometimes a group function for an afternoon, an evening, or a weekend on the site the group is trying to heal can accomplish this bonding. When you go onto the site of a particular problem it makes you deal with actual physical boundaries that test your ability to work together. For example, when my friends were healing a sick mountain forest they had to deal with the cold of the season, hiking up the paths, and communicating to the local rangers the gist of their "real" reason for being there. Their shared experience formed a bond of friendship, mutual respect, and understanding of one another's abilities that lasted them through many more Eco-Spirit projects.

"Reality is a collective hunch."

— Lily Tomlin
and Jane Wagner

21

THE ECO-SPIRIT
LIFESTYLE

Learning to use your spiritual ability and the natural essence of your energy self to heal the planet is more than simply enacting a series of mechanistic exercises. Working with your spirit is making a transformative statement in your life that actually takes your energy, grabs it, and imbues it with the conscious desire to change your inner self in order that you might be able to communicate with the greater powers at large. In other words, being the vehicle to transform natural energy towards a healing state also causes and enables you to change or heal yourself and to make an inner connection with the more powerful or essentially archetypal side of your self.

Eco-Spirit techniques for recharging an area, cleansing it, or redirecting the energy in an ecologically unbalanced area are easy to use and take little time to enact. When you use these exercises, you really have to use all of your self. All of your inner resources have to work in harmony with what you are doing at the time. You have to be able to have total focus. You cannot work on an area and be recharging the energy while at the same time you are thinking about what you are going to have for lunch, who you will see at the office, or what project you are currently working on. You must give all of your conscious and unconscious inner self totally into what you are doing at the moment. Energy workers call this "being in present time," in the here and now. Older established spiritual groups have called this "learning to focus." It is this inner directed focus that establishes your power to create a change in the energy flow.

As you learn to focus your energy in a cohesive fashion by using Eco-Spirit techniques you will discover that you can also learn to direct your energy in a more focused manner in accomplishing other tasks in your life. Once you learn these energy techniques on one level of awareness they usually spill over into all aspects of your lifestyle. It reminds me of what a friend who was studying Tai Chi described about his lessons in body awareness. For several months he concentrated on learning to make certain set moves with his arms and legs until he did them quite naturally without thought or concentration. One day a vase fell off of a shelf above him and he naturally moved the set movements he had learned and caught the vase. He did this without a conscious thought in his head by just allowing his body to move into the trained series of movements it had learned. It amazed him that his body worked so fluidly to catch the vase because for months all he understood himself doing was just practicing a very boring set of methodical movements. Suddenly he understood the inner resource he had developed by practicing this set of simple physical movements. He had now mastered the ability to move in harmony with his body and the surrounding environment. He was now able to direct his body movements without effort and to use the planet's power to ground himself. He had joined with a universal consciousness that would always work for him. What seemed like simple and trivial, boring exercises had become a doorway to a world of inner resources that changed his feeling about himself, his self reliance, his self image, and his ability to create his reality.

Eco-Spirit skills work much in the same way. If you use these skills they transform your natural inner ability to communicate with your inner intuitive transformative self, your Higher Self (the spiritual nature of your energy), and the structure of planetary energy we call Nature. If you practice these skills, one day you will be in an area finding out why it has an ecological problem and you will just **know** the problem and what you can **do** to change it. You will not have to concentrate on being Grounded, on being In the Center of Your Head, on being in touch with the Elementals, or on Being in Present Time because you will already be all of these things. As you work with these techniques they become one with you and become part of your personality and spiritual makeup. They become **you**. You will not have to pay attention to when you are grounding but only when you become ungrounded. You will not have to put special attention into centering because you will be centered all of the time. And because you will be centered all of the time you will easily converse with the elementals, the nature spirits, and the guardians of the planet because it is a natural extension of your abilities and awareness. In actuality Eco-Spirit skills are not a set of skills but a lifestyle of conscious awareness enabling you to pay attention to and acknowledge all of the life force on the planet as you interact with it. It is a lifestyle of discovering the harmony and beauty within all of Nature and learning to help recharge or redirect it when its natural harmony is out of balance.

When you are aware of what you are doing with your energy on the planet, both as a planetary user (a person who uses the resources of the planet) and as a planetary **healer** (a person who consciously uses his or her energy to recharge and rechannel the energy structure of Nature on the planet), then you will have learned to make a connection on a constant conscious and unconscious level to the inner core of planetary awareness. It is this constant inner connection that creates a lifestyle. By placing your awareness in synch and in harmony with the planetary consciousness you become as one with its energy system. You become one with the natural ecological system as human beings were meant to be. When you have fully developed your harmony with the planetary system, you have created a super conscious awareness of your actions, of the realm of cause and effect and of whether your actions aid or impede the natural harmony of nature. When you have developed this super consciousness you no longer need a book of rules and regulations about what is good and right for the environment or what is bad and destructive. You just **know**.

At the present time most of us are far from knowing, developing, owning, or using our planetary superconsciousness. Most of us are not aware that we have this ability or that we can develop it. The Native Americans are the best example of the use of superconsciousness of planetary awareness. The Indians worked with the spirit of the land and they understood it both intellectually and, far more importantly, on an intuitive and superconscious level. They perceived the land as a living spirit and they communicated with it, on both unconscious and conscious levels.

How do you relate to the planet now? Is it as a living being that we speak with and interact with and care about or is it as a non-entity that you just use, ignore, and take for granted? If you came home to dinner and a person was sitting at the dinner table waiting to have dinner with you, you would greet and interact with him or her. If, instead, you came home to dinner to find a plastic, inflated, life-size doll sitting at the table waiting to dine with you, you would probably not relate to it at all except, perhaps, for amusement. The manner in which you view and interact with the planet daily is the same manner you use to view and interact with your inner self. When everything is alive and crackling with life force and speaks to us, we, likewise, are alive, awake, and aware of ourselves and our environment. When everything around us is dead then part of our inner self is also dead.

The lifestyle of a planetary energy worker is a lifestyle of conscious awareness. It is the choice of using your inner energy self to create more life force on the planet and to further the life force that already exists. Each person can do this in his or her own way. The following sections of this chapter describe ways I fit this lifestyle into my own life.

Lifestyle at the Dinner Table

We have created the following saying as our before-dinner
ritual. Whenever we eat the main meal of the day we say this
small homemade message of thanks. It helps us to recharge by
making us aware of our oneness with the environment.

O Supreme Being,

*You can call upon your own
concept of the Higher, more
powerful nature of life force
here, or whatever your own
personal spiritual tradition is.
The Supreme Being is a
reference to the highest form of
God or oneness.*

Dear God and Goddess,

*The reference to the god and
goddess are as deities of nature
as seen in mythology.*

Thank you for the love, light, joy, and happiness that we
experience from day to day and moment to moment.

Thank you for the sun that shines each morning, the
moon that glows each night, and all the stars and planets
that twinkle bright.

And to all the little "wee" beings that nurture the planet,
we thank you for helping to create the food we are about to
eat.

We thank you for the birds and bees, the flowers and trees,
and all that there is.

Blessed be...

Ah _____.

Ah _____.

In this space I would say the name of the person I am having the meal with. Each person salutes the God force within the other person by saying his name, knowing that you are speaking to the higher force within that person.

When I say someone's name I create a golden light three feet above his or her head at about the eleventh chakra and another golden orb of light three feet in the ground below the person where his ninth chakra, the energy center relating to the earth is positioned. This is the olden blessing given by religious leaders to their followers to bestow light, love, and wisdom upon them.

Now that we live in an era when we are all "leaders", we can learn to bestow the gift of light to ourselves and to one another.

Just saying words does not actually hook you into an internal creative level or manifest anything in a practical way. I am sure many people have learned this lesson from saying prayers and feeling that they are unheard or that nothing happens. Asserting verbally that you are going to recharge yourself and the planet Earth is like reading a play aloud. It does not accomplish anything unless you also work to create the energy you need on an internal level. Your prayers could go "nowhere" unless you actually manage to communicate with the God force. Your manifesto of good ecological intentions for healing the planet must connect up with the larger macrocosm of the whole and it must be heard internally to create what you want. I have found that it is wise to keep connected with the energy of the Earth and so once a day I like to do at least one meditation to create a conscious connection with the planet. Scheduling a meditation or conscious creation during or before your big meal of the day allows you to share your feelings with the people closest to you while you can also make a conscious connection with the planet. This can be a verbal interaction, but for me it usually is a feeling, a sense of something, or an archetypal character enacting a vignette that shows or teaches me something.

Before the person at the dinner table speaks the message of thanks we always ground ourselves, get centered, and internally say hello to the earth. Many times I have done this at dinner time and had the earth speak back and tell me what is happening with it. The earth energy has told me about earthquakes ahead of time and has given me a sense of the season and the prevalent energy affecting the planet.

One night, about six years ago, I was about to have dinner with two close friends in the Bay Area in Northern California. My friend was saying our before-dinner meditational passage and I had automatically grounded and asked the earth how it was doing and what was happening with it when suddenly I felt this absolutely tremendous rush of energy that almost knocked me off my chair. It seemed like the entire fire energy within the planet had rushed by. At first I could not understand what it was since it was not an earthquake. And although it seemed like a volcano it was not really an exploding volcano. We turned on the radio and discovered that at that precise same time we were sitting down to dinner an underground atomic bomb was being exploded in Nevada. It has never ceased to amaze me, to this day, how powerfully a giant explosion an entire state away could affect the land directly beneath my feet. It made me realize the interconnected nature of our actions within the earth frame of awareness.

What You Eat Is An Ecological Statement

What you eat is probably the most personal statement you can make about yourself and your relationship with Nature. No one, outside of yourself, can decide what tastes good to you, how much of something you are going to ingest, and why and when you eat. You are the keeper of your body. Unfortunately most people do not realize that they are the ones in charge and that you can "choose" how you are going to treat and run this wonderful awesome creation of Mother Nature.

As an energy worker you will want to treat your body as a nurtured, loved, and cared for vehicle that enables you to have the highest amount of clear and intense energy for healing yourself and the Earth. And of course, how you deal with your body, how you feel about it and treat it, is how you also feel about yourself internally! Loving yourself and loving your body is actually loving the cellular part of the Earth that gives us the life force to enact our lives, our loves, and our karma. If you cannot love yourself you cannot possibly love the Earth enough to heal her.

Loving yourself can be paying attention to what you put into your body. No one can tell you what to eat. What you eat is the ultimate statement of your free will and of your individual right to define yourself as a special human being. But what you eat is also a statement of how you were brought up as a child, what you were taught, the particular culture you experienced as a child, the beliefs of the general society surrounding you, and the influence of your parents. True free will of the individual is making a determination based on facts and not on training or programming.

Some people say, "You are what you eat." Others say that what you eat determines the biological evolution of this planet.

In the United States we seem to pay more attention to medicines and cures and consulting doctors than to preventing or not causing the health problem in the first place. How much energy you have to use, whether for your daily actions or healing the planet, can be directly determined by what you ingest as food into your body. We are these wonderful cosmic spiritual beings who have to blend our higher knowledge and abilities with this practical earthly level of awareness that is the planetary sphere of the material basis of life.

Our spirit is made up of the cosmic but our bodies are created of the earth and it is our bodies that anchor us to this earthly plane and enable us to function on it. As we begin to better understand our relationship to our bodies we will become more able to communicate with the greater whole, the entire sphere of earth, and the Mother Nature that "created" our body on a cellular level. As we function through our physical vehicle we can more clearly understand and intuitively know our connection with the planetary eco-system. Our bodies are a microcosm of the greater macrocosm of the earth. We have, within our own small universal body system, a blueprint of how the processes of the earth works. If we can understand (whether it be scientifically, intellectually, or better yet, intuitively) the workings of our bodies we can understand the ecological workings of the entire sphere of energies we call the earth.

How we feed our bodies is part of how we understand the planet. Most people are creatures of habit. They eat the way they do because that is how they were taught as children. Our bodies are very "trainable" and very programmable. If you have control over a child for the first seven years of his or her life you can set the pattern for what that child will eat for the rest of his/her life unless he or she makes a conscious statement to change that. Have you ever noticed that when you are experiencing stress or encounter a difficult period of action in your life that you will want to eat whatever you ate as a child. Eating the foods from your childhood gives the body a natural feeling of security. Bodies, from an energy worker's point of view, are very easily programmed. If you eat a piece of chocolate today at 3 p.m. then tomorrow at the same time your body will expect to experience the same "sugar high." Matter of fact, your body will not just want the piece of chocolate that you had the day before, it will want a little more. Bodies are especially programmable to pleasurable experiences and this is why people can get easily hooked on drugs and foods. If you just listen to the body in the immediate, without weighing the facts about how you feel later on, you might become hooked on having your chocolate or your donut or your "little goody" every day.

Most people are "hooked" on food, using it as an escape from boredom, a path to instant pleasure, a means of belaying stress or insecurity, and a way of social interaction with their friends. However, the first and foremost reason for eating food is to sustain the body, to replenish its store of energy. It is this need for a high strong energy level that you need to pay attention to as a planetary energy worker.

As an energy worker I eat the foods that make my body feel good and strong "in the long run." I choose the foods I eat based on what makes me feel good both internally, as a spiritual person, and externally as an active human being. Therefore I eat organic foods not grown with pesticides and I am a vegetarian.

What you eat is ultimately up to you. I say ultimately, because you do have to rid yourself of your childhood programming, and your cultural training to find out what the "real" you is. You can do this by simply radically changing your diet for about four months. If for a period of four months you use a rotation diet eating pure and fairly simple foods you will be able to clean out your body. Rotation diets are used extensively by allergy doctors to clean out their patient's systems so that they can find out what specific food the person is allergic to. They rotate the food by species so that the person cleans out their entire system. Then foods are reintroduced, one by one, into that person's system and the doctor observes what they have a reaction to. Eating pure and simple food is simply eating the basics, eating food in its most natural state.

It is a simple and basic law of those who follow the system of food combining to eat one food at a time. Sometimes when you eat many different types of food at one time, such as three types of protein (meat, eggs, beans, and so on) the body has a difficult time processing each protein because they all digest in a different time sequence. This process is further complicated if you eat a piece of fruit or a piece of pie for dessert at the end of a rather large meal of proteins. The fruit, which usually can be digested in twenty minutes, sits at the end of the line of proteins that take eight hours to digest. While you are digesting the proteins the fruit begins to ferment and gives you gas and a feeling of being stuffed and uncomfortable. Your system might then digest your food somewhat incompletely as it attempts to deal with the myriad of messages giving priority to what should come first in the digestive process. Food combining states that there are certain foods that are best to digest or eat together while avoiding putting other foods together in the same meal.

Whether you wish to use the system of food combining or not as a lifestyle, you might want to try using it for three or four months to clear your system of toxins and clean up your system in general. The simple act of eating food in its basic form is one way of purging your system of all sorts of toxins. Eating the basic form of a food, the apple, the carrot, and so on, gives you its nourishment but also gives you the bulk or roughage that cleans your body. By eating low on the food chain you can also minimize the amount of heavy metals and pesticides that you ingest in your diet. If you allow yourself to simplify your diet for four months you will find out that you can then begin to reintroduce the foods "of pleasure" into your diet, one by one, and learn what you truly like and need to survive. If you do simplify your diet you will then learn how truly "addicted" you are to foods. Once you take away the tried and true foods of your childhood you may discover that you have cravings for foods simply because they represent security and love to you. If you can ignore these cravings for three or four months they will pass and you will enter the new world of free choice, the world of the true freedom as an individual to determine your own "food destiny."

Once you determine your food destiny you will be ready to also determine your relationship as an energy worker and an ecologically-concerned person to the food you eat. What you eat is a statement about how you relate to the planet as a whole. It signifies where your priorities are and how you feel about life force in general. Let's look at some facts and figures about the effects of what we eat are upon the environment.

Do you eat meat? Meat is the single most expensive protein on the planet. "Ninety percent of all the grains and legumes grown in the United States are fed to animals. Meanwhile, sixty million people on this planet Earth will starve to death this year, for lack of grains and legumes to eat. A child on Earth starves to death every two seconds."[14] In *Diet For A Small Planet*, Frances Moore Lapp tells us that "a cow must be fed 21 pounds of protein in order to produce one pound of protein for human consumption. One-half of our harvest acreage is fed to livestock."[15] Through the consumption of livestock we use up 18 million tons of protein that becomes inaccessible as food. "This is equivalent to 90 percent of the yearly protein deficit—enough protein to provide twelve grams a day for every person in the world."[16] According to Frances Lapp's computations, an acre of cereals can produce five times more protein than one acre devoted to meat production.[17] But one-third to one-half of the continental land surface is used for grazing. This land has been de-forested to allow it to be converted into beef grazing land. "Since 1967 the rate of deforestation in this country has been one acre every five seconds."[18] Two hundred sixty million acres of our forest have been clear-cut to create crop land for livestock.[19] It requires 2500 gallons of water to produce one pound of meat. Livestock production takes more than half of the water used in the United States today and causes 85% of our topsoil loss.[20] In the rainforest it takes 400 acres of land to feed one cow every year! "Every year the beef cattle in America eat ten times the protein and food calories than that consumed by the American people themselves. Just by decreasing their meat consumption by 10%, Americans would create a surplus of 12 million tons of grain each year, enough to eliminate the hunger problem in Africa and America, as well."[21] Much of the ecological damage could be reversed if we ate less meat. One acre of trees is saved each year by each individual who changes to a purely vegetarian diet.[22] A person eating a meat-based diet causes 6,000 gallons of water to be consumed every day, while a person on a vegetarian diet just requires 300 gallons of water each day. Raising livestock uses our natural resources very heavily. The statistics quoted above clearly show the ecological costs of a meat-based diet. When we raise livestock we have to give up our forests for grazing land which is denuded of all vegetation that could hold our soil in place, expend a great deal of water which then goes on to pollute the water table, and put a large percentage of our crops into production just to feed the livestock, and deal with the greenhouse affect, some of which is a direct cause of the methane released by livestock feces. It could be said that meat-eating is threatening to the very eco-system of our planet Earth!

No one can tell you what to eat, but if you are a meat eater you might consider cutting down on how much meat you eat. I chose to be a vegetarian many years ago, not based on ecological considerations, but based on the simple fact that my health improved and it made me feel great. By not eating meat, fish, or dairy foods I have discovered that I do not have the problem of consuming fat, so I do not have to deal with the "cholesterol problem", or any weight problem, or any karmic repercussions from killing a live animal either.

Many people will tell you that you need meat, fish, and dairy products for protein. This has been greatly exaggerated. Americans eat much more protein on a daily basis than we really need for our bodies to function well. Too much protein can be just as bad as too little protein. If you read some of the newer nutritional sources you will discover that beans and rice, tofu, many vegetables, and a variety of foods will give you adequate protein.

Our bodies use a great deal of energy to process the food that we eat. When we overeat, or eat too much protein at one time, our energy gets sluggish as our system slows down to use all of its energy to process the food. We all know this intuitively. You would not, for example, eat a large dinner before taking a test or doing something that requires exacting attention. You know from experience because your energy would be slow, both mentally and physically, and you would not be at your best. Many of us use food as an excuse to not face the boredom, fear of failure, or lack of love and light in our lives. We eat more than we need to slow ourselves down and to fill ourselves with the lowest energy type of nurturing. As you begin to eat light, energy foods you will discover that you have better health and much more energy. You will begin to "feel" your body from the inside and feel more in harmony and accord with it. You will begin to feel energized and more alive. This is something you have to experience and discover for yourself. No one can tell you what to eat and what is good for you. You have to experience it for yourself and then let that action inspire you.

Food With Life Force Energy

What you eat is not just what you ingest in your body. It is not just the "intake" of food that you experience. What you eat is also how you relate to the preparation of your food and how you relate to the act of eating it. If you grow your own food in a home organic garden you can ask the wee beings to fill your food with the life force of the earth. However, many people simply go to the grocery store to purchase their food then come home and stuff it in their refrigerators. The food you eat is not just an inanimate object that you consume when you are hungry. It is the very life force that gives you the energy to be alive. Food is alive. After food is picked from the vine it holds it life force for quite a while. This is why we refrigerate it and sometimes store it in water or in moist environments. We want the food to retain its life force.

Perhaps you have seen the difference in grocery stores between a vegetable that has been refrigerated or kept moist and a vegetable that has been shipped yet given no care. Broccoli, for example, when refrigerated or kept in ice, retains its crispness and is strong and firm. When broccoli is not kept cool or in ice it wilts and goes limp. Nutritionists would tell you that when it goes limp it has lost its vitamins and nutrients. Energy workers would say it has lost its spirit, its life force. You, of course, want to purchase your vegetables when they are ripe, firm, and alive. When you get home you can work with your energy to keep the vegetables alive until you eat them by simply speaking to the plant (subvocally if you wish) and asking it to stay alive and stay green so that it adds its life force back to the environment and to the earth. By asking the plant to stay green and hold its energy you will be keeping the energy there until you eat it. Experiments with prayer energy over plants have shown that the prayers can get a leaf that was separated from its stem and plant to remain green and vibrant for two weeks when people spoke to it and prayed over it. Leaves that were not spoken to or prayed over turned brown and withered away in a few days.[23] So, by speaking to your vegetables and paying attention to them you can help them to retain the valuable life force (and nutrients and vitamins) that you need to ingest as an energy worker. Eating food with life force creates vibrancy and an aliveness within your own system that you will pass on to whomever or whatever you are dealing with on the earth.

Eating food with life force is one step in consciousness. How you prepare your food is another. I like to cook. It is one of my favorite pastimes. And when I cook I also enjoy using all of my spiritual skills to create a dish filled with the energy of the earth. As I wash my vegetables I see them as being vibrant and full of energy. When I cut them I think loving warm thoughts. The energy going through you at the time you cook is what your food absorbs. When you are in harmony, at peace with yourself, and in a loving space, then this is what you fill your food with. When you are in disharmony, your food and whatever you touch or do vibrates with that disharmony. If you are in a hurry then the food has hurried energy. If you are unhappy or frustrated then the food has unhappy or frustration energy. What you are experiencing is what you are literally "feeding" yourself when you are the cook. Because I am ending the life of the vegetable to further my own life I like to envision life as a whole, of the plants being eaten, absorbed by my system, and of all of it being used by the interchange of energies. I like to be aware of the whole picture, of the full cycle of food, the full cycle of the life force energy on the planet.

When I use a pot I clean the energy of it by grounding it and filling it up with golden life force energy and asking whatever archetype I feel comfortable with to bless the pot or fill it with the energy of love and nurturing. I envision it as that cauldron of the never-ending abundance of the stream of life. Sometimes I call in life force energy to fill the food in my pot, or the food on my plate, in a similar manner as the Breath of Life exercise in the chapter by the same name where you call cellular life force to you.

You do not need to do a lot of complicated energy exercises to cook a meal in an energy-conscious manner. All you really have to do is be in a warm and loving space. But so often we are not in that type of space and we fill our foods and our stomachs with the tensions and energies of our frustrations, our confusions, and our hurts.

Food is sacred. It is a gift of the earth. If we treat it as such it will give us the high energy we need to live our lives. If we just take it for granted we might wake up one day to find out it does not exist.

Once you perceive the act of creating good food and the art of cooking as a sacred act you will also want to see the act of eating food as a sacred act. How you eat, the particular emotional and physical situation that you set for yourself when you are ingesting food, is the message you are giving to your body. If you are tense or in a hurry or in any way discordant with yourself, then your body has a difficult time digesting your food and experiencing that marvelous sensation of taste. When I eat I do an energy Creation at the beginning of the meal. I also take the time to taste the food I am eating and envision it as a gift of life force and enjoyment that I give my body.

My husband and I were having a guest come to visit and we decided to take him out for dinner to the local lodge. The lodge has wonderful ambience, it has been in existence for many years and has many fireplaces, log walls from an earlier era, wonderful nooks and crannies, good service, and quality gourmet food. I ordered a plate of vegetables and an enticing salad made of fresh baby carrots, wild lettuces, endives, radiccio, endoki mushrooms, and so on. When the waiter took the order he asked me what dressing I would like on my salad and I told him that I would like it plain, without any dressing. When the waiter came back to fill our water glasses he again asked if I wouldn't like some dressing on the salad. I declined. And again, before serving the salad, another waiter came to the table to ask if I was sure that I wouldn't like a dressing on my salad. I smiled and asked him if the salad was fresh. He assured me that the salad was fresh and had the best quality ingredients in it. Then I assured him that if the salad was indeed fresh I would want to eat it without dressing so that I could taste the ingredients. Even when the salad was finally served the waiter asked me if I would like some freshly ground pepper or a wedge of lemon. I graciously declined once again. The salad was indeed fresh and it tasted fantastic on its own, without being smothered in a dressing that would have hidden the actual taste of the vegetables.

You may not be a purist like me and enjoy having a dressing on your salad, a sauce on your vegetables, or a topping on your potatoes, but you might want to take the time to taste what you are eating. Tasting what you are eating is like listening to an orchestra. There is one whole sound and then there are the many instruments that make up that whole sound. You can hear the music but you can also, if you listen and train your ear, hear the individual instruments. Part of being spiritually ecologically aware is being aware of the whole and yet being able to know the individual parts that make up the whole.

Getting Information About Food

The following list contains societies and books from which you can get more information about food.

American Vegan Society, 501 Old Harding Highway, Malaga, N.Y. 08328.

Be Your Own Doctor. Ann Wigmore. (N.J.: Avery Publishing Group, 1982).

The Complete Vegetarian Cookbook. Karen Brooks. (N.Y.: Simonand Schuster, 1974).

Diet For A New America. John Robbins. (Walpole, NH: Stillpoint, 1987).

Diet For A Poisoned Planet. David Steinman. (N.Y.: Harmony Books, 1990).

Diet For A Small Planet. Frances Moore Lappe. (N.Y.: Ballantine Books, 1971).

Fit For Life. Harvey and Marilyn Diamond. (N.Y.: Warner Books, 1985).

Moon Sign Book and Lunar Planting Guide. (MN: Llewellyn Publications,1990).

North American Vegetarian Society, P.O. Box 72, Dolgeville, N.Y. 13329

Pregnancy, Children, and the Vegan Diet. Michael Klaper, M.D. (Umatilla, Florida: Gentle World Inc. 1987).

Sprout For The Love of Every Body. Viktoras Kulvinskas M.S. (IA: 21st Century Publications, 1972).

The Farm Vegetarian Cookbook. Louise Hagler, editor. (Summertown, TN: The Book Publishing Co.).

PRACTICAL WAYS TO DO ENERGY WORK

Like everyone else who lives in our modern society I am always pressed for time. It seems like we are always trying to do today what we should have done yesterday. Because of this, or in spite of it, I try to really use my time wisely. Whenever I have a spare moment I apply myself to the ecological task at hand. Normally, when I am very busy and have a small amount of free time I do not want to engage it doing something, because that free time is my relaxation time, the moments I cherish to be still and know that I can reconnect with the internal side of my self and just be at peace. But when I take these small amounts of "extra" time to do planetary healing work I actually feel more recharged than if I just took this time to relax. That is because when I am energy working to heal the planet I am connecting with the whole, the oneness of nature. It is like doing yoga or meditation or Tai Chi or getting a massage or any number of things that take you into that marvelous place where you are doing something, being totally relaxed, and yet completely charged with energy. So I hope that, like me, you can find your way to experiment with your time to add in little bits and pieces of energy work throughout the day. These bits and pieces of energy work will recharge the planet and also give you more energy, better health, and a sense of being a part of a greater wholeness, the totality of Mother Nature.

There are some days when I spend the entire day on the phone doing spiritual counseling. When I do phone counseling from my office in my home in the mountains I take the time, in between calls, to heal my plants and to talk to them. For some reason the practice of speaking to plants makes people nervous. My theory is that people suspect that they are going batty if they are speaking to themselves. But when you speak to a plant you are **not** speaking to yourself, you are speaking to a live entity that is a plant and it does hear you.

During the 1960s and 1970s many studies were done on the response of plants to all forms of energy: music, prayer, speech, love, and various behaviors.[24] The scientists discovered many interesting things, such as that plants grow larger and fuller while Indian or classical music is played and seem to die and wither away from rock and roll. They also discovered that prayer or love can influence seeds to grow and that asking seeds not to grow can cause them to not grow and that thoughts of harm or pain can affect the plant negatively.[25] Energy workers have known many of these things for centuries but it is valuable to have scientists document it!

When I speak with my plants I tell them how beautiful they are, how much I enjoy their presence, and I ask them to grow in specific ways. I also ask them if they need anything. But most of all I like to use an archetype creation and hook the plant into the oneness of nature or the higher source of natural knowledge. I have always had this idea that it must be more lonely being in a pot of soil, rather than being in the earth where there is a natural feeling of connection with all other living things. I call to the wee devas or plant fairies to come and tend my plants so that they will get loving care. The plant fairies usually come to the plants in the outdoor gardens but they shy away from indoor plants unless they happened to come in with them originally. Sometimes this is because they do not know how to take care of different and exotic species that are not native to their area. I know that if a plant has plant fairies taking care of it the plant will usually do well so I attempt to make this connection. Sometimes I just sing a song to my plants, incorporating my own invented lyrics encouraging them to grow and be green. Speaking to your plants and hooking into the archetypal resource that touches all of us is a good way of warming up your planetary healing abilities. After speaking with my plants I am usually ready to do other, more advanced works.

During the day, as my time permits, I sit down and ground, run energy, and clear myself of any excess emotions or extraneous feelings. I make the connection between my inner intuitive self, my Higher Self, and that vast oneness of nature or specific archetype pattern I have chosen. Then I pick something to work on. You can work on healing the planet as a whole but I have found that specific energy projects seem to get quicker, more measurable results. So I pick a particular problem area to work on: a polluted body of water, a neighborhood piece of land in dispute with developers, an endangered species, a dying forest, and so on. When I am working by myself I tend to choose areas or problems that are close by and that I relate to because it affects my direct reality. When I am more directly involved with an energy project I seem to get better results. When I work with a group of people I often vote to choose larger problems that are more universal.

As I work I keep a journal or other specific record. Keeping an actual written record helps you because it encourages you to believe in what you are doing as it reinforces the reality of your work. It allows you to notice if there are any measurable changes in what you are working on and gives you a chronological record of what you did and how you did it. If you have done planetary energy work and have kept written records of measurable or noticeable changes please send us a copy at Eco-Spirit. We are beginning to document the power of our human planetary healing abilities. The more that we document and share this information with one another the more that we can access our true potential as planetary healers and the more we can learn from one another's experiences. (We are going to start a nation-wide phone tree this year to encourage all planetary healers to work on a specific "trouble spot" each week.) As we learn to use our focused energy we can change the face of the planet Earth to mirror Mother Nature's original intention.

Wherever I go, and whatever I do, I like to communicate with the elementals and fairies and devas and earth nature spirits. As I speak to the earth spirits I learn what is happening with them. When I encounter an imbalance I try to find the time to do a Creation to work to clear it.[26] Please do not misunderstand my use of the term "speaking" to the elementals or earth nature spirits. It is not that little beings come and speak to me in English—although this has happened. Most of the time my speech is subvocal and their reply is in images, pictures, move-ments and a sort of internal understanding or knowing that is beyond words or explanations.

In the morning when I walk down my driveway I speak to the tree spirits. As I drive off from my house to teach classes I speak to the mountains, the lake, the sky, and the clouds. Wherever you live you can find something of nature to speak with, whether it be the land under your feet or the sky above your head.

When I drive through Malibu Canyon towards the ocean there is a tunnel cut through the mountain to reach the coast. As I drive through the tunnel I speak with the mountain and to the nature elementals who live in the mountain. I open up my system and for the few minutes I spend within the mountain as I drive through the tunnel I can feel my energy centers open up as a rush of energy passes through them. I see and hear the elementals speak to me of the world they live in and inhabit. It is a precious few minutes that I treasure.

When there are many cars driving through this tunnel I can see the elemental degenerative beings devouring oxygen at the top of the tunnel. These degenerative beings dwell above crowded freeways or inhabit garbage cans or live wherever waste is present. I usually view them as ugly, although actually these degenerative beings are just energy eaters and transformers! These beings are necessary to the survival of the ecology of the planet. They eat energy and cause all energy around them to degenerate or die. They help to degenerate and recycle matter back to another form. Unfortunately, their numbers are increasing as we pollute the air with too much gasoline use and overload the planet with too much garbage. It is unfortunate to drive through the canyon tunnel and find these beings but this is the price we pay for driving cars.

When you see these beings where there is not supposed to be decay then you know that somehow pollution is destroying the system and an imbalance has occurred. Life on the planet is a fine web of birth, growth, and decay, and the planet needs to always complete the entire cycle. You can work to clear or clean a space and send the degenerative beings away but you would not want to come into direct contact with the decay beings nor work with them directly as they cause whatever they come in contact with to decay. This can effect body functions or specific internal organs, so I recommend you always work through another being that knows how to handle these degenerative beings. One of the best ways I have found is to call in other elementals to rebalance an area so that it does not degenerate so quickly. I repeat, it is always wise to work through another being—an elemental or archangel or planetary healer—when you are dealing with the degenerative beings.

When we first moved to Los Angeles my husband and I rented a very nice apartment in Beverly Hills. It was convenient to our jobs and had a wonderful view of the green Beverly Hills High School stadium with the lights of the Century City complex behind it. Both of us, enjoying nature, wanted to gaze out of the window and see green so we did not really pay attention to the rest of the apartment, although it seemed fine. One night, three or four months later, I was awakened from my sleep with an underlying bad feeling, an unease that I was sharing the room with another entity. Because I teach meditation I am consciously open to communication with entities but I prefer to live in a "clean" house where I do not encounter "spirits" unless I choose. As I sat up in bed I suddenly realized that a degenerative-type elemental was hanging half in and half out of the wall between the bedroom and the outside hallway. This seemed strange, so I got up and walked outside of our apartment to see what was on the other side of the wall of our bedroom. And right there was the garbage shoot. I remembered the building manager telling us how wonderful and convenient it was to be near the trash shoot, that we could easily dump our garbage without having to walk far. But what did not register with me was that the garbage shoot was right next to our bedroom wall. It appeared that degenerative "garbage" elementals were congregating over the garbage on the first floor and were rising up to the third floor (where we were located) and spreading out from there. I immediately filled our bedroom wall with life force energy and created a wall of life force energy between our bed and the wall to push them back to their garbage, and then I got a better night's sleep. While degenerative beings are necessary to help disintegrate garbage and help all matter return to another form, they are not good to have around your physical body. This is why we have many innate health precautions about garbage. Our "rules" about garbage on a scientific level refer to "germs" and on a spiritual level mean not associating with the degenerative elementals which can cause the body to decay and thus become diseased. Needless to say, I was happier and more relieved when we moved from this apartment. Not wishing to associate with degenerative beings is one of the reasons for always putting your garbage outside of your living abode and for always placing a cover on your garbage pail and for not leaving raw sewage or decaying matter in the open.

I have found that the more that I work doing my Creations or energy work to heal the planet, the more energy I have to do anything else. Energy work seems to charge and energize my system. And of course, it does make me feel like I am doing something and accomplishing something.

ENERGY BROADCASTING

Recharging the Planet

You will find that there are special times of the day when it is easier to communicate with the archetypes of the planet and the flow of energy. By using these special times you will create a more powerful link with the planet.

I like to do an energy working for healing the planet at least once a day. I see this as kind of using the power of positive reinforcement. There are so many systems created by human-kind that are constantly destroying or endangering the essence of our ecological system that I see it as a small effort to spend at least ten or twenty minutes in a twenty-four hour period to try to readjust energy or broadcast some positive energy to the planet.

Broadcasting energy is not broadcasting your own wishes and thoughts to the planet or Mother Nature. It is creating an energy flow that allows the higher energies to come into the planet and rebalance the energy flow. If you broadcast yourself at 6 a.m. Mother Nature might get the idea that she is hungry for breakfast. If you broadcast the higher level of cosmic energy she will feel balanced with the Universe and recharged with life force.

The best times to broadcast energy are at 6 a.m., noon, 6 p.m., or midnight. These are the most powerful times on the planet for broadcasting energy outwards to reach Mother Nature. If you wish to reach or broadcast to people you would use a different time system. This is because at these times you have the tides of energy beginning to flow and the use of both the sun and moon energy. One of the most powerful times of the day is when you can see both the sun and the moon, when one is rising and the other is setting. At 6 a.m., noon, 6 p.m., and midnight you have the natural turns of energy when the flow begins to rebalance and move in a new direction. It is then you can balance both the internal and external energy of the moon and the sun to charge your broadcast with power. It is not important which one of these times you use as long as you are centered within yourself.

When I perform an energy broadcasting exercise I sit down in a chair, breathe deeply, relax, ground myself, and check in with my internal self. I find out who I am at the present moment and clear any strong emotions or ruts or repetitive patterns I am running on an unconscious level. Clearing charged emotions or internal patterns allows me to have the space to do a higher mode of energy work and also makes me feel good and at peace with myself. I allow myself to totally enter present time so that I am not reworking the day I experienced or anticipating my next meal but am just totally, entirely in the moment.

Energy Broadcasting is very easy. All you have to remember is that you are working with actual energy and to not get involved. You want to keep your ego and desires out of the process. When we humans get in between Mother Nature and the higher powers of the universal life force we create an imbalance that results in discordance. So it is best to just channel the energy to recharge and not to "direct" it in any way. You are simply connecting one end of the universal frame—the Universal Life Force (or God consciousness as some people call it)—with the eco-system of the planet (or Mother Nature, Gaia, or the Goddess as other people call it). It is the same as plugging in your stereo. When you put the plug into the wall socket you do not exclaim what type of energy or current you want. This is predetermined. In the case of your stereo it has been decided by engineers, electricians, and the particular system that your country has set up to "broadcast" electricity. In the case of energy working with the planet it is also determined by what the universal life force energy is and you do not need to influence it for these purposes, just channel it. Mother Nature can rebalance herself given the proper amount of energy.

Imagine speaking with the highest life force energy that exists, whether this is your personal concept of God or the oneness of the Universe. Ask this life force to give you some energy to recharge the planet. I visualize the Universal Life Force as giving me a glowing ball of powerful golden light energy. I pull that golden ball into a column of energy that stretches down from the heavens to the earth and into the earth where it goes directly into the center of the earth to form another golden powerful ball of light. Here the energy glows and pulsates and begins to radiate outwards. Remember, all you are doing is directing this energy from one place to another. You are not telling it what to do or leaving any imprint on it. This energy is the clear cleansing and recharging light of the universe. It will charge and nourish anything that it comes into contact with.

A Column of Golden Light Coming into the
Earth and Going Back to Where It Came from

Our planet is made up of a series of energy levels in concentric circles. As this energy radiates outward from the center of the planet it travels through these different energy levels. If you can see these different levels of energy that are the physical, emotional, mental, and spiritual boundaries of our planet you would notice that the golden energy travels through some boundaries quickly and easily while it encounters resistance at other boundaries. Some of the energy levels that create our planet are made up of the karma and life force agreements of people, spiritual beings, and nature beings. One time when I worked with this particular exercise the golden energy would not go directly through one particular boundary. I kept checking in with it all day to see what happened. About eight hours later it had completely permeated through the boundary. To the best of my knowledge I discerned that this particular boundary seemed to represent war and aggression on the planet. This seemed to be confirmed by the Iraq-Kuwait Gulf incident heating up at that time. Hopefully though, the golden energy you direct will permeate through all of the planetary boundary levels filling the planetary energy level with a clear high energy that rebalances and thus heals the planet.

The energy levels around our planet extend outward over a large amount of space. If you do not "see" where or how the golden light travels it is all right. As an energy worker you will be able to feel or know what is happening. As you practice broadcasting energy, knowledge of what is happening will just come to you. When the energy has thoroughly permeated through the planetary levels you then see the golden light as extending to the edge of our galaxy and then being called back or returning to the Universal Life Force from whence it came. This is like a boomerang. The energy goes directly to the center of the planet where it recharges the actual essence of it, then radiates through it to connect with all life force energy beaming itself outward to fill the entire galaxy, and then comes back to its original source. You are just the facilitator. Usually you can accomplish this in ten or twenty minutes. If it does get stuck in some area, it will patiently work its way through. When you are done broadcasting energy, send the energy back to its original source.

For ecological healing or cleansing or recharging the planet, pure golden light works best. When I wish to charge the planet with peace and good will I use a cosmic love energy. You could use whatever your higher concept of cosmic love is—often it is seen as rose in color or pink or peach. If you are not sure what color or vibration to use ask your Higher Self for the information or simply ask for a certain type of energy and see what you get. Of course, the more specific you are when you work, the more directly the energy vibration works. It is however, best to use a color. White light, which many of the older energy workers from the Christian tradition use, is a combination of all of the colors. It is a very high vibration of energy that is used more to protect than to change. White light energy is very much like snow in that it freezes or protects whatever it surrounds or goes through. In order to change or cleanse the planet you need a lower vibration of energy that easily permeates every level. White light is the energy of the heavens, while gold, bright blue, green, and rose light are the energies of the more earthly plane. When you wish to work with or heal the earthly plane you have to work with energy that can reach or vibrate on the same frequency. This is akin to traveling and doing as the natives do. When in heaven you would use white or high vibration, heavenly energy and while on earth you would use gold, sunshine yellow, green, orange or rose, the more earthly energies to transform the earthly level quickly.

Recharging the planet with pure golden light is easy and simple to do and you could do it before breakfast, on your lunch break, at your desk before you go home, or in the evening before going to bed.

A LIFESTYLE IS WHAT YOU DO

Obviously most of us cannot spend every waking moment healing the planet. Nor would we want to as we need to spend a good deal of time just enjoying the act of being here on it. But we can choose to take a little time, whether it be five, ten, or twenty minutes in the morning, afternoon, or evening to make a connection with the Earth and to help heal her. In order to heal the planet you do not have to be consumed by a passion to work on it every minute of every day but you do have to spend a little bit of time to just broadcast specific energy in a loving manner. This can make a tremendous change. And it takes so little effort. Believe it or not, twenty minutes of specifically focused energy on a Saturday night could make a difference towards saving our ecological system. And doing this, would of course, change your lifestyle because lifestyle is not what you think or believe but what you actually do or accomplish with your life's energy.

We are now at a crossroads in history. We can no longer wait for someone else to come along whose lifestyle is "planetary saving" who can bail us out of the situation. There is no one or no energy to save us. We are the energy makers that created this disastrous situation and we are the only ones who can save ourselves. Even though the Native American Indian and other Indian tribes and nations throughout the world are the keepers of the earth, we cannot now expect them to come and save us and take "care" of the earth. We, as a race of "colonial Americans" have separated the Native American Indian from their natural place in the planetary affairs of nature. We have "conquered" them, killed them with our foreign diseases, reneged on treaties, and forced their children into our "white man's" form of education. We have separated them from their heritage and from their land. To the Indian their land is what *is* sacred and alive. They do not value the material goods of our culture but only seek to live in freedom and harmony in peace with the land.

Unfortunately, as a race of beings we colonialist "newcomers" to America have robbed the Native American Indian of the one thing that is priceless and has meaning to their lives, their land. In making treaties with the Native Americans we moved them, sometimes 2,000 miles, to a land and climate hostile to their lifestyle. We enacted laws that forced their children to be taken to boarding schools for nine or ten months out of the year. We locked them into specific plots of land so that they could not roam from winter to summer camping grounds or follow the herds. We broke treaties so we could mine their sacred mountains, dam their sacred rivers, pollute their sacred air, chop down their sacred trees, and we completely killed off the herds of animals and flocks of birds that they hunted and relied upon as a food source. Our forbears devastated everything that was sacred to the Native American not realizing that one day, two hundred or more years later, their children would wake up to realize that it also was sacred to them. But now it is sacred no longer because it does not exist, except as the remnants of a once flourishing land. The symbols of our country, our cars, and our money and coins—the eagle, the jaguar, and the buffalo—will soon be just symbols with new generations never being able to see the original wild animal that portrayed the strength, tenacity, courage these things were named for because we are destroying the sacredness of the life force of this planet with our unconscious lifestyle.

In 1877, the United States government broke the treaty with the Sioux Nation to grab the Black Hills where gold was discovered. The Sioux have fought in the courts for the return of their sacred land, sacred center of their culture. The United States government has offered the Sioux Indians $122 million in compensation for the Black Hills but the Sioux have rejected it, demanding the land instead. To the Sioux the Black Hills is the most special place on Earth.[27] Unlike our "white man's culture" the Native Americans would not erect housing developments, hotels, and condominiums on their land. To them, the land is sacred and needs to breathe and live and it is there for humankind to care for and live on, not to suffocate.

But the Indians are prevented from acting upon their heritage as the planetary saviors because they are struggling to rebalance and save themselves and their traditional cultures. The Native Americans are divided among themselves about how they should retain their heritage and their dignity and still find a means of support for their families. It is often the Native American Indian tribes who must contend with some of the worst cases of America's pollution. Many of the promoters of facilities for toxic waste disposal see Indian reservations as prime locations since Indian reservations are not governed by the same laws as elsewhere in the United States. These isolated reservations are semi-sovereign and are free from state and federal regulation and political pressures. Ventures that create jobs are appealing to tribes who are searching for alternatives to the traditional fishing, hunting, and farming economy that no longer supports them.

For example, the building of the St. Lawrence Seaway in the 1950s destroyed the fishing grounds and changed the way of life for the Mohawk Indians forever. The new channel and inexpensive hydroelectric power brought companies like Reynolds, General Motors, Alcoa, and others to build shoreline factories. While environmental law enforcement was still in its infancy these companies poured enormous amounts of waste into the riverside lagoons, created landfills, and even polluted the river itself. By the 1960s cattle grazing upwind of the Reynolds smoke stacks had developed brittle bones, loose teeth, and some died while giving birth. Fish caught in the river had deformed spines and skin ulcers. In 1978, scientists from Cornell and other universities discovered that the cattle were suffering from fluoride poisoning. They also found high levels of polychlorinated biphenyls (PCBs) and other toxins in the flora and fauna. Taking these cases to court has been costly and almost bankrupted some Indian tribes. The pollution became so extreme that some Akwesasne Indian residents were warned to avoid eating lettuce and tomatoes from their own gardens. Women of child bearing age and children were advised to stop eating fish, their main source of protein. Now they buy fish from New England vendors who sell it from refrigerated trucks! It is no wonder that some of the more radical Indians have threatened to occupy factories to stop pollution! They speak of remembering the river when it had a stronger spirit. "If they stopped polluting today, the river would heal itself. I know the river still has the spirit. It is waiting," said Mark Narsissian who lives in a small cabin near the General Motors plant.[28]

There is a good deal that we can learn from the Native American Indians and other Indians throughout the world if we put our cultural egos aside long enough to listen and learn and hear them. But they, alone, can not tend nor keep nor save the land now. Their spokespeople are wise and learned with an innate understanding of the earth that is the result of their genetic heritage and centuries of living in a culture "in harmony" with the earth, but the problem is too large and too vast for just one people to accomplish. All of us, all of us human beings on the good ship Earth have to get together to solve this problem.

I do not feel that I am responsible for what the generations before me did when they settled this country. But I can be responsible for my lifestyle, for what I do now in the time of my life. This is the decision, a conscious decision, that all of us must come to make. The decision is to do something, to promote what is real and sacred, what makes the quality of your life worth something. A lifestyle is what gives meaning to who you are. Right now we are in an era of getting back to the basics. Of finding what is really meaningful within us. In the 1980s many people viewed collecting the "good things in life", the consumption of material items: the cars, homes, and material goods as what was meaningful in life. We labeled the American dream as the image of that well to do person who could afford a good home and all of the things that go with it. We judged people by how much money they made, what they wore, what kind of car they drove, what type of work they did, and what they owned. But then, many people who realized the American dream and were successful began to understand that something was lacking, that ownership of material goods, the security of money, and the status of clothes, cars and home weren't enough. Some people began to realize that there was more to life, that the bountifulness of life was in the very process of living. We are beginning to see that life has to have meaning besides the accumulation of goods, and that some values such as love, friendship, and family and the quality of life—good air, safe neighborhoods, healthy food, natural surroundings—far surpassed the banal collecting of material possessions. We are finally coming to value the things that we cannot purchase—clean air to breathe, healthy food to eat, forests to walk in, rivers to fish in, and wilderness to hike and revel in. These are the sacred things which money cannot buy. We are finally coming full circle to value that which the Native American always held in the highest regard: Mother Nature.

In the 1990s, as we begin to return to the basics of our natural heritage and to rediscover what really gives meaning to our lives, we have the chance to choose a lifestyle that expresses this meaning. Now we can choose whether we want life in the fast lane with disposable products or whether we are willing to slow down a bit to preserve the ecology of our planet. We can choose the lifestyle of irresponsibility and of waiting for someone else to enact laws to preserve the land or we can take action to save the planet by being politically active and using our spirit to cause a positive statement upon the Earth.

This is a special time. It is a time when many of us will begin to question what our true purpose is and why we are here upon this beautiful bright green planet. And as we begin to question our personal purpose in life we will begin to comprehend what our higher purpose is and how we fit into the planetary scheme of things.

LIFESTYLE IS WHAT REFLECTS THE MEANING IN YOUR LIFE

The way you live your life, your lifestyle, is a matter of choice. You choose what you eat, what you wear, how you work, how you dispose of your garbage, what you do in your spare time, and how you celebrate your life force on a daily level. These are choices made by habits, learned patterns, accepted programs, or conscious awareness. It takes only a little energy and forethought to use your conscious awareness to assess what you are doing in this lifetime. In order to preserve this planet Earth as a viable life form we need to use all of the awareness we can possibly muster to question what we do. Yes, it does take a little more time and energy to deviate from the habitual patterns of our daily lifestyles to question what to do and how to improve our actions to create a more balanced environment. But the result is that it gives us so much more in return!

Begin by questioning everything that you do, then see what interesting answers you come up with. The questions are simple and the answers are common sense or can be found in any of the newer ecological books. However, there are many areas in your life that only you can formulate an answer for. These questions and answers are a new area of consciousness. There are no tried and true answers. It is up to each one of us to find a way to deal with our lifestyles to create a world in which we have a loving and nurtured planet and a healthy happy environment.

Start with the questions and answers below then move on to question other areas in your life, home, job, etc.

Question: How can I save water?

Answer: By washing my dishes in a sink full of soapy water instead of running the tap and washing the dishes one by one. By getting new water saving toilets (or putting a brick or plastic bottle in the tank to take up some space to use less water). By taking shorter showers and using energy saver shower heads that use less water. By watering the yard before 6 a.m. or after 6 p.m. so that the water does not evaporate. By collecting and using grey water (water recycled from the washing machine for example) to water the yard.

Question: How can I continue the tradition of a real Christmas tree without having to cut one down?

Answer: You can now rent a live tree that will be delivered to your house. You can water it, decorate it, and return it to the grower after Christmas and even reserve it for the next year when it will have grown an extra foot. (The first of these rental services was started by Loyd R. Johnson in Alpine, California. If you do not have this service in your hometown ask the growers to start one and spread the concept of living trees. Johnson rents and delivers trees that range from 2–3 feet to 5–6 feet for $20 to $32 a tree.)

Question: When someone dies why do they have to be put in a concrete-lined grave? Even if they are in a wooden casket, once they are in a concrete lined grave they can never truly decompose and release their body nutrients and body energy back to the earth where it came from.

Answer: I have yet to get a satisfactory answer to this—other than it aids in stopping disease and that we have to abide by the local health statutes—and perhaps this will become another ecological issue soon.

Question: Why must we put up with "fancy" packaging that we throw away almost immediately?

Answer: We accept fancy packaging, it looks nice, and corporations feel that it sells their product. To change these situations we must make it known to businesses that we will purchase their product in simpler and recycled containers, and that given a choice of products, you would not purchase ones that are over packaged.

Question: How can I make recycled paper products less expensive?

Answer: Recycled paper, as used in the printing of this book, costs much more because it is less readily available. Through the simple process of demand and supply, if more people demand more of a product more will be produced and the cost will decrease. This has already begun to happen with paper towels, toilet paper, and so on because enough people have asked for it. This, of course, leads us to the philosophical and practical question of how can we be a consumer society without devouring all of our natural resources. Many ecologists believe that we can do it, but it does take some planning and forethought.

Question: How can I put meaning and environmental consciousness into my life?

Answer: You will have to figure this one out for yourself as you live your life in day-to-day existence. But let me tell you, as a planetary energy worker, how I have added this to my lifestyle.

I believe that environmental consciousness does not come naturally to inhabitants of the modern world. I had to school myself to take my carryall bags into the grocery store, to save water, to separate garbage and recycle, and to always look for alternatives. Like anything else that is learned, it takes some time until these conscious efforts become second nature.

Including this awareness into my life has added joy and an immense amount of fun and pleasure to my daily existence. Rather than allowing myself to join the daily grind of bowing down to the mundane rituals of life, I have allowed myself to become as the child within and to constantly "play" with my actions. I take the time, and it really is only a few minutes, to allow myself to make the inner connection with my body and the outer connection with life force spirit, to be connected on every level that I can be. With spirit in body, as energy workers refer to it, I find life is fun. I view everything as sacred. Drinking a glass of water is imbibing the sacred life stream of Mother Earth, feeling the water as it courses through my body, seeing the water through the distortion of the glass, and feeling the strength and solidity of the glass in my hand. Sometimes I fill my glass of water with the cosmic archetypal energy of love or of strength or of courage or of humor. And then I drink my water as if it is a fine liquor (which to me it truly is!).

Each thing that I do in life I do with the joy of being alive, in present time, as if I have never done it before and I am here to experience what it means to do it now. And thus, each thing that I do is the sacred expression of my life and my reason for being alive to interact with everything around me. Planting a tree or a plant is sacred. Cleaning the beach or cleaning up after myself in the outdoors is sacred.

There is an old Native American song, part of which states, "In a sacred manner I live. To the heavens I gazed. In a sacred manner I live."[29]

It seems that if we are going to turn around the awful environmental devastation taking place on Earth we are going to have to learn to value the Earth which we have taken for granted, to find the spiritual part of ourselves that takes form on the earth, and to live in a sacred manner.

 ## A PLANETARY HEALING CREATION

Find yourself a comfortable chair to sit in. Take a nice deep breath, loosen any tight clothing and allow yourself to relax. Put a grounding cord from the bottom of your First Chakra down to the center of the Earth and hook yourself on to the planet.

Close your eyes and find the center of your head and place your consciousness in it so that you can have the full total use of your awareness. Now take another deep breath and send any tension or anything that you would like to let go of down your grounding cord. It will go down to the center of the Earth and be released as new life force energy.

Take another deep breath and say hello to yourself. Say hello to your body and ask your body right now what it would like. Bodies are fun vehicles and if you ask your body what it wants you will probably get a long list of things, such as your favorite foods, a massage, a hot tub, some hugs or loving, and so on. If you do get a long list of requests from your body take one item on that list and promise it to your body in the next week. Just promise one thing to your body. If you promise everything on your list to your body and you forget to give it one of those things your body will not trust you. So just promise it one thing that you know you will give your body in the next week's time.

Now tell your body that you will be going on a trip and will leave for a few minutes but that you will return soon. Bodies are nature's machines. They get nervous if you pull out your consciousness for too long and do not tell it that you are going. Also tell it that you will return. You want your body to feel safe, secure, and relaxed. Now triple ground your body, and just give your body an extra strong grounding cord.

Open your eyes for a minute and find an upper corner of the room. Now close your eyes and be in the center of your head and say hello to your body.

Now take your consciousness and **be** in the upper corner of the room. Look at your body from the upper corner of the room and know where it is and that it is safe and well. Now take your consciousness and go from the upper corner of the room to the roof of the building you are in. Be aware of yourself on the roof. Then look around and find the moon. Now take your consciousness and go up to the moon. And place your consciousness on the moon. Look around you. You can see the stars in the deep black void.

From the moon you can survey the planet Earth. You can look down upon it and see what is happening to it. So, make yourself comfortable on the moon and begin to look at the Earth. There are many ways to view the Earth. It can seem like a bright green-blue planet or you could see it on an energy level, as bright bands of energy surrounding, enveloping, and protecting the Earth. If you can see the planet as an energy sphere begin to look for bright and dark spots. These often look like chakras or appear as tornados or water spouts or funnels of energy.

The red energy centers often represent hot spots where there are wars or disputes on the planet. When you look closely and know some geography you will be able to see what country is located beneath the funnel of energy. You can drain out the martial "fight" energy by sending it down the grounding cord, down to the center of the Earth and there it gets released to come back as life force energy in a new form. As you release energy from these red "hot" areas you need to fill them up with some cosmic gold light or rose love energy so that a new and higher vibration fills the area. If you do not replace the energy of the area the people in that area will just continue to fill their area with the blind fury of hate and hot passion.

The darker, blue-black or dark green, energy centers often represent cool spots where the ecology energy of the area is sinking or being destroyed or folding in on itself. You can begin to help to heal these areas by taking some cosmic neutral life force energy and placing a grounding cord on the energy centers and drain them out to the center of the earth then fill them up with cosmic gold or bright green (a growth energy). You can also connect them to an abundance or growth archetype.

Now look for cracks in the energy field or dark areas where the energy has lost its vibrance. You can fill these in with some soft cosmic gold energy, interlacing the energy field of the planet with the pure gold sunlight of life force. You can also bring in some cosmic gold life force energy and fill in the center of the planet with it. If you can see any holes in the ozone layer you can knit or "fold" these together with some soft bright blue "air" energy.

When you have finished observing the Earth it is time to find your bearings and go home. Look down at the planet and find the continent that you live on. Find the country or state you live in and see the area you come from. Then bring your consciousness back, all the way back, to the roof of the house your body is located in. From the roof come back inside to the corner of the room and find your body. From the corner of the room come into your body. Make sure that you are completely in your body with your astral or energy head in your head, your hands in your hands, and your feet in your feet. Feel your body, make sure that you are facing forward, and take a nice deep breathe. Wiggle your toes, move your fingers, open your eyes and take a good look around you and check out what your version of reality is right now. Then bend over, with your head and arms reaching towards the ground and let any excess energy run from the top of your head and also through your arms out into the earth. Now come back up to a sitting position, take a deep breath, and welcome yourself home to the planet Earth.

May your feet always touch the ground,
May you reach for the stars,
May you know the heavens,
May the winds of nature caress you,
and May you always know the wonderment and awe
of being in harmony with the earth,
and May all good things come your way.

22

DOING IT
WITH SPIRIT

What can you do as a spiritual being to help preserve the planet and to help change the spiraling downward trend of destruction?

I believe that if you do define yourself as a spiritual person, that you must work with your spirit. If, as yet, you do not define yourself as a spiritual person, you may find that working with your spirit is getting in touch with the one part of yourself that does indeed have the most power to transform the planetary energy level at this time. Your spirit is your Life Force, the part of you that is almost immortal, knows no boundaries, believes that anything can be accomplished, and has a tremendous capacity to love. If we have such a wonderful tool at our disposal how do we use it?

On a spiritual level you use the following abilities:

Will: Using your will power is the act of being able to direct your energy in a given manner to get a desired end.

339

Intention: You must know what you want. You cannot just say, "I wish the earth to be green and beautiful and balanced." You must be specific and work on one very specific situation at a time, knowing exactly what you wish to create.

Directing the Energy: You must be able to get in touch with your innate higher energy source, know what you wish to do, and be able to guide the energy in a given form or direction. It is not enough to just love the planet. You must be able to direct that love in a way that the planet can receive it, accept it, and use it.

Throughout this book you have been given specific exercises and ways to work with your energy. Some of these exercises will help you develop your own personal power as a spiritual being in a physical body so that you can be in touch and balanced enough within yourself to be a capable energy worker. Other exercises are specifically aimed at healing different situations on a planetary level so that you can help to heal the Earth. At all times, of course, you must remember to use your will, know your intention, and direct the energy towards where it is needed.

23
EPILOG

The decision of whether or not to use your energy to help heal the Earth is up to you.

Even if you only spend ten minutes a day or one hour a week using your spiritual nature to directly help to rebalance Mother Nature, you will accomplish something. You do not have to become an Eco-Spirit Energy Worker or follow the entire system presented in this book to have an affect upon the energy of the Earth. Whatever it is that you can willingly and lovingly give to Mother Earth she will accept.

But, the more that you can give to Mother Earth the more you in return will receive. This is not a law of energy workers but the simple law of logic. If you replenish your source, it continues.

In general, I would define us, the race of humanity, as a race of takers. We have taken so much from Mother Nature that now we must not only learn how to give back but must increase our efforts twofold just to hold on to what we have. In the ecological scheme of things, using all of our conscious environmental efforts, we are barely treading water to stay abreast of environmental catastrophe. This means that we cannot put off to tomorrow what we can do today.

If you find that the information and skills presented by Eco-Spirit in this book have relevance, please use them. Unfortunately just having knowledge is not enough. We have to put that knowledge into action. We are now in the stage of the environmental movement called Earth Work. This means that many people are educated and informed about the problem and that the time has come to go into action to work to alleviate the situation.

If you know of a better or different way to use your spirit, mind, heart, and body to heal the Earth, or a way to combine the Eco-Spirit skills with other spiritual, psychological, environmental, or scientific skills that you already have, I hope you will do so. Most of all, I hope you will answer this call to action.

ECO-SPIRIT WORKSHOPS

The Eco-Spirit Dream

Eco-Spirit was devised as a set of concepts and practical exercises that all people, of various beliefs, religions and conceptual and spiritual practices, can use to help heal the Earth.

The practical aims of Eco-Spirit are:

1. To educate people to use their most valued resource—their spirit—to heal the Earth.

2. To heal Mother Earth using every means possible including: spiritual, educational, scientific, and political.

3. To bring together people of diverse cultural, spiritual, religious, and conceptual beliefs to work together in harmony to further the healing of the Earth.

4. To research and demonstrate that ecological spiritual skills can be used to increase crop yields, protect crops

from pests, and improve organic and other farming methods.

5. To research and demonstrate that ecological spiritual skills can be used to heal the Earth, rebalance the environment, and protect natural resources.

6. To create an archive of traditional earth healing skills of all traditions, and to accumulate and preserve the ancient folklore of all natural energy workers.

7. To create a communication channel between the spiritual, scientific, and ecological communities to enable everyone to work as a unified force in time of need.

8. To show the connection between humankind and the earth, the true inter-connectedness of the life force of this planet.

9 To raise the life force energy of the Earth so that the harmony of life can be restored.

10. To awaken and re-establish the world-wide ley lines and Chakra power centers of the planet.

11. To find the new natural centers of earth energies and open these to use by energy workers to heal the Earth.

12. To reclaim all land as sacred.

Our down-to-earth simple goals this year are:

1. To create a telephone tree that will enable large numbers of people to work on a different environmental problem each week. This will enable us to put a focused energy source on each ecological problem facing us.

2. To raise money in order to purchase land to create an Eco-Spirit retreat to study the effects of using the Eco-Spirit techniques to farm and preserve the environment and for use as a base to hold workshops to teach all who are interested in how to heal the planet with spirit.

3. To experiment with the power of spirit to affect the growth and quality of plants, trees, and all living creatures.

4. To culturally archive and preserve the quickly dwindling oral tradition of spiritual earth energy workers.

5. To create a communication channel between diverse spiritual and religious groups, the scientific community, and the ecological community in order to further community effort.

ECO SPIRIT WORKSHOP FOLDER

A workshop to explore being a planetary healer

Morning Introductions

Meeting and greeting one another.

The Morning Creation

A movement Creation to begin the day and the Energy Worker Way. A celebration of life and the rising sun.

Grounding, Center of the Head, Running Energy

A class in the use and concepts of Grounding, Centering, and Running Your Own Life Force Energy through you. Using trance as a skill for everyday life.

Mid-morning break

Refreshments and socializing.

The Elements

An introduction to the concepts of the elements of Earth, Air, Fire, and Water and how we can be cognizant of them and use them in an Earth-healing manner.

Earth – A movement Creation in manifesting the elemental energy of the Earth—using the body, sound, movement, and spiritual awareness.

Air – A movement Creation in manifesting the elemental energy of the air—using the body, sound, movement and spiritual awareness.

Lunch

The Eating Creation

Developing Clarity

Learning the skills of transforming energy to clear yourself.

Breathing for life energy

An exercise in learning to absorb dynamic life force energy as breath.

The Elements

Fire – A movement Creation in manifesting the elemental energy of Fire—using the body, sound, movement, and spiritual awareness.

Water – A movement Creation in manifesting the elemental energy of Water—using the body, sound, movement, and spiritual awareness.

Mid-afternoon break

Refreshments and socializing.

Being the Archetype

An exercise in becoming a chosen Archetype.

Discussion-Seminar

Discussing our goals as planetary energy workers.

Healing the Earth

We will pick a specific goal and use the elemental, archetypal and movement skills we have learned to do a Creation to heal this particular situation.

Evening Creation

A movement Creation to end the day and welcome the Moon and the evening.

Parting Creation

We meet in joy and we part in joy.

ECO-SPIRIT TAPES

The following tapes of the Eco-Spirit skills are available.

Making the Connection

Learn the skills of Grounding, Running Your Own Life Force Energy, Centering and finding the inner peace within you and the connection to Mother Earth.

MAKING THE CONNECTION $10

Change

Learn the skills of how to release and let go of patterns, programs, and unwanted emotions. Develop clarity in your life with these simple easy skills.

CHANGE $10

Life force

Working with the exercises of The Breath of Life and the Exercise of the Rose, learn to focus your energy to achieve your goals.

LIFE FORCE...$10

Working with the Elements

Learn what the elements are and how to balance yourself according to the elements of earth, air, fire and water. As you work with the elements and begin to understand them you can begin to rebalance the planet.

WORKING WITH THE ELEMENTS $10

Earth

An explanation of the element of Earth with different exercises for learning to expand your consciousness to be the Earth and to communicate with Earth energy and the elementals, the Gnomes of the Earth.

EARTH $10

Air

Experience being in touch with the element of Air. In this tape you will use several exercises to learn to expand consciousness to be the air and to communicate with the air elementals, the Sylphs.

AIR $10

Fire

Learn about the element of Fire and how you can use different Creation exercises to be one with the fire element. On this tape you explore communicating with the fire elementals, the Salamanders.

FIRE $10

Water

Explore the element of Water by using several different Creation exercises to be one with the water element. Experience communicating with the water elementals, the Undines.

WATER $10

Introducing the Archetypes

This tape delves into what archetypes are and how you can use them to heal the planet and yourself. Included on this tape are archetypal creations for getting in touch with Mother Earth, the Goddess, the God force, the animals, the forces of nature, and the Supreme Being.

INTRODUCING THE ARCHETYPES $10

Healing the Planet

This tape contains Creations that lead you into different states of awareness and action to heal the planet.

HEALING THE PLANET $10

The Morning and Evening Creation

In the morning, begin the day by doing a Creation to greet the rising of the Sun and the raising up of life force energy for the day to come. In the evening, end the day by doing a Creation for ending the day and greeting the night and rising of the Moon.

THE MORNING AND EVENING CREATION $10

TO ORDER TAPES

You can order Eco-Spirit Tapes by sending a check or money order to:

ECO-SPIRIT
140 S. Beverly Drive, Suite 200
Beverly Hills, CA 90212

Shipping and handling costs are $2.00 for the first tape and an additional .75 for each additional tape. California residents must include the appropriate tax. Please make your check or money order payable to Eco-Spirit.

You can also order tapes using a credit card by calling Eco-Spirit at (310) 275–5859.

ECO-SPIRIT T-SHIRTS

Wear a T-Shirt that speaks your mind!

ECO-SPIRIT T-Shirts are available for $19.95 each. The Eco-Spirit logo is printed on the front of the 100% cotton T-shirts in full color—just as it appears on the front cover of this book. Printed in green on the back of the shirt is the saying "*healing the planet with spirit.*"

You can order these T-Shirts by calling (310) 275-5859 and using a visa or mastercard, or you can order them by mailing a check or money order to:

ECO-SPIRIT
140 S. Beverly Drive, Suite 200
Beverly Hills, CA 90212

If paying by check please include $19.95 plus $2.50 postage and packaging, also tax if you are in California. Please specify small, medium, large, or X-large.

THE SACRED
PLANT PROGRAM

For many of us the act of seeing is believing. People who have worked using their spiritual skills to affect the growth of plants will be the first ones to tell you that these simple experiments changed their lives and their inner concepts about themselves.

The Eco-Spirit Sacred Plant Program has been created to fulfill two needs:

1. to create a bank of scientific intuitive information about the power of spirit in regard to growing plants and trees.

2. to further demonstrate in hands-on fashion how powerful spirit work can be.

The Sacred Plant Program is open to everyone. For $12 (plus $3 postage, packaging, and handling) anyone can join. As a member of the Sacred Plant Program you will receive a Sacred Plant Kit which includes organic seeds, growing paraphernalia, and instructions. The instructions guide you in a scientific experiment of using energy to raise plants. Because this is a scientific experiment you will be asked to follow the instructions as closely as possible. As a Sacred Plant grower you will place sterilized soil in two containers, plant your seeds, and water. Both containers will receive the same soil, water, and light. One container of seeds, however, will be just physically cared for and then ignored emotionally and spiritually while the other will be showered with energy salutations, love, Eco-Spirit techniques, and/or prayer (whatever you are comfortable with). In your notebook you will keep a journal of everything that you do or that happens in your home near the plants. At the end of the experiment you will send us a copy of your notes.

All members of the Sacred Plant Program will also receive a quarterly newsletter describing the progress of other members and any pertinent information regarding any new processes being developed for healing the planet.

To join the Sacred Plant Program please send $15 to:

ECO-SPIRIT
Sacred Plant Program
140 S. Beverly Drive, Suite 200
Beverly Hills, CA 90212

or call (310) 275-5859 or (310) 859-0869 11 a.m. to 4 p.m. California time to order by credit card.

APPENDIX A
THE ELEMENTS

The following are some descriptive aspects of the elements.

THE EARTH ELEMENT

The Elemental Beings   Gnomes – Gnome has come to mean earth dweller. This is from the ancient name for them, although they have also been called trolls, pygmies, satyrs, pans, dryads, hamadryads, elves, brownies, tree spirits or forest sprites, sylvestres, goblins, and little old men of the woods.

Direction   North – North has come to be where the Astral Doorway to the Higher planes of consciousness and other dimensions is located.

Physical Body	Hands, thighs and lower part of body, and ring finger.
Spiritual Body	First Chakra, the energy center located at base of spine, used for earth information and survival.
Planetary Body	Salt (used as a purification symbol and tool)
Tattva Symbol	

□

Astrological Signs	Capricorn Virgo Taurus

Elemental Colors	Yellow
	Colors of the earth—
	    bright green – growth and change
	    deep brown – solid deep earth
	    black – decay or death of earth

Senses	Odor-smelling
Food	Bread and Grains
Attribute	Feminine

Symbol

Pentacle—representing human person on earth. It has five points—two arms, two legs, and a head which represents spirit.

The pentacle, or five-pointed star, is a design that naturally occurs in nature—you can see it in seeds, flowers (many petunias, for example, have a five pointed star pattern), and fruits (if you cut an apple across the middle you will see a five-pointed star.)

Earth = Physical Life

THE AIR ELEMENT

The Elemental Beings Sylphs, Beings of Air

Direction

East – The sun rises in the East and the Air element is seen as the element of movement and of enlightenment or under-standing.

Physical Body	Mind: the analyzer (to think, discriminate, analyze, or have knowledge). Chest, heart and throat, and fifth finger (the pinky).
Spiritual Body	Fifth Chakra, the energy center located at the base of the throat used for communication, clairaudience, inner voice, telepathy, and precognition.
Planetary Body	Smoke (on a spiritual level = incense) Fresh Air; Energy of Air
Tattva Symbol	

Astrological Signs	Gemini Libra Aquarius
Elemental Color	Blue or pale light blue
Senses	Touch and feeling. Air can be heard and felt.
Food	Seeds, sprouts, and berries
Attribute	Masculine
Symbol	Wand, staff, and tree branch. Symbol of directing energy and being able to send

energy outwardly. The wand is a symbol of energy and creative will power.

Air = Intuition

THE FIRE ELEMENT

The Elemental Beings	Salamanders. Spirits of Fire. Also known as Angels of the Sun, Will-O-Wisps, and small balls of light.

Direction

South. Fire is the great transformer that moves everyone and everything irrevocably forward. It is the great purifying element that causes the evolution of heat and light during combustion.

Physical Body

Head and forefinger

Spiritual Body

Third Chakra, the energy center located at the solar plexus, focuses mental energy and brings it down to earth, controls how much energy is used through the body; location where the "silver cord" attaches the Astral Body of Light to the physical body.

Seventh or Crown Chakra, the energy center located at the top of the head, the big control center for the entire body, enables you to have and own your free will and use your ability to know.

Planetary Body	Fire. The element of action, the principle of light, the great purifyer, the process of transmutation. Igne Natura renovatur integra – "All Nature is renewed by fire."

Life Force Energy

Tattva Symbol

Astrological Signs	Aries Leo Sagittarius
Elemental Colors	Physical plane – red Spiritual plane – sun golden yellow
Senses	Sight – to be able to see
Food	All red- or orange-colored foods
Attribute	Masculine

Symbol   Sword or knife

Fire = Mind

THE WATER ELEMENT

The Elemental Beings Undines, Water Spirits. Also known as: nymphs, oceanids, oreades, nereides, limoniades, potamides, sea maids, mermaids, and water sprites.

Direction

(W)

West. West is where the sun sets and represents the deep, the internal, and the emotions.

Physical Body   Abdomen and internal organs, and thumb

Spiritual Body   Second Chakra, the energy center located in the abdomen, governs feelings, emotions, sensuality, and sexuality. The "I feel" center.

Planetary Body   Water: a universal cleanser and transformative medium.

Tattva Symbol

Astrological Signs	Cancer Scorpio Pisces
Elemental Colors	Blue (deep blue, navy blue, or blue-green)
Senses	Taste, Perceptions. Water can be heard, felt, seen, and tasted.
Food	Fruits, vegetables, juices; high water content foods
Attribute	Feminine
Symbol	Cup (holder of water), Chalice (symbol of eternal life, love, and the bountiful creative feminine principle), and Cauldron (symbol of the feminine meaning to cook and feed, both spiritually and physically, and representing the needs of the people). A pond, a lake, or a very fertile valley is a natural cup or chalice.

Water = Feeling

APPENDIX B
ASTROLOGICAL TERMS

EARTH

♍ Virgo –
the Virgin

August 24th through September 23rd

♉ Taurus –
the Bull

April 21st through May 21st

♑ Capricorn –
the Goat

December 22nd through January 20th

AIR

♊ Gemini –
the Twins

May 22nd through June 21st

♎ Libra –
the Scales

September 24th through October 23rd

♒ Aquarius –
the Waterbearer

January 21st through February 19th

APPENDIX B – ASTROLOGICAL TERMS

FIRE

♈ Aries –
the Ram
March 21st through April 20th

♌ Leo –
the Lion
July 24th through August 23rd

♐ Sagittarius –
the Archer
November 23rd through December 21st

WATER

♋ Cancer –
the Crab
June 22nd through July 23rd

♏ Scorpio –
the Scorpion
October 24th through November 22nd

♓ Pisces –
the Fish
February 20th through March 20th

APPENDIX C
SOURCE ORGANIZATIONS

American Forestry Association, Global Releaf Program, P.O. Box 2000, Washington, DC 20013.

Animal Legal Defense Fund, 333 Market St. San Francisco, CA 94105.

Animal Rights International, Box 214, Planetarium Station, New York, N.Y. 10024.

The Bio-Integral Resource Center, P.O. Box 7242, Berkeley, CA 94707.

Center for Marine Consrvation, 1725 DeSales St. NW, Washington, DC 20036.

Center for Environmental Education, 1725 DeSales St. NW, Washington, DC 20036.

Citizen's Clearinghouse for Hazardous Waste, P.O. Box 926, Arlington, VA 22216.

Citizens for a Better Environment, 33 East Congress, Suite 523, Chicago, IL 60605.

Compassion in World Farming, 20 Lavant Street, Petersfield, Hants, England

Earth Island Institute, 300 Broadway, Suite 28, San Francisco, CA 94133.

Environmental Action, 1525 New Hampshire NW,
   Washington, D.C. 20036.
Environmental Defense Fund, 1616 P St., NW, Suite 150,
   Washington DC 20036.
Friends of Animals, Inc., 11 West 60th St., New York,
   N.Y. 10023
Friends of the Earth,U.S., 218 D St. SE,
   Washington, DC 2003.
Garbage Magazine, P.O. Box 56519, Boulder, CO 80322.
Global Tomorrow Coalition, 1325 G St. NW, Suite 915,
   Washington, DC 20005.
Greenhouse Crisis Foundation, 1130 17th St. NW,
   Suite 630, Washington DC 20036.
Greenpeace, 1436 U St. NW, Washington, DC 20009.
Humane Farming Association, 1550 California St., Suite 6,
   San Francisco, CA 94109.
International Society for Animal Rights, Inc.,
   421 South State St., Clarks Summit, PA 18411
International Union for the Conservation of Nature and
   Natural Resources, Avenue Mont Blanc, 1196 Gland,
   Switzerland.
Mothers and Others for Pesticide Limits, 40 West 20th St.,
   New York, N.Y. 10011.
National Audubon Society, 645 Pennsylvania Ave. SE,
   Washington, DC 20003.
National Coalition Against the Misuse of Pesticides,
   530 7th St. SE, Washington, DC 20003.
National Museum of Natural History/Smithsonian
   Institution, Washington, DC 20008.
National Wildlife Federation, 1400 16th St. NW,
   Washington, DC 20036.
Natural Resources Defense Council, 40 W. 20th St.,
   New York, N.Y. 10011.

Nature Conservancy, 1800 North Kent. St., Arlington,
VA 22209.

Oceanic Society, 218 D St. SE, Washington, D.C. 20003.

Peace Seeds, 2385 SE Thompson St., Corvallis, OR 97333

Pele Defense Fund, P.O. Box 404, Volcano, HI 96875.

People for the Ethical Treatment of Animals,
P.O. Box 42516, Washington, DC 20015

Population Crisis Committee, 1120 19th St. NW, Suite 550,
Washington, DC 20036.

Progressive Animal Welfare Society (PAWS), P.O. Box 1037,
Lynnwood, WA 98046.

Rainforest Action Network, 301 Broadway, Suite A,
an Francisco, CA 94133.

Rainforest Alliance, 270 Lafayette St., Suite 512, New York,
N.Y. 10012.

The Rainforest Foundation, Inc., 1776 Broadway,
14th Floor, New York, N.Y. 10019.

Renew America, 1001 Connecticut Ave. N.W, Suite 1719,
Washington, DC 20036.

Rocky Mountain Institute, 1739 Snowmass Creek Road,
Snowmass, CO 81654.

Sierra Club, 730 Polk St., San Francisco, CA 94109.

Seeds of Change (catalogue), 621 Old Santa Fe Trail No.10,
Santa Fe, N.M. 87501.

Seed Savers Exchange, Rural Route 3, Box 239, Decorah,
IA 52101.

The Fund for Animals, 200 West 57th St., New York, N.Y.

TreePeople, 12601 Mulholland Dr., Beverly Hills,
CA 90210.

Trees for the Future, 11306 Estona Dr., P.O. Box 1786,
Silver Spring, MD 20915.

Wilderness Society, 1400 Eye St. NW,
Washington, D.C. 20005.

World Rainforest Movement, 87 Contonment Road, 10250 Penang, Malaysia.

World Resources Institute, 1735 New York Ave. NW, Washington, DC 20008.

World Wildlife Fund/Conservation Foundation, 1250 24th St. NW, Washington, DC 20037.

Worldwatch Institute, 1776 Massachusetts Ave. NW, Washington, DC 20036.

•

APPENDIX D
SUGGESTED READING
BIBLIOGRAPHY

Allen, Marcus. *Astrology for the New Age.* Mill Valley, CA: Whatever Publishing, 1979.

Allen, Paula Gunn. *The Sacred Hoop.* Boston, Mass.: Beacon Press, 1986.

Arroyo, Stephen. *Astrology, Psychology and the Four Elements.* Sebastopol, CA: CRCS Publications, 1975.

Bord, Janet and Bord, Colin. *Mysterious Britain.* New York: Doubleday and Co., 1973.

Brown, Beth. E.S.P. *With Plants and Animals.* New York: Simon and Schuster; Essandes Special Editions, 1971.

Brown, Dee. *Bury My Heart at Wounded Knee.* New York: Washington Square Press, 1970.

Briffault, Robert. *The Mothers.* New York: Grosset and Dunlap, 1959.

Campbell, Joseph. *The Inner Reaches of Outer Space.* New York: Harper and Row Publishers, 1988.

_____, *The Power of Myth.* New York: Doubleday, 1988.

Dames, Michael. *The Silbury Treasure: The Great Goddess Rediscovered.* England: Thames and Hudson, 1976.

_____, *The Avebury Cycle*. England: Thames and Hudson, 1976.

Doyle, Arthur Conan, Sir. *The Coming of the Fairies*. New York: Samuel Weiser, Inc., 1975.

Durdin-Robertson, Lawrence. *The Year of the Goddess*. Wellingborough Northamptonshire, England: The Aquarian Press, 1990.

Earth Works Group, the. *50 Simple Things You Can Do to Save the Earth*. Berkeley: Earthworks Press, 1989.

Erdoes, Richard and Ortiz, Alfonso. *American Indian Myths and Legends*. New York: Pantheon Books,1984.

Fowler, Cary and Mooney, Pat. *Shattering: Food, Politics, and the Loss of Genetic Diversity*. North Carolina: RAFI, 1991.

Frazer, James George, Sir. *The New Golden Bough*. New York: S.G. Phillips, Inc., 1968.

Gimbutas, Marija. *The Language of the Goddess*. San Francisco: Harper and Row Publishers, 1989.

Ginn, Victoria. *The Spirited Earth*. New York: Rizzoli International Publications, Inc., 1990.

Hall, Manley P. *An Encyclopedic Outline of Masonic, Hermetic, Quabbalistic, and Rosicrucian Symbolic Philosophy*. Los Angeles, CA: The Philosophical Research Society Inc., 1968.

Hamaker-Zondag, Karen. *Astro Psychology*. New York: Samuel Weiser Inc., 1980.

Jung, C.G. *Man and His Symbols*. New York: Dell Publishing,1964.

_____, *The Basic Writings of C.G. Jung ed. Violet de Laszlo*. New York: Random House, 1959.

Leadbeater, C.W. *The Astral Plane*. Adyar, Madras, India: The Theosophical Publishing House, 1973.

Lewis, Scott. *The Rainforest Book*. Living Planet Press, 1990.

Lemesurier, Peter. *The Healing of the Gods.* Dorset, England: Element Books,1988.

Loehr, Franklin, Rev. *The Power of Prayer on Plants.* New York: Signet Books, 1969.

Michell, John. *The Earth Spirit.* New York: Avon Books, 1975.

Miller, David Humphreys. *Ghost Dance.* Duell, Sloan and Pearce, 1959. (also by Bison Books)

Neuman, Eric. *The Great Mother.* Princeton, N.J.: Princeton University Press, 1963.

One Earth. Collins Publishers, 1990.

Pearson, Carol S. *The Hero Within.* San Francisco: Harper and Row Publishers, 1989.

Powell, T.G.E. *Prehistoric Art.* New York: Frederick A. Praeger, 1967.

Screeton, Paul. *Quicksilver Heritage: The Mystic Leys – Their Legacy of Ancient Wisdom.* England: Thorsons, Wellingborough, 1974.

Sharkey, John. *Celtic Mysteries: The Ancient Religion.* New York: Crossroad, 1981.

Silverberg, Robert. *Mound Builders of Ancient America.* New York: Graphic Society, 1968.

Strachan, Francoise. *Natural Magic.* New York: Blackwatch, 1974.

Tompkins, Peter and Bird, Christopher. *The Secret Life of Plants.* New York: Harper and Row Publishers, 1973.

_____, *Secrets of the Great Pyramid.* New York: Harper and Row Publishers, 1971.

Tyler, Edward Burnett. *Religion in Primitive Culture.* New York: Harper and Row Publishers, 1958.

Watkins, Alfred. *The Old Straight Track.* England: Methuen, 1926.

Weatherford, Jack. *Indian Givers.* New York: Ballantine Books, 1988.

Weiner, Jonathan. *The Next One Hundred Years.* New York: Bantam Books, 1990.

Wentz, W.Y. *The Fairy Faith in Celtic Countries.* England: Oxford University Press, 1911.

Whitman, John. *The Psychic Power of Plants.* New York: New American Library, Signet, 1974.

CHAPTER NOTES
LIST OF REFERENCES

Chapter One – Saving the Planet and Ourselves

1. Jerry Baker. *Talk To Your Plants* (New York: Pocket Books, 1973). Thank you Grandma Putt for your wise concepts in regard to living in harmony with the land: p. 28.

Chapter Two – Your Ecological Mirror

2. Rev. Franklin Loehr, *The Power of Prayer on Plants* (New York: Signet Books, 1969, pp 46–56.

3. Scott Lewis, *The Rainforest Book* (Los Angeles: Living Planet Press, 1990), p. 10.

4. Karen Foley, "Community in Focus: The Earth," *Lifestyle Magazine* Vol. 5, No. 11 [Calabasas, California] (October 1990): p. 15.

5. "Rubber Duck", *The PennySaver* [San Fernando Valley, L.A.. Zone 237] (Dec. 5, 1990).

Chapter Three – The Four Elements

6. The Cup of Cerridwen, unlike the Holy Grail of Jesus, was seen as an immense bowl three feet across. You can see copies of this bowl in museums.

Chapter Five – It's Very Elemental

7. Gary Larson, "The Far Side," *Los Angeles Times* (June 26, 1991): p. E6.

Chapter Fifteen – Archetypal Excursions

8. Edith Hamilton, *Mythology* (New York: Mentor: The New American Library, Inc., 1942), p. 64

9. "River," *Encyclopedia Britannica* (1972 edition), s.v. "river."

10. "Johnny Appleseed, known as John Chapman," *Encyclopedia Britannica* (1972 edition).

Chapter Sixteen – The Dance of the Trees

11. Victoria Ginn, *The Spirited Earth* (New York: Rizzoli International Publications, Inc., 1990), p. 55.

12. Loehr, op. cit., pp. 104–107.

Peter Tompkins and Christopher Bird, *The Secret Life of Plants* (New York: Harper and Row, 1973), p. 38.

John Whitman, *The Psychic Power of Plants* (New York: Signet, 1974), pp. 17–20.

13. Loehr, op. cit., pp. 46–56.

Chapter Twenty-One – The Eco-Spirit Lifestyle

14. Michael Klaper, M.D., *Pregnancy, Children and the Vegan Diet* (Umatilla Florida: Gentle World, Inc.,1987), p. 71.

15. Ann Wigmore, *Be Your Own Doctor* (New Jersey: Avery Publishing Group,1982), p. 66.

16. Ibid.

17. Ibid. Quoting Frances Moore Lappe, *Diet for a Small Planet* (New York: Ballantine Books, 1975).

18. Klaper, op. cit., p. 71.

19. Pat Stone, "John Seed and the Council of All Beings," *Mother Earth Magazine* 117 (May–June, 1989): p. 61.

John Robbins, *Diet for a New America*, (Walpole, N.H.: Stillpoint Publishing,1987), p. 367.

20. Foley, op. cit., p. 15.

21. Klaper, op. cit., p. 71.

22. Robbins, op. cit., p. 363.

23. Loehr, op. cit., p. 47.

24. Whitman, op. cit., pp. 56–63.

25. Loehr, op. cit., pp. 46–56.

Whitman, op. cit., pp. 17–20.

26. Creation: an energy working using an archetype. See Archetype chapters "Finding Your Archetype" and "Archetypal Excursions."

27. Howard Rosenberg, "Frontline Touches Spirit of the Sioux" *Los Angeles Times* (December 17, 1990): p. 10, Calendar. Quote from article: "Charlotte Black Elk says: 'We're created and spread out from the Black Hills... This is the most special place on Earth.' "

28. Robert Tomsho, "Dumping Grounds: Indian Tribes Content With Some of Worst of America's Pollution" *The Wall Street Journal* [New York], November 29, 1990: p. 1, A 9.

29. Dee Brown, *Bury My Heart At Wounded Knee* (New York: Washington Square Press, 1970), p. 36. Courtesy of the Bureau of American Ethnology Collection.

INDEX

ECO-SPIRIT

About the Author...

Levanah Shell Bdolak has been speaking with plants, animals, and the wee nature creatures since she can remember having consciousness in this body. In 1967 she began to do formal earth nature rituals to heal the Earth and make the connection between spirit and body. Levanah is one of the founding members of the Clearsight Program, an intuitive center teaching Meditation, Healing, Clairvoyancy, Intuitive Weight Control, and Stress Reduction. She has been teaching people how to connect with the intuitive transformational side of themselves for the past twenty years. Levanah is also the author of *The Aura Coloring Book.*

She has ministerial degrees from the Church of the Divine Within and the Church of Divine Man, as an Elder in the Covenant of the Goddess, and has a B.S. from Antioch College. Today she has a private spiritual counseling practice in Beverly Hills, California, and lives in the Santa Monica mountains where she spends her spare time communicating with the realms of nature.

Voyant

VOYANT BOOKS AND PRODUCTS

If you have enjoyed this book and found it useful you may wish to order one for your friends or several for your group.

ECO-SPIRIT, A Spiritual Guide to Healing the Planet $9.95
Special discounts are available for bulk orders. Call (310) 275-5859 or (818) 707-6448. If you are ordering individual books by mail, please include $2.00 for postage and handling.

The Eco-Spirit T-Shirt $19.95
Specify size, S, M, L, X-L. Please add $2.50 postage and handling.

The Sacred Plant Program $15.00
You will receive seeds, a guide to speaking with plants and how to do the Sacred Plant Program experiments plus a quarterly news-letter chronicling the Program.

Eco-Spirit Tapes .... $10.00 each
Making the Connection – *Grounding, Centering, Running Energy, and finding the inner peace within you and your connection to Mother Earth.*
Change – *Achieving clarity by releasing patterns, programs, and old emotions.*

Life force – *Exercises with The Breath of Life and The Exercise of the Rose.*

Working with the Elements – *How to use earth, air, fire, and water to rebalance ourselves and the planet.*

Earth – *Exercises for getting in touch with the Earth element and speaking with the Earth elementals.*

Air – *Exercises for getting in touch with the Air element and speaking with the Air elementals.*

Fire – *Exercises for getting in touch with the Fire element and speaking with the Fire elementals.*

Water – *Exercises for getting in touch with the Water element and speaking with the Water elementals.*

Introducing The Archetypes – *What archetypes are and how we can use them to heal the planet and ourselves.*

Healing The Planet – *Creations that lead you into different states of awareness and action to heal the planet.*

The Morning And Evening Creation – *The greeting of the sun and the moon and the rising up of life force energy.*

To order tapes please include $2.00 for postage and handling for the first tape and .75 for each additional tape. California residents must include the appropriate tax.

The Aura Coloring Book $11.95
Please include $1.50 for fourth class mail or $3.50 for first class mail to cover postage and packaging.

Clearsight Tapes

Meditation – *Grounding, Centering, Running Energy, and finding a quiet inner space within yourself.*

Change – *Letting go of patterns, programs, and old emotions. Giving yourself permission to change.*

Meet Your Higher Self – *Exercises for speaking with the Higher Self.*

Chakras—Doorways of Perception – *What the chakras (energy centers) are, where they are located, how to use them to create your own reality, and how to clean them.*

Creating a Safe Space – *Learn to clean your home, office, car, or special space of unwanted entities and energy.*

The Abundance Tape – *Create the reality you wish with health, happiness, success, and the abundance of life force energy.*

To order tapes please include $2.00 for postage and handling for the first tape and .75 for each additional tape. California residents must include the appropriate sales tax.

VOYANT BOOKS AND PRODUCTS
Ordering Instructions

When ordering by check or money order, please make payable to:

Voyant
1515 Lookout Drive
Malibu Lake, Agoura, CA 91301

To order by credit card call any of the following numbers:

(818) 707-6448
(310) 859-0869
(310) 275-5859